CENSUS OF INDIA 1891

Census of India 1871-1951, 9 Sets In 384 Bindings (9788121258876) Rs. 700000

Census of India 1891, 28 Vols. In 49 Bindings (978-81-212-7129-5) Rs. 125000

1. General Report (9788121269834) Rs. 1450
2. General Tables For British Provinces And Feudatory States (9788121269810) Rs. 2710 (Vol. I)
3. General Tables For British Provinces And Feudatory States (9788121269797) Rs. 950 (Vol. II)
4. Assam - Report (9788121269773) Rs. 2390 (Vol. I, V.1)
5. Assam - Tables (9788121269759) Rs. 2210 (Vol. II, V.2)
6. Assam - Provincial Tables (9788121269735) Rs. 1310 (Vol. II, V.3)
7. The Lower Provinces of Bengal and their Feudatories - The Report (9788121269711) Rs. 1660 (Vol. III)
8. The Lower Provinces of Bengal and their feudatories - The Administrative Tables (9788121269698) Rs. 4200 (Vol. IV)
9. The Lower Provinces of Bengal and their feudatories - The Caste Tables (9788121269674) Rs. 2600 (Vol. V, Pt. 1)
10. Lower Provinces of Bengal - The Provincial Tables (9788121269650) Rs. 1980 (Vol. V, Pt. 2)
11. Berar or the Hyderabad Assigned Districts (9788121269636) Rs. 3360 (Vol. VI)
12. Bombay and Its Feudatories - Report (9788121269612) Rs. 4010 (Vol. VII, Pt. 1)
13. Bombay And Its Feudatories - Imperial Tables (9788121269599) Rs. 790 (Vol. VIII, Pt. 2)
14. Imperial Series - Burma Report (9788121269575) Rs. 2320 (Vol. IX-V.1)
15. Imperial Tables - Burma Report (9788121269551) Rs. 3360 (Vol. X-V.2)
16. Provincial Tables Burma Report (9788121269537) Rs. 3510 (Vol. X-V.3)
17. Provincial Tables Burma Report (9788121269513) Rs. 3630 (Vol. X-V.4)
18. The Central Provinces And Feudatories - The Report (9788121269490) Rs. 2290 (Vol. XI, Pt. 1)
19. The Central Provinces And Feudatories - Imperial tables and supplementary returns (9788121268936) Rs. 2010 (Vol. XII)
20. Madras The Report On The Census (9788121269476) Rs. 2870 (Vol. XIII)
21. Madras - Tables I to XVII-C, British Territory (9788121269452) Rs. 3490 (Vol. XIV)
22. Madras - Tables A TO E, British Territory. Tables for feudatory States and A Caste Index (9788121269438) Rs. 2820 (Vol. XV)
23. The North Western Provinces and Outh - Report and Provincial Tables (9788121268912) Rs. 3100 (Vol. XVI, Pt. 1)
24. The North - Western Provinces and Oudh- Imperial Tables (9788121269414) Rs. 2000 (Vol. XVII, Pt. 2)
25. The North - Western Provinces and Oudh- Imperial Caste Tables (9788121269391) Rs. 3020 (Vol. XVIII, Pt. 3)
26. Punjab and Its Feudatories - The Report on the Census (9788121269377) Rs. 2710 (Vol. XIX, Pt. 1)
27. Punjab and Its Feudatories - Imperial Tables and Supplementary Returns for the British Territory (9788121269353) Rs. 1370 (Vol. XX, Pt. 2)
28. Punjab and Its Feudatories - Imperial Tables and Supplementary Returns for the Native States, Together With A Caste Index (9788121269339) Rs. 4910 (Vol. XXI, Pt. 3)
29. Report on The Census of The Districts of Ajmere-Merwara (9788121269056) Rs. 720 (Vol. XXII)
30. His Highness The Nizam's Dominions - Report (9788121269315) Rs. 2240 (Vol. XXIII, Pt. 1)
31. His Highness The Nizam's Dominions - Report (9788121269292) Rs. 2410 (Vol. XXIII, Pt. 2)
32. His Highness The Nizam's Dominions - Imperial And Supplementry Tables and Caste Index (9788121269278) Rs. 3390 (Vol. XXIII, Pt. 3)
33. Baroda - Report (9788121269254) Rs. 3810 (Vol. XXIV, Pt. 1)
34. Baroda - Tables (9788121269230) Rs. 2620 (Vol. XXIV, Pt. 2)
35. Mysore - Report (9788121269216) Rs. 2590 (Vol. XXV, Pt. 1)
36. Mysore - Imperial Tables (9788121269193) Rs. 1600 (Vol. XXV, Pt. 2)
37. Mysore - Tables (9788121269179) Rs. 5320 (Vol. XXV, Pt. 3)
38. Mysore - Supplementary Tables (9788121269155) Rs. 3590 (Vol. XXV, Pt. 4)
39. Mysore- Supplement to the Mysore census report of 1891 being a list of villages in the Mysore province and : comparing the population as per Censuses of 1891, 1881 & 1871 (9788121279024) Rs. 5350 (Vol. XXV, Pt. 5)
40. Rajputana - The Report, Imperial Tables And Supplementary Returns (9788121269131) Rs. 2330 (Vol. XXVI, Pt. 1)
41. Rajputna - The Provincial Tables and Remarks (9788121269117) Rs. 550 (Vol. XXVI, Pt. 2)
42. Central India (9788121269094) Rs. 2000 (Vol. XXVII)
43. Kashmir State - The Report on the census and Imperial and supplementary Tables (9788121269070) Rs. 2290 (Vol. XXVIII)
44. The Census of Calcutta (9788121269032) Rs. 890
45. Report on the census of Cochin (9788121269018) Rs. 790 (Pt. 1)
46. Report on the census of Cochin - The Final Census Tables with Appendices (9788121268998) Rs. 910 (Pt. 2)
47. Report on the Census of Coorg (9788121268974) Rs. 730
48. Report on the census of Travancore -Report (9788121274029) Rs. 4220 (Vol. I)
49. Report on the census of Travancore -Appendix (9788121268950) Rs. 5300 (Vol. II)

Owing to the antiquity and rarity of this book, certain pages are regrettably absent, and readability is compromised due to the blurring of the original text. If you possess any insights regarding the availability of these missing sections, kindly inform us. Your assistance is crucial in ensuring the completion of this significant work for the benefit of future generations.

CENSUS OF INDIA, 1891

BOOK-46

REPORT ON THE CENSUS OF COCHIN

1891 A.D.—1066 M.E.

PART II.—THE FINAL CENSUS TABLES WITH APPENDICES

C. ACHYUTA MENON

GYAN

Published by

Gyan Publishing House
5, Ansari Road
Daryaganj, New Delhi-110002
Phone: 011-47034999, 9811692060
E-mail: books@gyanbooks.com

Distribution Network
gyanbooks.com
India, USA, Canada, UK, Australia

ISBN: 978-81-212-7129-5 (Set) 28 Vols. In 49 Bindings
978-81-212-6899-8 (PB) Book-46, Pt. II

First Published, 1893

2nd Impression 2024

Printed at: Gyan Press, Delhi.

CENSUS OF INDIA 1891

REPORT

ON THE

Census of Cochin

1891 A. D. — 1066 M. E.

BY

C. Achyuta Menon B. A.

SUPERINTENDENT OF CENSUS OPERATIONS.

PART II.—*THE FINAL CENSUS TABLES, WITH APPENDICES.*

PRINTED AT THE COCHIN GOVERNMENT PRESS.

1893.

CONTENTS.

ERRATA IN PART II.

Page	8	column	11	line	3	for	487	read	113
,,	8	,,	12	,,	3	,,	270	,,	60
,,	8	,,	13	,,	3	,,	217	,,	53
,,	12	,,	12	,,	18	,,	3318	,,	3388
,,	19	,,	25	,,	9	,,	88	,,	38
,,	19	,,	33	,,	1	,,	12566	,,	13506
,,	20	,,	4	,,	6	,,	4245	,,	4524
,,	20	,,	8	,,	10	,,	2121	,,	3121
,,	20	,,	11	,,	6	,,	246	,,	256
,,	21	,,	22	,,	15	,,	2655	,,	2654
,,	21	,,	28	,,	13	,,	19	,,	18
,,	21	,,	28	,,	15	,,	56	,,	55
,,	23	,,	30	,,	8	,,	3224	,,	3225
,,	24	,,	13	,,	13	,,	255	,,	525
,,	26	,,	16	,,	15	,,	27200	,,	27230
,,	28	,,	8	,,	2	,,	152	,,	162
,,	28	,,	18	,,	3	,,	23	,,	93
,,	31	,,	33	,,	15	,,	4206	,,	3550
,,	84	,,	6	,,	2	,,	845	,,	835
,,	138	,,	19	,,	4	,,	2874	,,	2374
,,	143	,,	36	,,	11	,,	984	,,	986
,,	143	,,	38	,,	9	,,	14367	,,	14267
,,	143	,,	39	,,	7	,,	100	,,	110
,,	144	,,	3	,,	1	,,	10499	,,	10449
,,	147	,,	6	,,	2	,,	203	,,	2203

TABLE I.

Area, Houses and Population.

TABLE I.

Area, Houses and Population.

Taluq.	Area.	Number of		Occupied Houses.			Population.								
							Total			Males.			Females.		
	In square miles.	Towns	Villages.	Total.	Towns.	Villages.	Total	Towns	Villages.	Total.	Towns.	Villages	Total.	Towns.	Villages.
1	2	3	4	5	6	7	8	9	10	11	12	13	14	15	16
1. Kanayannur ...	**80 ¾**	1	87	**19,281**	1,124	18,157	**102,033**	7,283	94,750	**52,454**	4,083	48,371	**49,579**	3,200	46,379
2. Cochin ...	**62 ¾**	1	54	**20,714**	2,978	17,736	**105,582**	17,254	88,328	**54,396**	9,028	45,368	**51,186**	8,226	42,960
3. Kotungallur ...	**18 ¾**	...	7	**5,056**	...	5,056	**27,965**	...	27,965	**14,111**	...	14,111	**13,854**	...	13,854
4. Mukundapuram.	**418 ¼**	1	142	**26,380**	869	25,511	**145,690**	5,217	140,473	**72,814**	2,638	70,176	**72,876**	2,579	70,297
5. Trichur ...	**225**	1	174	**21,401**	2,070	19,331	**128,957**	12,945	116,012	**63,980**	6,592	57,388	**64,977**	6,353	58,624
6. Talappilli ...	**271**	...	164	**23,160**	...	23,160	**133,894**	...	133,894	**65,719**	...	65,719	**68,175**	...	68,175
7. Chittur ...	**281**	1	25	**17,197**	1,472	15,725	**78,785**	7,848	70,937	**38,430**	3,737	34,693	**40,355**	4,111	36,244
Total...	**1,361 ½**	5	653	**133,189**	8,513	124,676	**722,906**	50,547	672,359	**361,904**	26,078	335,826	**361,002**	24,469	336,533

TABLE II.

Variation in the Enumerated Population since last Census.

TABLE II.

Variation in the Enumerated Population since last Census.

Taluq.	Total.			Males.			Females.		
	1891.	1881.	Increase.	1891.	1881.	Increase.	1891.	1881.	Increase.
1	2	3	4	5	6	7	8	9	10
1 Kanayannur	**102,033**	88,847	13,186	**52,454**	45,587	6,867	**49,579**	43,260	6,319
2 Cochin	**105,582**	89,758	15,824	**54,396**	45,879	8,517	**51,186**	43,879	7,307
3 Kotungallur	**27,965**	20,950	7,015	**14,111**	10,634	3,477	**13,854**	10,316	3,538
4 Mukundapuram	**145,690**	115,212	30,478	**72,814**	58,351	14,463	**72,876**	56,861	16,015
5 Trichur	**128,957**	104,695	24,262	**63,980**	51,766	12,214	**64,977**	52,929	14,048
6 Talapilli	**133,894**	113,114	20,780	**65,719**	56,528	9,191	**68,175**	56,586	11,589
7 Chittur	**78,785**	67,702	11,083	**38,430**	38,070	5,360	**40,355**	34,632	5,723
Total...	**722,906**	600,278	122,628	**361,904**	301,815	60,089	**361,002**	298,463	62,539

TABLE III.

Towns and Villages classified by Population.

TABLE III.

Towns and Villages Classified by Population.

Taluq.	Total number of towns and Villages.	Total Population.	1—199		200—		500—		1,000—		2,000—		3,000—		5,000—		10,000—		15,000—	
			No.	Population.	No.	Population.	No.	Population.	No.	Population.	No.	Population.	No.	Population.	No.	Population.	No.	Population.	No.	Population.
1	2	3	4	5	6	7	8	9	10	11	12	13	14	15	16	17	18	19	20	21
1. Kanayannur ...	88	102,033	13	1,739	28	9,254	13	9,716	20	28,790	5	11,985	6	22,483	3	18,066	...	...	...	...
2. Cochin ...	55	105,582	3	211	9	3,410	13	9,474	15	22,047	5	12,517	7	28,090	2	12,579	...	...	1	17,254
3. Kotungallur ...	7	27,965	...	...	1	437	...	...	...	...	1	2,094	3	11,711	2	13,723	...	...	...	...
4. Mukundapuram ...	143	145,690	8	916	35	11,752	40	29,530	47	63,945	9	22,232	3	12,098	1	5,217	...	...	...	...
5. Trichur ...	175	128,957	20	2,312	68	23,185	52	36,994	27	37,160	7	16,361	...	...	...	...	1	12,945	...	...
6. Talappilli ...	164	133,894	15	2,137	49	16,581	58	41,164	31	43,467	7	16,032	4	14,513	...	...	...	...	...	...
7. Chittur ...	26	78,785	1	182	2	795	2	1,513	5	8,066	6	13,896	5	20,853	5	33,480	...	...	...	...
Total...	658	722,906	60	7,497	192	65,414	178	128,391	145	203,475	40	95,117	28	109,748	13	83,065	1	12,945	1	17,254

TABLE IV and TABLE V.

Towns.

Towns were not separately censused on any previous occasion. The Manual of Cochin for the Imperial Gazetteer, however, gives their population in 1875, as shown in Table IV, but no sexual distribution is given. As the areas of Towns were defined only recently, the areas for which the returns of 1875 were made were apparently much larger than these censused on the present occasion, especially in the case of Chittur, Ernakulam and Irinjalakuta.

TABLE IV.

Towns according to Population, compared with the Census of 1875.

Towns.	Taluq.	Total Population.			Males.			Females.		
		1891.	1875.	Variation.	1891.	1875.	Variation.	1891.	1875.	Variation.
1	2	3	4	5	6	7	8	9	10	11
1. Mattanchery ...	Cochin ...	17,254	13,775	+3,479	9,028	...	...	8,226	...	...
2. Trichur ...	Trichur ...	12,945	11,109	+1,836	6,592	...	...	6,353	...	...
3. Chittur ...	Chittur ...	7,848	11,103	—3,255	3,737	...	...	4,111	...	...
4. Ernakulam ...	Kanayannur ...	7,283	14,038	—6,755	4,083	...	...	3,200	...	...
5. Irinjalakuta ...	Mukundapuram ...	5,217	6,326	—1,109	2,638	...	...	2,579	...	...
Total.		50,547	56,351	—5,804	26,078	...	...	24,469	...	...

TABLE V.

Towns, with Population by Religion.

Towns.	Total Population.			Hindu.			Mussalman.			Christian.			Jew.		
	Total.	Males.	Females.	Total.	Males.	Females.	Total.	Males.	Females.	Total.	Males.	Females.	Total.	Males.	Females.
1	2	3	4	5	6	7	8	9	10	11	12	13	14	15	16
1. Mattanchery ...	17,254	9,028	8,226	8,461	4,581	3,880	3,504	1,751	1,753	4,821	2,490	2,331	468	206	262
2. Trichur ...	12,945	6,592	6,353	6,884	3,574	3,310	858	459	399	5,203	2,559	2,644	...	...	...
3. Chittur ...	7,848	3,737	4,111	7,582	3,598	3,984	153	79	74	487	270	217	...	...	...
4. Ernakulam ...	7,283	4,083	3,200	3,720	2,172	1,548	487	270	217	2,649	1,420	1,229	427	221	206
5. Irinjalakuta ...	5,217	2,638	2,579	3,137	1,625	1,512	253	120	133	1,827	893	934	...	...	...
Total.	50,547	26,078	24,469	29,784	15,550	14,234	5,255	2,679	2,576	14,987	7,632	7,355	895	427	468

TABLE VI.

Religions.

TABLE VI.

Religions.

Taluq.	Total Population.			Hindu.			Mussalman.			Christian.			Jew		
	Total.	Males.	Females.	Total.	Males.	Females.	Total.	Males.	Females.	Total.	Males.	Females.	Total.	Males.	Females.
1	2	3	4	5	6	7	8	9	10	11	12	13	14	15	16
1. Kanayannur ...	**102,033**	52,454	49,579	**63,723**	32,703	31,020	**5,082**	2,656	2,426	**32,801**	16,874	15,927	**427**	221	206
2. Cochin ...	**105,582**	54,396	51,186	**52,238**	26,973	25,265	**5,598**	2,847	2,751	**47,121**	24,280	22,841	**625**	296	329
3. Kotungallur ...	**27,965**	14,111	13,854	**20,056**	10,064	9,992	**6,483**	3,288	3,195	**1,426**	759	667	...	...	...
4. Mukundapuram...	**145,690**	72,814	72,876	**98,995**	49,312	49,683	**7,041**	3,581	3,460	**39,564**	19,872	19,692	**90**	49	41
5. Trichur ...	**128,957**	63,980	64,977	**93,149**	46,127	47,022	**4,374**	2,206	2,168	**31,434**	15,647	15,787	...	...	...
6. Talappilli ...	**133,894**	65,719	68,175	**104,484**	50,931	53,553	**11,752**	5,972	5,780	**17,658**	8,816	8,842	...	...	...
7. Chittur ...	**78,785**	38,430	40,355	**68,899**	33,556	35,343	**6,059**	2,988	3,071	**3,827**	1,886	1,941	...	...	...
Total...	**722,906**	361,904	361,002	**501,544**	249,666	251,878	**46,389**	23,538	22,851	**173,831**	88,134	85,697	**1,142**	566	576

TABLE VII.

Ages by Religions.

Persons whose ages are not returned are incluled in this Table. The following Statement gives their number distributed Talukwar by Religion.

Taluq.	All Religions.			Hindu.			Mussalman.			Christian.			Jew.		
	Total.	Males.	Females.	T.	M.	F.	T.	M.	F.	T.	M.	F.	T.	M.	F.
Kanayannur ...	**14**	13	1	**5**	4	1	**2**	2	...	**7**	7	...	...	...	...
Cochin ...	**5**	3	2	**2**	1	1	...	...	...	**3**	2	1	...	...	...
Kotungallur ...	...	...	...	...	...	...	...	...	...	...	...	...	...	...	...
Mukundapuram ...	**34**	16	18	**18**	10	8	**2**	1	1	**14**	5	9	...	...	...
Trichur ...	**15**	5	10	**9**	4	5	**2**	1	1	**4**	...	4	...	...	...
Talappilli ...	**65**	33	32	**54**	26	28	**10**	7	3	**1**	...	1	...	...	...
Chittur ...	**7**	4	3	**4**	2	2	**3**	2	1	...	...	...	...	...	...
Total...	**140**	74	66	**92**	47	45	**19**	13	6	**29**	14	15	...	...	...

TABLE VII.

Ages by Religions. Part (A):—**Total Population.**

	State Total.			Distribution by Taluq.													
				Kanayannur.		Cochin.		Kotungallur.		Mukunda-puram.		Trichur.		Talappilli.		Chittur.	
	Total.	Males.	Females.	Males.	Females.	Males.	Females.	Males.	Females.	Males.	Females.	Males.	Females.	Males.	Females.	Males.	Females.
1	2	3	4	5	6	7	8	9	10	11	12	13	14	15	16	17	18
Under 1 year ...	18,151	8,525	9,626	1,087	1,042	1,006	1,141	452	461	1,781	1,953	1,337	1,546	1,796	2,089	1,066	1,394
1 year ...	18,999	9,260	9,739	1,224	1,312	1,291	1,433	433	429	1,788	1,902	2,069	2,163	1,760	1,757	695	743
2 years ...	23,130	11,249	11,881	1,531	1,648	1,662	1,760	530	499	2,419	2,515	2,120	2,172	1,965	2,146	1,022	1,141
3 Do. ...	23,301	11,282	12,019	1,607	1,685	1,835	1,798	465	486	2,184	2,308	1,979	2,189	2,056	2,172	1,156	1,281
4 Do. ...	19,553	9,499	10,054	1,316	1,387	1,452	1,475	419	439	2,027	2,305	1,670	1,758	1,611	1,688	1,004	1,002
Total 0—4 ...	103,134	49,815	53;319	6,765	7,074	7,246	7,707	2,299	2,314	10,199	10,983	9,175	9,828	9,188	9,852	4,943	5,561
5—9 ...	96,288	48,955	47,333	7,360	6,790	7,061	7,005	2,099	1,924	10,417	10,363	8,496	8,310	8,734	8,312	4,788	4,629
10—14 ...	87,312	45,887	41,425	6,722	5,821	6,645	5,937	1,729	1,559	9,743	8,656	8,428	7,846	8,084	7,364	4,536	4,242
15—19 ...	68,329	34,170	34,159	4,798	4,522	5,087	4,760	1,256	1,346	6,759	6,835	6,208	6,025	6,189	6,602	3,873	4,069
20—24 ...	63,695	298,29	33,866	4,246	4,720	4,598	4,934	1,169	1,284	5,408	6,362	5,542	6,286	5,098	6,203	3,568	4,077
25—29 ...	65,736	31,665	34,071	4,460	4,524	4,516	4,893	1,138	1,249	6,102	6,768	5,658	5,825	6,120	6,695	3,671	4,117
30—34 ...	56,254	28,267	27'987	4,009	3,671	4,560	4,188	1,053	1,003	5,451	5,358	4,976	5,032	5,104	5,220	3,114	3,515
35—39 ...	45,862	24,894	20,968	3,662	2,865	3,784	2,833	866	751	5,044	4,192	4,263	3,633	4,693	4,203	2,782	2,491
40—44 ...	40,646	21,122	19,524	3,093	2,574	3,356	2,783	734	640	4,112	3,762	3,475	3,359	3,821	3,956	2,531	2,450
45—49 ...	25,671	13,768	11,903	2,185	1,859	2,382	1,674	516	438	2,723	2,333	2,054	2,052	2,491	2,333	1,417	1,214
50—54 ...	25,770	12,625	13,145	1,877	1,804	1,886	1,557	408	438	2,489	2,563	2,211	2,484	2,416	2,703	1,338	1,596
55—59 ...	13,002	6,725	6,277	1,058	976	1,052	802	217	293	1,428	1,295	1,054	1,100	1,242	1,112	574	699
60 and over ...	31,067	14,108	16,959	2,206	2,378	2,220	2,111	527	615	2,923	3,318	2,435	3,187	2,506	3,588	1,291	1,692
All ages. ...	722,766	361,830	360,936	52,441	49,578	54,393	51,184	14,111	13,854	72,798	72,858	63,975	64,967	65,686	68,143	38,426	40,352

Table VII.

AGES BY RELIGIONS.

TABLE VII.—*Continued.*

Ages by Religions. PART (B):—**Hindu.**

AGE-PERIOD.	State Total.			Distribution by Taluq.													
				Kanayannur.		Cochin.		Kotungallur.		Mukundapuram.		Trichur.		Talapilli.		Chittur.	
	Total.	Males.	Females.	Males.	Females.	Males.	Females.	Males.	Females.	Males.	Females.	Males.	Females.	Males.	Females.	Males.	Females.
1	2	3	4	5	6	7	8	9	10	11	12	13	14	15	16	17	18
Under 1 year ...	12,777	5,916	6,861	673	664	446	556	333	330	1,221	1,329	961	1,114	1,362	1,657	920	1,211
1 year ...	12,396	6,061	6,335	700	764	557	598	306	298	1,150	1,234	1,451	1,514	1,305	1,300	592	632
2 years ...	15,418	7,486	7,932	225	984	737	809	362	361	1,603	1,678	1,513	1,492	1,473	1,613	873	995
3 do. ...	15,727	7,552	8,175	984	1,019	852	888	338	355	1,445	1,549	1,407	1,569	1,542	1,686	984	1,109
4 do. ...	13,108	6,370	6,738	809	856	708	687	290	290	1.333	1,535	1,163	1,214	1,217	1,272	850	884
Total 0—4 ...	69,426	33,385	36,041	4,091	4,287	3,300	3,538	1,629	1,634	6,752	7,325	6,495	6,903	6,899	7,528	4,219	4,831
5—9 ...	64,479	32,914	31,565	4,377	4,009	3,309	3,141	1,492	1,379	6,845	6,804	6,056	5,866	6,657	6,367	4,178	3,999
10—14 ...	58,699	30,839	27,860	4,079	3,501	3,106	2,720	1,201	1,100	6,405	5,641	5,923	5,583	6,209	5,619	3,916	3,696
15—19 ...	47,677	23,517	24,160	2,964	2,894	2,468	2,421	873	950	4,542	4,631	4,464	4,416	4,811	5,247	3,395	3,601
20—24 ...	44,919	21,001	23,918	2,693	2,966	2,396	2,605	845	956	3,826	4,399	4,075	4,518	4,028	4,905	3,136	3,569
25—29 ...	46,426	22,437	23,989	2,876	2,837	2,364	2,404	823	888	4,231	4,725	4,089	4,237	4,809	5,317	3,245	3,581
30—34 ...	40,086	20,032	20,054	2,598	2,365	2,411	2,192	759	724	3,832	3,825	3,667	3,733	4,047	4,123	2,718	3,092
35—39 ...	32,387	17,402	14,985	2,361	1,840	1,953	1,407	632	549	3,296	2,907	3,069	2,695	3,665	3,379	2,426	2,208
40—44 ...	28,931	14,883	14,048	1,936	1,678	1,716	1,448	521	463	2,902	2,705	2,573	2,484	2,996	3,188	2,239	2,137
45—49 ...	17,929	9,515	8,414	1,393	1,210	1,227	893	371	316	1,895	1,550	1,470	1,507	1,926	1,856	1,233	1,082
50—54 ...	18,757	9,064	9,693	1,212	1,169	1,039	889	299	329	1,765	1,844	1,662	1,875	1,904	2,192	1,18[illegible]	1,395
55—59 ...	9,242	4,689	4,553	692	649	529	429	228	224	949	895	794	804	989	924	518	628
60 and over ...	22,494	9,941	12,553	1,427	1,619	1,152	1,182	396	480	2,062	2,424	1,786	2,396	1,965	2,930	1,158	1,522
All ages...	501,452	249,619	251,833	32,699	31,019	26,972	25,264	10,064	9,992	49,302	49,675	46,123	47,017	50,905	53,525	3,3554	35,341

TABLE VII.—*Continued.*

Ages by Religions PART (C):—Mussalman.

Age-period.	State Total.			Distribution by Taluq.													
				Kanayannur.		Cochin.		Kotungallur.		Mukunda-puram.		Trichur.		Talapilli.		Chittur.	
	Total.	Males.	Females.	males.	Females.	Males.	Females.	Males.	Females.	Males.	Females.	Males.	Females.	Males	Females.	Males.	Females.
1	2	3	4	5	6	7	8	9	10	11	12	13	14	15	16	17	18
Under 1 year ...	1,306	636	670	65	53	61	55	101	105	81	96	41	56	196	208	91	97
1 year ...	1,388	655	733	67	58	71	80	107	109	111	121	74	103	174	205	51	57
2 years ...	1,656	795	861	80	91	89	97	138	122	131	143	64	103	197	219	96	86
3 do. ...	1,497	756	741	55	72	83	98	105	99	126	114	65	81	218	182	104	95
4 do. ...	1,407	705	702	66	77	73	50	111	120	123	139	68	66	170	181	94	69
Total 0—4	7,254	3,547	3,707	353	351	377	380	562	555	572	613	312	409	955	995	436	404
5—9 ...	6,516	3,356	3,160	394	329	307	333	508	447	555	546	325	314	885	789	382	402
10—14 ...	5,692	3,043	2'649	368	307	276	282	433	382	471	419	306	253	805	669	384	337
15—19 ...	4,353	2,157	2,196	249	215	253	310	315	324	320	311	218	181	532	568	270	287
20—24 ...	4,105	1,930	2,175	210	262	287	294	261	270	279	296	164	200	435	539	294	314
25—29 ...	4,108	1,931	2,177	193	219	253	269	230	308	273	290	197	198	528	576	257	317
30—34 ...	3,512	1,766	1,746	200	189	260	252	239	239	237	215	171	159	435	417	224	275
35—39 ...	2,791	1'550	1,241	176	128	211	164	178	159	223	190	152	107	389	302	221	191
40—44 ...	2,564	1,369	1,195	182	127	212	173	176	148	190	165	105	95	323	299	181	188
45—49 ...	1,554	873	681	122	79	117	73	106	102	127	121	82	61	203	164	116	81
50—54 ...	1,503	767	736	98	83	110	78	88	92	113	98	62	78	200	189	96	118
55—59 ...	731	408	323	40	45	65	33	78	59	76	56	30	28	86	55	33	47
60 and over ...	1,687	828	859	89	92	119	110	114	110	144	139	81	84	189	215	92	109
All ages...	4,6370	23,525	22,845	2,654	2,426	2,847	2,751	3,288	3,195	3,580	3,459	2,205	2,167	5,965	5,777	2,986	3,070

TABLE VII. —*Continued.*

Ages by Religions. PART (D):—**Christians.**

Age-period.	State Total			Distribution by Taluq.													
	Total.	Males.	Females.	Kanayannur.		Cochin.		Kotungallur.		Mukunda-puram.		Trichur.		Talappilli.		Chittur.	
				Males.	Females.	Males.	Females.	Males.	Females.	Males.	Females.	Males.	Females.	Males.	Females.	Males.	Females.
1	2	3	4	5	6	7	8	9	10	11	12	13	14	15	16	17	18
Under 1 year ...	**4,041**	1,963	2,078	316	321	493	518	18	26	478	527	335	376	238	224	55	86
1 do. ...	**5,197**	2,535	2,662	452	486	659	755	20	22	527	547	544	546	281	252	52	54
2 years ...	**6,032**	2,955	3,077	520	569	830	848	30	16	684	693	543	577	295	314	53	60
3 do. ...	**6,046**	2,959	3,087	562	586	894	906	22	32	610	648	507	539	296	304	68	77
4 do. ...	**5,010**	2,407	2,603	434	451	661	731	18	29	571	630	439	478	224	235	60	49
Total 0— 4 ...	**26,326**	12,819	13,507	2,314	2,413	3,537	3,758	108	125	2,870	3,040	2,368	2,516	1,334	1,329	288	326
5— 9 ...	**25,146**	12,619	12,527	2,563	2,423	3,416	3,488	99	98	3,006	3,004	2,115	2,130	1,192	1,156	228	228
10—14 ...	**22,816**	11,948	10,868	2,258	1,992	3,225	2,915	95	77	2,865	2,589	2,199	2,010	1,070	1,076	236	209
15—19 ...	**16,178**	8,430	7,748	1,561	1,396	2,328	1,996	68	72	1,893	1,868	1,526	1,428	846	787	208	181
20—24 ...	**14,563**	6,848	7,715	1,318	1,474	1,897	1,998	63	58	1,494	1,664	1,303	1,568	635	759	138	194
25—29 ...	**15,105**	7,250	7,855	1,372	1,450	1,871	2,190	85	53	1,595	1,751	1,372	1,390	783	802	169	219
30—34 ...	**12,574**	6,435	6,139	1,199	1,101	1,868	1,716	55	40	1,381	1,314	1,138	1,140	622	680	172	148
35—39 ...	**10,614**	5,904	4,710	1,110	882	1,600	1,246	56	43	1,322	1,094	1,042	831	639	522	135	92
40—44 ...	**9,077**	4,834	4,243	960	764	1,409	1,139	37	29	1,018	887	797	780	502	519	111	125
45—49 ...	**6,141**	3,358	2,783	660	559	1,030	694	39	20	697	662	502	484	362	313	68	51
50—54 ...	**5,469**	2,770	2,699	557	546	723	579	21	17	611	621	487	531	312	322	59	83
55—59 ...	**2,998**	1,609	1,389	322	277	446	333	16	10	400	344	230	268	167	133	28	24
60 and over. ...	**6,795**	3,296	3,499	673	650	925	788	17	25	715	825	568	707	352	443	46	61
All ages ...	**173,802**	88,120	85,682	16,867	15,927	24,278	22,840	759	667	19,867	19,683	15,647	15,783	8,816	8,841	1,886	1,941

TABLE VII.—*Continued.*

Ages by Religions. PART (E):—Jew.

AGE-PERIOD.	State Total.			Distribution by Taluq.													
				Kanayannur.		Cochin.		Kotungallur.		Mukundapuram.		Trichur.		Talappilli.		Chittur.	
	Total.	Males.	Females.	Males.	Females.	Males.	Females.	Males.	Females.	Males.	Females.	Males.	Females.	Males.	Females.	Males.	Females.
1	2	3	4	5	6	7	8	9	10	11	12	13	14	15	16	17	18
Under 1 year ...	27	10	17	3	4	6	12	...	...	1	1	...	...	...	...	...	...
1 year ...	18	9	9	5	4	4	5	...	...	...	...	...	...	...	...	...	...
2 years ...	24	13	11	6	4	6	6	...	...	1	1	...	...	...	...	...	...
3 do. ...	31	15	16	6	8	6	6	...	...	3	2	...	...	...	...	...	...
4 do. ...	28	17	11	7	3	10	7	...	...	...	1	...	...	...	...	...	...
Total 0—4 ...	128	64	64	27	23	32	36	...	...	5	5	...	...	...	...	...	...
5—9 ...	147	66	81	26	29	29	43	...	...	11	9	...	...	...	...	...	...
10—14 ...	105	57	48	17	21	38	20	...	...	2	7	...	...	...	...	...	...
15—19 ...	121	66	55	24	17	38	33	...	...	4	5	...	...	...	...	...	...
20—24 ...	108	50	58	25	18	16	37	...	...	9	3	...	...	...	...	...	...
25—29 ...	97	47	50	19	18	25	30	...	...	3	2	...	...	...	...	...	...
30—34 ...	82	34	48	12	16	21	28	...	...	1	4	...	...	...	...	...	...
35—39 ...	70	38	32	15	15	20	16	...	...	3	1	...	...	...	...	...	...
40—44 ...	84	36	38	15	10	19	23	...	...	2	5	...	...	...	...	...	...
45—49 ...	47	22	25	10	11	8	14	...	...	4	...	...	...	...	...	...	...
50—54 ...	41	24	17	10	6	14	11	...	...	...	...	...	...	...	...	...	...
55—59 ...	31	19	12	4	5	12	7	...	...	3	...	...	...	...	...	...	...
60 and over ...	91	43	48	17	17	24	31	...	...	2	...	...	...	...	...	...	...
All ages ...	1,142	566	576	221	206	296	329	...	...	49	41	...	...	...	...	...	...

TABLE VIII.

Civil Condition by Religion and Age.

Persons whose Civil Condition is not returned are not included in this Table. The following Statement gives their number distributed Talukwar by Religion.

Age-period	State Total.									Kanayannur.						Mukundapuram.		Trichur.				Talappilli.		Chittur.	
	All Religions.			Hindu.		Mussalman.		Christian.		Hindu.		Mussalman.		Christian.		Hindu.		Hindu.		Christian.		Hindu.		Hindu.	
	Total.	Males.	Females.	Males.	Females.	Males.	Females.	Males.	Females.	Males.	Females.	Males.	Females.	Males.	Females.	Males.	Females.	Males.	Females.	Males.	Females.	Males.	Females.	Males.	Females.
0— 4 ...	1	1	...	1	...	...	...	...	...	...	...	...	...	...	...	1	...	...	...	...	...	...	...	...	...
5— 9 ...	...	...	...	...	...	...	...	...	...	...	...	...	...	...	...	...	...	...	...	...	...	...	...	...	...
10—14 ...	1	1	...	1	...	...	...	...	...	...	...	...	...	...	...	1	...	...	...	...	...	...	...	...	...
15—19 ...	1	...	1	...	...	...	...	...	1	...	...	...	...	...	...	...	...	...	...	...	1	...	...	...	...
20—24 ...	1	...	1	...	1	...	...	...	...	...	...	...	...	...	...	...	1	...	...	...	...	...	...	...	...
25—29 ...	1	1	...	1	...	...	...	...	...	...	...	...	...	...	...	1	...	...	...	...	...	...	...	...	...
30—34 ...	1	1	...	1	...	...	...	...	...	...	...	...	...	...	...	1	...	...	...	...	...	...	...	...	...
35—39 ...	...	...	...	...	...	...	...	...	...	...	...	...	...	...	...	...	...	...	...	...	...	...	...	...	...
40—44 ...	...	...	...	...	...	...	...	...	...	...	...	...	...	...	...	...	...	...	...	...	...	...	...	...	...
45—49 ...	...	...	...	...	...	...	...	...	...	...	...	...	...	...	...	...	...	...	...	...	...	...	...	...	...
50—54 ...	2	...	2	...	1	...	...	...	1	...	...	...	...	...	...	...	...	...	1	...	1	...	...	...	...
55—59 ...	...	...	...	...	...	...	...	...	...	...	...	...	...	...	...	...	...	...	...	...	...	...	...	...	...
60 and over.	...	...	...	...	...	...	...	...	1	...	...	...	...	...	...	...	...	...	...	...	1	...	...	...	...
Not Stated.	68	37	31	34	30	1	...	2	...	1	...	1	...	2	...	3	3	4	1	...	...	25	26	1	...
All ages ...	76	41	35	38	32	1	...	2	3	1	...	1	...	2	...	7	4	4	2	...	3	25	26	1	...

Table VIII.

CIVIL CONDITION.

TABLE VIII.

Civil Condition by Religion and Age.—State Total.

Age-period.	All Religions.												Hindu.							
	Total.			Unmarried.			Married.			Widowed.			Total.		Unmarried.		Married.		Widowed.	
	Total.	Males.	Females.	Total.	Males.	Females.	Total.	Males.	Females.	Total.	Males.	Females.	Males.	Females.	Males.	Females.	Males.	Females.	Males.	Females.
1	2	3	4	5	6	7	8	9	10	11	12	13	14	15	16	17	18	19	20	21
0—4 ...	103,133	49814	53319	102,960	49810	53150	171	4	167	2	...	2	33,384	36,041	33380	35873	4	166	...	2
5—9 ...	96,288	48955	47333	95,445	48870	46575	836	84	752	7	1	6	32,914	31,565	32853	30887	60	674	1	4
10—14 ...	87,311	45886	41425	80,454	45198	35256	6,819	683	6136	38	5	33	30,838	27,860	30380	22923	454	4911	4	26
15—19 ...	68,328	34170	34158	40,198	29022	11176	27,880	5125	22755	250	23	227	23,517	24,160	20303	7656	3200	16327	14	177
20—24 ...	63,694	29829	33865	141,85	11905	2280	48,653	17808	30850	886	121	735	21,001	23,917	8973	1672	11946	21698	82	547
25—29 ...	65,735	31664	34071	5,379	4265	1114	58,499	27057	31442	1,857	342	1515	22,436	23,989	3348	836	18860	22075	222	1078
30—34 ...	56,253	28266	27987	2,435	1660	775	50,485	25996	24489	3,333	610	2723	20,031	20,054	1359	635	18247	17475	425	1944
35—39 ...	45,862	24894	20968	1,496	901	595	40,583	23288	17295	3,783	705	3078	17,402	14,985	[illegible]	444	16176	12382	478	2159
40—44 ...	40,646	21122	19524	1,163	567	596	32,845	19562	13283	6,638	993	5645	14,883	14,048	463	438	13737	9652	683	3958
45—49 ...	25,671	13768	11903	778	392	386	19,970	12591	7379	4,923	785	4138	9,515	8,414	301	286	8719	6265	495	2863
50—54 ...	25,768	12025	13143	753	294	459	16,850	11026	5824	8,165	1305	6860	9,064	9,692	234	322	7951	4296	879	5074
55—59 ...	13,002	6725	6277	434	184	250	8,295	5724	2571	4,273	817	3456	4,689	4,553	142	177	4000	1865	547	2511
60 and over.	31,066	14108	16958	1,052	389	663	13,258	10138	3120	16,756	3581	13175	9,941	12,553	312	505	7140	2316	2489	9732
Not stated.	73	37	36	37	20	17	29	16	13	7	1	6	13	15	4	5	9	7	...	3
All ages ...	722,830	361863	360967	346,769	193477	153292	325,173	159097	166076	50,888	9289	41599	249,628	251,846	132800	102659	110509	119109	6319	30078

Table VIII.

CIVIL CONDITION.

TABLE VIII.—*Continued.*

Civil Condition by Religion and Age.—State Total.

Age-period.	Mussalman.								Christian.								Jew.							
	Total.		Unmarried.		Married.		Widowed.		Total.		Unmarried.		Married.		Widowed.		Total.		Unmarried.		Married.		Widowed.	
	Males.	Females.	Males.	Females.	Males.	Females.	Males.	Females.	Males.	Females.	Males.	Females.	Males.	Females.	Males.	Females.	Males.	Females.	Males.	Females.	Males.	Females.	Males.	Females.
	22	23	24	25	26	27	28	29	30	31	32	33	34	35	36	37	38	39	40	41	42	43	44	45
0— 4 ...	3,547	3,707	3547	3707	...	...	...	...	12,819	13,507	12819	12566	...	1	...	...	64	64	64	64	...	...	...	...
5— 9 ...	3,356	3,160	3355	3144	1	16	...	...	12,619	12,527	12596	12464	23	61	...	2	66	81	66	80	...	1	...	...
10—14 ...	3,043	2,649	3031	2433	12	215	...	1	11,948	10,868	11730	9854	217	1006	1	6	57	48	57	46	...	2	...	...
15—19 ...	2,157	2,196	1927	836	229	1337	1	23	8,430	7,747	6726	2654	1696	5067	8	20	66	55	66	30	...	24	...	1
20—24 ...	1,930	2,175	852	195	1066	1921	12	59	6,848	7,715	2045	407	4776	7180	27	128	50	58	35	6	15	51	...	1
25—29 ...	1,931	2,177	303	88	1606	1965	22	124	7,250	7,855	594	188	6558	7355	98	312	47	50	20	2	27	47	...	1
30—34 ...	1,766	1,746	80	54	1660	1507	26	185	6,435	6,139	220	86	6059	5465	156	588	34	48	1	...	30	42	3	6
35—39 ...	1,550	1,241	29	33	1491	985	30	223	5,904	4,710	123	117	5585	3900	196	693	38	32	1	1	36	28	1	3
40—44 ...	1,369	1,195	16	88	1308	768	45	389	4,334	4,243	86	120	4484	2834	264	1289	36	38	2	...	33	29	1	9
45—49 ...	873	681	14	19	820	390	33	272	3,358	2,783	77	80	3026	1707	255	906	22	25	...	1	20	17	2	7
50—54 ...	767	736	4	17	712	304	51	415	2,770	2,698	54	120	2346	1216	370	1362	24	17	2	...	17	8	5	9
55—59 ...	408	323	3	5	375	128	30	190	1,809	1,389	39	68	1331	572	239	749	19	12	...	...	18	6	1	6
60 and over	828	859	12	35	647	117	169	707	3,296	3,498	65	122	2314	671	917	2705	43	48	...	1	37	16	6	31
Not Stated.	12	6	10	4	1	...	1	2	12	15	6	8	6	6	...	1	...	...	...	...	...	...	...	...
All ages ...	23,537	22,851	13183	10608	9934	9653	420	2590	88,132	85,694	47180	39704	38421	37043	2531	8857	566	576	314	231	233	271	19	74

TABLE VIII. —*Continued.*

Civil Condition by Religion and Age:—Kanayannur Taluq.

Age-period.	All Religions.												Hindu.							
	Total.			Unmarried.			Married.			Widowed.			Total.		Unmarried.		Married.		Widowed.	
	Total.	Males.	Females.	Total.	Males.	Females.	Total.	Males.	Females.	Total.	Males.	Females.	Males.	Females.	Males.	Females.	Males.	Females.	Males.	Females.
1	2	3	4	5	6	7	8	9	10	11	12	13	14	15	16	17	18	19	20	21
0—4 ...	**13,839**	6765	7074	13786	6765	7021	53	...	53	...	...	...	4091	4287	4091	4234	...	53	...	...
5—9 ...	**14,150**	7360	6790	13831	7340	6491	318	20	298	1	...	1	4377	4009	4363	3732	14	277	...	...
10—14 ...	**12,543**	6722	5821	11020	6560	4460	1521	160	1361	2	2	...	4079	3501	3989	2424	88	1077	2	...
15—19 ...	**9,320**	4798	4522	5252	4064	1188	4039	733	3306	29	1	28	2964	2894	2577	641	387	2232	...	21
20—24 ...	**8,966**	4246	4720	2147	1897	250	6710	2334	4376	109	15	94	2693	2966	1298	133	1390	2771	5	62
25—29 ...	**8,984**	4460	4245	958	836	122	7770	3572	4198	246	52	204	2876	2837	602	71	2244	2633	30	133
30—34 ...	**7,680**	4009	3671	351	288	63	6878	3618	3260	451	103	348	2598	2365	226	51	2297	2090	75	224
35—39 ...	**6,527**	3662	2865	252	182	70	5693	3354	2339	582	126	456	2361	1840	146	31	2131	1529	84	280
40—44 ...	**5,667**	3093	2574	198	113	85	4576	2803	1773	893	177	716	1936	1673	84	56	1749	1159	103	458
45—49 ...	**4,044**	2185	1859	113	64	49	2121	1966	1155	810	155	655	1393	1210	47	37	1248	736	98	437
50—54 ...	**3,681**	1877	1804	140	60	80	2431	1606	825	1110	211	899	1212	1160	49	45	1048	522	115	602
55—59 ...	**2,034**	1058	976	72	31	41	1322	894	428	640	133	507	692	649	22	30	583	278	87	341
60 and over	**4,585**	2207	2378	150	52	98	2094	1593	501	2341	562	1779	1427	1619	50	77	1013	310	364	1232
Not Stated.	**9**	8	1	3	3	...	6	5	1	...	...	...	3	1	1	...	2	1	...	...
All ages	**102,029**	52450	49579	48273	28255	20018	46532	22658	23874	7224	1537	5687	32702	31020	17545	11562	14194	15668	963	3790

TABLE VIII.—*Continued.*

Civil Condition by Religion and Age:—KANAYANNUR TALUQ.

Age-period.	Mussalman. Total. Males.	Mussalman. Total. Females.	Mussalman. Unmarried. Males.	Mussalman. Unmarried. Females.	Mussalman. Married. Males.	Mussalman. Married. Females.	Mussalman. Widowed. Males.	Mussalman. Widowed. Females.	Christian. Total. Males.	Christian. Total. Females.	Christian. Unmarried. Males.	Christian. Unmarried. Females.	Christian. Married. Males.	Christian. Married. Females.	Christian. Widowed. Males.	Christian. Widowed. Females.	Jew. Total. Males.	Jew. Total. Females.	Jew. Unmarried. Males.	Jew. Unmarried. Females.	Jew. Married. Males.	Jew. Married. Females.	Jew. Widowed. Males.	Jew. Widowed. Females.
	22	23	24	25	26	27	28	29	30	31	32	33	34	35	36	37	38	39	40	41	42	43	44	45
0—4 ...	**333**	**351**	333	351	...	...	...	...	**2,314**	**2,413**	2,314	2,413	...	...	...	...	**27**	**23**	27	23	...	...	...	...
5—9 ...	**394**	**329**	394	327	...	2	...	...	**2,563**	**2,423**	2,557	2,403	6	19	...	1	**26**	**29**	26	29	...	...	...	...
10—14 ...	**368**	**307**	365	287	3	20	...	...	**2,258**	**1,992**	2,189	1,729	69	263	...	...	**17**	**21**	17	20	...	1	...	...
15—19 ...	**249**	**215**	223	93	25	122	1	...	**1,561**	**1,396**	1,240	446	321	944	...	6	**24**	**17**	24	8	...	8	...	1
20—24 ...	**210**	**262**	87	23	122	237	1	2	**1,318**	**1,474**	492	94	817	1350	9	30	**25**	**18**	20	...	5	18	...	...
25—29 ...	**193**	**219**	47	7	143	202	3	10	**1,372**	**1,450**	177	44	1176	1346	19	60	**19**	**18**	10	...	9	17	...	1
30—34 ...	**200**	**189**	5	6	193	171	2	12	**1,199**	**1,101**	57	6	1117	985	25	110	**12**	**16**	...	...	11	14	1	2
35—39 ...	**176**	**128**	4	3	168	108	4	17	**1,110**	**882**	32	36	1041	689	37	157	**15**	**15**	...	...	14	13	1	2
40—44 ...	**182**	**127**	1	2	173	78	8	47	**960**	**764**	28	27	867	529	65	208	**15**	**10**	...	...	14	7	1	3
45—49 ...	**122**	**79**	2	...	115	49	5	30	**660**	**559**	15	11	594	362	51	186	**10**	**11**	...	1	9	8	1	2
50—54 ...	**98**	**83**	1	2	86	43	11	38	**557**	**546**	9	33	463	258	85	255	**10**	**6**	1	...	9	2	...	4
55—59 ...	**40**	**45**	...	...	38	22	2	23	**322**	**277**	9	11	269	124	44	142	**4**	**5**	...	...	4	4	...	1
60 and over.	**89**	**92**	1	9	70	16	19	67	**673**	**650**	1	12	494	165	178	473	**17**	**17**	...	...	16	10	1	7
Not Stated.	...	...	...	...	...	...	...	...	**5**	...	2	...	3	...	...	...	...	...	...	...	...	...	...	...
All ages ...	**2,655**	**2,426**	1,463	1,110	1136	1070	56	246	**16,872**	**15,927**	9,122	7,265	7237	7034	513	1628	221	206	125	81	91	102	5	23

TABLE VIII. —*Continued.*

Civil Condition by Religion and Age:—Cochin Taluq.

Age-period.	All Religions.												Hindu.							
	Total.			Unmarried.			Married.			Widowed.			Total.		Unmarried.		Married.		Widowed.	
	Total.	Males.	Females.	Total.	Males.	Females.	Total.	Males.	Females.	Total.	Males.	Females.	Males.	Females.	Males.	Females.	Males.	Females.	Males.	Females.
1	2	3	4	5	6	7	8	9	10	11	12	13	14	15	16	17	18	19	20	21
0—4 ...	14,953	7,246	7,707	14,951	7,246	7,705	2	...	2	...	...	...	3,300	3,533	3,300	3,531	...	2	...	...
5—9 ...	14,066	7,061	7,005	14,028	7,050	6,978	36	10	26	2	1	1	3,309	3,141	3,303	3,128	5	13	1	...
10—14 ...	12,582	6,645	5,937	11,921	6,563	5,358	656	81	575	5	1	4	3,106	2,720	3,066	2,363	40	354	...	3
15—19 ...	9,847	5,087	4,760	6,069	4,403	1,666	3,750	683	3,067	28	1	27	2,468	2,421	2,129	798	338	1,606	1	17
20—24 ...	9,532	4,598	4,934	2,307	1,975	332	7,061	2,601	4,460	164	22	142	2,398	2,605	1,085	207	1,300	2,306	13	92
25—29 ...	9,409	4,516	4,893	787	632	155	8,275	3,818	4,457	347	66	281	2,364	2,404	388	81	1,939	2,163	37	160
30—34 ...	8,748	4,560	4,188	416	295	121	7,727	4,134	3,593	605	131	474	2,411	2,192	181	82	2,166	1,838	64	272
35—39 ...	6,617	3,784	2,833	193	121	72	5,823	3,526	2,297	601	137	464	1,953	1,407	79	38	1,797	1,131	77	238
40—44 ...	6,139	3,356	2,783	184	96	88	4,880	3,060	1,820	1075	200	875	1,716	1,448	63	47	1,543	953	110	448
45—49 ...	4,056	2,382	1,674	145	76	69	3,091	2,149	942	820	157	663	1,227	893	47	49	1,113	497	67	347
50—54 ...	3,443	1,886	1,557	108	43	65	2,239	1,614	625	1096	229	867	1,039	889	20	29	905	344	114	516
55—59 ...	1,854	1,052	802	67	25	42	1,156	886	270	631	141	490	529	429	14	20	454	144	61	265
60 and over ...	4,331	2,220	2,111	145	70	75	1,887	1,559	328	2299	591	1708	1,152	1,182	42	33	826	181	284	968
Not Stated ...	5	3	2	4	3	1	1	...	1	...	...	...	1	1	1	...	...	1	...	...
All ages ...	105,582	54,396	51,186	51,825	28,598	22,727	46,584	24,121	22,463	7673	1677	5996	26,973	25,265	13,718	10,406	12,426	11,533	829	3326

TABLE VIII.—*Continued.*

Civil Condition by Religion and Age.—Cochin Taluq.

Age-period.	Mussalman. Total. Males.	Mussalman. Total. Females.	Mussalman. Unmarried. Males.	Mussalman. Unmarried. Females.	Mussalman. Married. Males.	Mussalman. Married. Females.	Mussalman. Widowed. Males.	Mussalman. Widowed. Females.	Christian. Total. Males.	Christian. Total. Females.	Christian. Unmarried. Males.	Christian. Unmarried. Females.	Christian. Married. Males.	Christian. Married. Females.	Christian. Widowed. Males.	Christian. Widowed. Females.	Jew. Total. Males.	Jew. Total. Females.	Jew. Unmarried. Males.	Jew. Unmarried. Females.	Jew. Married. Males.	Jew. Married. Females.	Jew. Widowed. Males.	Jew. Widowed. Females.
	22	23	24	25	26	27	28	29	30	31	32	33	34	35	36	37	38	39	40	41	42	43	44	45
0— 4 ...	**377**	**380**	377	380	...	...	...	...	**3,537**	**3,758**	3,537	3,758	...	...	...	...	**32**	**36**	32	36	...	...	...	...
5— 9 ...	**307**	**333**	307	331	...	2	...	...	**3,416**	**3,488**	3,411	3,477	5	10	...	1	**29**	**43**	29	42	...	1	...	...
10—14 ...	**276**	**282**	276	242	...	39	...	1	**3,224**	**2,915**	3,183	2,733	41	182	1	...	**38**	**20**	38	20	...	...	...	...
15—19 ...	**253**	**310**	212	98	41	208	...	4	**2,328**	**1,996**	2,024	749	304	1241	...	6	**36**	**33**	38	21	...	12	...	...
20—24 ...	**287**	**294**	106	20	177	265	4	9	**1,897**	**1,998**	773	99	1,119	1859	5	40	**16**	**37**	11	6	5	30	...	1
25—29 ...	**253**	**269**	33	12	220	239	...	18	**1,874**	**2,190**	201	60	1,644	2027	29	103	**25**	**30**	10	2	15	28	...	...
30—34 ...	**260**	**252**	16	6	240	220	4	26	**1,868**	**1,716**	97	33	1,710	1511	61	172	**21**	**28**	1	...	18	24	2	4
35—39 ...	**211**	**164**	4	7	203	130	4	27	**1,600**	**1,246**	37	26	1,507	1022	56	198	**20**	**16**	1	1	19	14	...	1
40—44 ...	**212**	**173**	3	10	200	105	9	58	**1,409**	**1,139**	28	31	1,300	744	81	364	**19**	**23**	2	...	17	18	...	5
45—49 ...	**117**	**73**	2	5	108	36	7	32	**1,030**	**694**	27	15	921	400	82	279	**8**	**14**	...	...	7	9	1	5
50—54 ...	**110**	**78**	...	4	97	35	13	39	**723**	**579**	22	32	604	240	97	307	**14**	**11**	1	...	8	6	5	5
55—59 ...	**65**	**33**	...	...	59	11	6	22	**446**	**333**	11	22	362	113	73	198	**12**	**7**	...	...	11	2	1	5
60 and over.	**119**	**110**	1	3	86	11	32	96	**925**	**788**	27	38	628	130	270	620	**24**	**31**	...	1	19	6	5	24
Not Stated.	...	...	...	...	...	...	...	...	2	1	2	1	...	...	...	...	...	...	...	...	...	...	...	...
All ages ...	**2,847**	**2,751**	1,337	1,118	1431	1301	79	332	**24,280**	**22,841**	13,380	11,074	10,145	9479	755	2,288	**296**	**329**	163	129	119	150	14	50

TABLE VIII.

Civil Condition by Religion and Age.—Kotungallur Taluq.

Age-period.	All Religions. Total. Total.	Males.	Females.	Unmarried. Total.	Males.	Females.	Married. Total.	Males.	Females.	Widowed. Total.	Males.	Females.	Hindu. Total. Males.	Females.	Unmarried. Males.	Females.	Married. Males.	Females.	Widowed Males.	Females
1	2	3	4	5	6	7	8	9	10	11	12	13	14	15	16	17	18	19	20	21
0— 4 ...	4,613	2,299	2,314	4,612	2,299	2,313	1	...	1	...	...	...	1,629	1,634	1,629	1,633	...	1	...	...
5— 9 ...	4,023	2,099	1,924	4,014	2,098	1,916	9	1	8	...	...	...	1,492	1,379	1,492	1,374	...	5	...	...
10—14 ...	3,288	1,729	1,559	3,135	1,720	1,415	151	8	143	2	1	1	1,201	1,100	1,193	970	7	129	1	1
15—19 ...	2,602	1,256	1,346	1,696	1,149	547	895	107	788	11	...	11	873	950	790	361	83	582	...	7
20—24 ...	2,453	1,169	1,284	747	634	113	1,664	531	1,133	42	4	38	845	956	444	76	398	855	3	25
25—29 ...	2,387	1,138	1,249	264	206	58	2,055	923	1,132	68	9	59	823	888	150	32	667	816	6	40
30—34 ...	2,056	1,053	1,003	131	87	44	1,801	945	856	124	21	103	759	724	67	30	677	624	15	70
35—39 ...	1,617	866	751	53	36	17	1,411	812	599	153	18	135	632	549	33	17	585	425	14	107
40—44 ...	1,374	734	640	37	18	19	1,097	687	410	240	29	211	521	463	17	17	480	288	24	158
45—49 ...	954	516	438	19	8	11	724	478	246	211	30	181	371	316	7	7	338	164	26	145
50—54 ...	846	408	438	13	6	7	554	366	188	279	36	243	299	329	5	7	264	149	30	173
55—59 ...	610	317	293	16	13	3	368	270	98	226	34	192	223	224	12	2	183	76	28	146
60 and over.	1,142	527	615	20	17	3	485	398	87	637	112	255	396	480	16	1	291	70	89	409
Not stated.	...	...	...	...	...	...	...	...	...	...	...	...	...	...	...	...	...	...	...	...
All ages ...	27,965	14,111	13,854	14,757	8,291	6,466	11,215	5,526	5,689	1,903	294	1,609	10,064	9,992	5,855	4,527	3,973	4,184	236	1,281

TABLE VIII.—*Continued.*

Civil Condition by Religion and Age:—Kotungallur Taluq.

Age-period.	Mussalman.								Christian.								Jew.							
	Total.		Unmarried.		Married.		Widowed.		Total.		Unmarried.		Married.		Widowed		Total.		Unmarried.		Married.		Widowed.	
	Males.	Females.	Males.	Females.	Males.	Females.	Males.	Females.	Males.	Females.	Males.	Females.	Males.	Females.	Males.	Females.	Males.	Females.	Males.	Females.	Males.	Females.	Males.	Females.
	22	23	24	25	26	27	28	29	30	31	32	33	34	35	36	37	38	39	40	41	42	43	44	45
0— 4 ...	562	555	562	555	...	...	...	...	108	125	108	125	...	...	...	...	...	...	...	...	...	...	...	...
5— 9 ...	508	447	507	444	1	3	...	...	99	98	99	98	...	...	...	...	...	...	...	...	...	...	...	...
10—14 ...	433	382	432	370	1	12	...	...	95	77	95	75	...	2	...	...	...	...	...	...	...	...	...	...
15—19 ...	315	324	298	155	17	165	...	4	68	72	61	31	7	41	...	...	...	...	...	...	...	...	...	...
20—24 ...	261	270	158	34	102	223	1	13	63	58	32	3	31	55	...	...	...	...	...	...	...	...	...	...
25—29 ...	230	308	42	25	186	266	2	17	85	53	14	1	70	50	1	2	...	...	...	...	...	...	...	...
30—34 ...	239	239	16	13	218	198	5	28	55	40	4	1	50	34	1	5	...	...	...	...	...	...	...	...
35—39 ...	178	159	3	...	172	133	3	26	56	43	...	...	55	41	1	2	...	...	...	...	...	...	...	...
40—44 ...	176	148	1	2	170	104	5	42	37	29	...	...	37	18	...	11	...	...	...	...	...	...	...	...
45—49 ...	106	102	...	4	105	68	1	30	39	20	1	...	35	14	3	6	...	...	...	...	...	...	...	...
50—54 ...	88	92	...	...	84	34	4	58	21	17	1	...	18	5	2	12	...	...	...	...	...	...	...	...
55—59 ...	78	59	...	1	73	18	5	40	16	10	1	...	14	4	1	6	...	...	...	...	...	...	...	...
60 and over.	114	110	1	2	93	16	20	92	17	25	...	...	14	1	3	24	...	...	...	...	...	...	...	...
Not-Stated.	...	...	...	...	...	...	...	...	...	...	...	...	...	...	...	...	...	...	...	...	...	...	...	...
All ages ...	3,288	3,195	2,020	1,605	1,222	1,240	46	350	759	667	416	334	331	265	12	68	...	...	...	...	...	...	...	...

Table VIII.

CIVIL CONDITION.

TABLE VIII.—*Continued.*

Civil Condition by Religion and Age:—Mukundapuram Taluq.

Age-period.	All Religions.												Hindu.							
	Total.			Unmarried.			Married.			Widowed.			Total.		Unmarried.		Married.		Widowed.	
	Total.	Males.	Females.	Total.	Males.	Females.	Total.	Males.	Females.	Total.	Males.	Females.	Males.	Females.	Males.	Females.	Males.	Females.	Males.	Females.
1	2	3	4	5	6	7	8	9	10	11	12	13	14	15	16	17	18	19	20	21
0—4 ...	21,181	10,198	10,983	21,156	10,198	10,958	24	...	24	1	...	1	6,751	7,325	6,751	7,300	...	24	...	1
5—9 ...	20,780	10,417	10,363	20,628	10,392	10,236	149	25	124	3	...	3	6,845	6,804	6,830	6,693	15	108	...	3
10—14 ...	18,398	9,742	8,656	17,411	9,628	7,783	980	114	866	7	...	7	6,404	5,641	6,323	4,897	81	737	...	7
15—19 ...	13,594	6,759	6,835	8,853	5,962	2,891	4,700	791	3,909	41	6	35	4,542	4,631	4,074	1,926	464	2,675	4	30
20—24 ...	11,969	[illegible]	6,361	2,855	2,345	510	9,013	3,251	5,762	101	12	89	3,826	4,398	1,779	360	2,039	3,974	8	64
25—29 ...	12,869	6,101	6,768	1,139	848	291	11,448	5,199	6,249	282	54	228	4,230	4,725	681	234	3,516	4,333	33	158
30—34 ...	10,808	5,450	5,358	513	338	175	9,795	5,011	4,784	500	101	399	3,831	3,825	300	150	34,60	3,397	71	278
35—39 ...	9,036	4,844	4,192	355	184	171	8,057	4,534	3,523	624	126	498	3,296	2,907	149	128	3,072	2,456	75	323
40—44 ...	7,874	4,112	3,762	270	124	146	6,542	3,830	2,712	1062	158	904	2,902	2,705	106	115	2,689	1,967	107	623
45—49 ...	5,056	2,723	2,333	179	77	102	4,051	2,518	1,533	826	128	698	1,895	1,550	62	72	1,769	1,032	64	446
50—54 ...	5,052	2,489	2,563	209	66	143	3,515	2,220	1,295	1328	203	1125	1,765	1,844	56	107	1,575	946	134	791
55—59 ...	2,723	1,428	1,295	102	47	55	1,831	1,241	590	790	140	650	949	895	36	46	826	418	87	431
60 and over ...	6,311	2,923	3,388	321	94	227	2,827	2,166	661	3163	663	2500	2,062	2,424	82	180	1,530	468	450	1,776
Not Stated ...	28	13	15	10	4	6	17	9	8	1	...	1	7	5	1	2	6	2	...	1
All ages ...	145,679	72,807	72,872	74,001	40,307	33,694	62,949	30,909	32,040	8729	1591	7138	49,305	49,679	27,200	22,210	21,042	22,537	1033	4,932

TABLE VIII.—*Continued.*

Civil Condition by Religion and Age.—Mukundapuram Taluq.

Age-period.	Mussalman.								Christian.								Jew.							
	Total.		Unmarried.		Married.		Widowed.		Total.		Unmarried.		Married.		Widowed.		Total.		Unmarried.		Married.		Widowed.	
	Males.	Females.	Males.	Females.	Males.	Females.	Males.	Females.	Males.	Females.	Males.	Females.	Males.	Females.	Males.	Females.	Males.	Females.	Males.	Females.	Males.	Females.	Males.	Females.
	22	23	24	25	26	27	28	29	30	31	32	33	34	35	36	37	38	39	40	41	42	43	44	45
0—4 ...	572	613	572	613	...	...	...	...	2,870	3,040	2,370	3,040	...	...	...	...	5	5	5	5	...	...	...	...
5—9 ...	555	546	555	545	...	1	...	...	3,006	3,004	2,996	2,989	10	15	...	...	11	9	11	9	...	...	...	...
10—14 ...	471	419	471	410	...	9	...	...	2,865	2,589	2,832	2,470	33	119	...	...	2	7	2	6	...	1	...	...
15—19 ...	320	311	300	156	20	153	...	2	1,893	1,888	1,584	808	307	1,077	2	3	4	5	4	1	...	4	...	...
20—24 ...	279	296	161	49	118	241	...	6	1,494	1,664	401	101	1,089	1,544	4	19	9	3	4	...	5	3	...	...
25—29 ...	273	290	57	12	213	262	3	16	1,595	1,751	110	45	1,467	1,652	18	54	3	2	...	...	3	2	...	...
30—34 ...	237	215	6	8	230	183	1	24	1,381	1,314	32	17	1,320	1,200	29	97	1	4	...	...	1	4	...	...
35—39 ...	223	190	6	7	213	156	4	27	1,322	1,094	29	36	1,246	910	47	148	3	1	...	...	3	1	...	...
40—44 ...	190	165	4	8	180	122	6	35	1,018	887	14	23	959	619	45	245	2	5	...	...	2	4	...	1
45—49 ...	127	121	...	2	122	80	5	39	697	662	15	28	623	421	59	213	4	...	...	...	4	...	...	...
50—54 ...	113	98	1	5	109	49	3	44	611	621	9	31	536	300	66	290	...	...	...	...	...	...	...	...
55—59 ...	76	56	3	1	71	22	2	33	400	344	8	8	341	150	51	186	3	...	...	...	3	...	...	...
60 and over.	144	139	1	7	116	23	27	109	715	825	11	40	518	170	186	615	2	...	...	...	2	...	...	...
Not Stated.	1	1	1	1	...	...	...	...	5	9	2	3	3	6	...	...	...	...	...	...	...	...	...	...
All ages ...	3,581	3,460	2,138	1,824	1,392	1,301	51	335	19,872	19,692	10,913	9,639	8,452	8,183	507	1,870	49	41	26	21	23	19	...	1

TABLE VIII.

Civil Condition by Religion and Age.—Trichur Taluq.

Age-period.	All Religions. Total. Total.	Total. Males.	Total. Females.	Unmarried. Total.	Unmarried. Males.	Unmarried. Females.	Married. Total.	Married. Males.	Married. Females.	Widowed. Total.	Widowed. Males.	Widowed. Females.	Hindu. Total. Males.	Total. Females.	Unmarried. Males.	Unmarried. Females.	Married. Males.	Married. Females.	Widowed Males.	Widowed Females.
1	2	3	4	5	6	7	8	9	10	11	12	13	14	15	16	17	18	19	20	21
0— 4 ...	19,003	9,175	9,828	18,960	9,171	9,789	43	4	39	...	...	...	6,495	6,903	6,491	6,864	4	39	...	...
5— 9 ...	16,806	8,496	8,310	16,644	8,480	8,164	152	16	146	...	...	...	6,056	5,866	6,042	5,728	14	138	...	...
10—14 ...	16,274	8,428	7,846	15,012	8,288	6,724	1,258	140	1,118	4	...	4	5,923	5,583	5,830	4,688	23	892	...	3
15—19 ...	12,232	6,208	6,024	7,034	5,120	1,914	5,161	1,082	4,079	37	6	31	4,464	4,416	3,814	1,445	648	2,947	2	24
20—24 ...	11,828	5,542	6,286	2,234	1,831	403	9,483	3,679	5,804	111	32	79	4,075	4,518	1,556	320	2,495	4,148	24	50
25—29 ...	11,483	5,658	5,825	813	638	175	10,428	4,964	5,464	242	56	186	4,089	4,237	562	140	3,491	3,965	36	132
30—34 ...	10,008	4,976	5,032	402	244	158	9,140	4,658	4,482	466	74	392	3,667	3,733	223	138	3,392	3,325	52	270
35—39 ...	7,896	4,263	3,633	256	147	109	7,153	4,028	3,125	487	88	399	3,069	2,695	134	97	2,880	2,308	55	290
40—44 ...	6,834	3,475	3,359	157	70	87	5,657	3,277	2.380	1,020	128	892	2,573	2,484	66	65	2,420	1,797	87	622
45—49 ...	4,106	2,054	2,052	132	63	69	3,276	1,901	1,375	698	90	608	1,470	1,507	52	51	1,355	1,052	63	404
50—54 ...	4,693	2,211	2,482	146	57	89	3,112	1,943	1,169	1,435	211	1,224	1,662	1,874	46	74	1,464	866	152	934
55—59 ...	2,154	1,054	1,100	77	29	48	1,390	904	486	687	121	566	794	804	21	36	691	351	82	417
60 and over	5,821	2,435	3,186	231	86	145	2,306	1,716	590	3,084	633	2,451	1,786	2,396	62	112	1,269	442	455	1842
Not Stated.	10	1	9	6	...	6	3	1	2	1	...	1	...	4	...	1	...	2	...	1
All ages ...	128,948	6,3976	64,972	62,104	34,224	27,880	58,572	28,313	30,259	8,272	1,439	6,833	46,123	47,020	24,899	19,759	20,216	22,272	1,008	4989

Table VIII.

CIVIL CONDITION.

TABLE VIII.—*Continued.*

Civil Condition by Religion and Age.—Trichur Taluq.

AGE-PERIOD.	Mussalman.								Christian.								Jew.							
	Total.		Unmarried.		Married.		Widowed.		Total.		Unmarried.		Married.		Widowed		Total.		Unmarried.		Married.		Widowed	
	Males.	Females.	Males.	Females.	Males.	Females.	Males.	Females.	Males.	Females.	Males.	Females.	Males.	Females.	Males.	Females.	Males.	Females.	Males.	Females.	Males.	Females.	Males.	Females.
	22	23	24	25	26	27	28	29	30	31	32	33	34	35	36	37	38	39	40	41	42	43	44	45
0— 4 ...	**312**	**409**	312	409	...	...	...	...	**2,368**	**2,516**	2,368	2,516	...	...	...	...	...	...	...	...	...	...	...	...
5— 9 ...	**325**	**314**	325	313	...	1	...	...	**2,115**	**2,130**	2,113	2,123	2	7	...	...	...	...	...	...	...	...	...	...
10—14 ...	**306**	**253**	305	236	1	17	...	...	**2,199**	**2,010**	2,153	1,800	46	209	...	1	...	...	...	...	...	...	...	...
15—19 ...	**218**	**181**	191	64	27	116	...	1	**1,526**	**1,427**	1,115	405	407	1016	4	6	...	...	...	...	...	...	...	...
20—24 ...	**164**	**200**	67	14	96	180	1	6	**1,303**	**1,568**	208	69	1088	1476	7	23	...	...	...	...	...	...	...	...
25—29 ...	**197**	**198**	25	7	171	186	1	5	**1,372**	**1,390**	51	28	1302	1313	19	49	...	...	...	...	...	...	...	...
30—34 ...	**171**	**159**	9	5	160	142	2	12	**1,138**	**1,140**	12	15	1106	1015	20	110	...	...	...	...	...	...	...	...
35—39 ...	**152**	**107**	3	2	146	88	3	17	**1,042**	**831**	10	10	1002	729	30	92	...	...	...	...	...	...	...	...
40—44 ...	**105**	**95**	...	2	102	68	3	25	**797**	**780**	4	20	755	515	38	245	...	...	...	...	...	...	...	...
45—49 ...	**82**	**61**	1	2	77	29	4	30	**502**	**484**	10	16	469	294	23	174	...	...	...	...	...	...	...	...
50—54 ...	**62**	**78**	...	1	58	47	4	30	**487**	**530**	11	14	421	250	55	260	...	...	...	...	...	...	...	...
55—59 ...	**30**	**28**	...	...	25	12	5	16	**230**	**268**	8	12	188	123	34	133	...	...	...	...	...	...	...	...
60 and over...	**81**	**84**	6	4	57	10	18	70	**568**	**706**	18	29	390	138	160	539	...	...	...	...	...	...	...	...
Not Stated...	**1**	**1**	...	1	1	...	...	...	...	**4**	...	4	...	...	...	...	...	...	...	...	...	...	...	...
All ages ...	**2,206**	**2,168**	1,244	1,060	921	896	41	212	**15,647**	**15,784**	8,081	7,061	7176	7091	390	1632	...	...	...	...	...	...	...	...

Table VIII.

CIVIL CONDITION.

TABLE VIII. —*Continued.*

Civil Condition by Religion and Age:—Talappilli Taluq.

Age-period.	All Religions.												Hindu.							
	Total.			Unmarried.			Married.			Widowed.			Total.		Unmarried.		Married.		Widowed.	
	Total.	Males.	Females.	Total.	Males.	Females.	Total.	Males.	Females.	Total.	Males.	Females.	Males.	Females.	Males.	Females.	Males.	Females.	Males.	Females.
1	2	3	4	5	6	7	8	9	10	11	12	13	14	15	16	17	18	19	20	21
0— 4 ...	**19,040**	**9,188**	**9,852**	19,001	9,188	9,813	39	...	39	...	...	...	**6,899**	**7,528**	6·899	7,489	...	39	...	...
5— 9 ...	**17,046**	**8,734**	**8,312**	16,916	8,723	8,193	129	11	118	1	...	1	**6,657**	**6,367**	6,646	6,263	11	103	...	1
10—14 ...	**15,448**	**8,084**	**7,364**	13,749	7,932	5,817	1,692	152	1,540	7	...	7	**6,209**	**5,619**	6,090	4,382	119	1,235	...	2
15—19 ...	**12,791**	**6,189**	**6,602**	6,495	4,831	1,664	6,255	1,351	4,904	41	7	34	**4,811**	**5,247**	3,857	1,337	949	3,891	5	19
20—24 ...	**11,301**	**5,098**	**6,203**	1,908	1,530	378	9,278	3,555	5,723	115	13	102	**4,028**	**4,905**	1,300	311	2,720	4,511	8	83
25—29 ...	**12,815**	**6,120**	**6,695**	804	611	193	11,760	5,461	6,299	251	48	203	**4,809**	**5,317**	525	162	4,257	5,002	27	153
30—34 ...	**10,324**	**5,104**	**5,220**	358	239	119	9,511	4,782	4,729	455	83	372	**4,047**	**4,123**	212	101	3,775	3,756	60	266
35—39 ...	**8,896**	**4,693**	**4,203**	256	155	101	8,106	4,429	3,677	534	109	425	**3,665**	**3,379**	143	83	3,442	2,984	80	312
40—44 ...	**7,777**	**3,821**	**3,956**	208	104	104	6,531	3,575	2,956	1038	142	896	**2,996**	**3,138**	96	90	2,797	2,392	103	656
45—49 ...	**4,824**	**2,491**	**2,333**	133	79	54	3,892	2,288	1,604	799	124	675	**1,926**	**1,856**	70	46	1,773	1,310	83	500
50—54 ...	**5,119**	**2,416**	**2,703**	102	50	52	3,454	2,164	1,290	1563	202	1361	**1,904**	**2,192**	45	46	1,715	1,085	144	1,061
55—59 ...	**2,354**	**1,242**	**1,112**	71	31	40	1,570	1,064	506	713	147	566	**989**	**924**	30	35	852	423	107	466
60 and over ...	**6,094**	**2,506**	**3,588**	154	60	94	2,546	1,811	735	3394	635	2759	**1,965**	**2,930**	55	86	1,424	653	486	2,191
Not Stated ...	**14**	**8**	**6**	8	2	1	2	1	1	4	...	4	**1**	**2**	...	...	1	1	...	1
All ages ...	**133,843**	**65,694**	**68,149**	60,163	33,535	26,623	64,765	30,644	34,121	8915	1510	7405	**50,906**	**53,527**	25,968	20,431	23,835	2,7385	1103	5,711

TABLE VIII.—*Continued.*

Civil Condition by Religion and Age:—Talapilli Taluq.

Age-period.	Mussalman.								Christian.								Jew.							
	Total.		Unmarried.		Married.		Widow-ed.		Total.		Unmarried.		Married.		Widow-ed		Total.		Unmarried.		Married.		Widowed.	
	Males.	Females.	Males.	Females.	Males.	Females.	Males.	Females.	Males.	Females.	Males.	Females.	Males.	Females.	Males.	Females.	Males.	Females.	Males.	Females.	Males.	Females.	Males.	Females.
	22	23	24	25	26	27	28	29	30	31	32	33	34	35	36	37	38	39	40	41	42	43	44	45
0— 4 ...	955	995	955	995	...	...	...	...	1,334	1,329	1,334	1,329	...	...	...	...	...	...	...	...	...	...	...	...
5— 9 ...	885	789	885	784	...	5	...	...	1,192	1,156	1,192	1,146	...	10	...	...	...	...	...	...	...	...	...	...
10—14 ...	805	669	798	582	7	87	...	...	1,070	1,076	1,044	853	26	218	...	5	...	...	...	...	...	...	...	...
15—19 ...	532	568	453	172	79	386	...	10	846	787	521	155	323	627	2	5	...	...	...	...	...	...	...	...
20—24 ...	435	539	141	39	290	489	4	11	635	759	89	28	545	723	1	8	...	...	...	...	...	...	...	...
25—29 ...	528	576	60	19	458	532	10	25	783	802	26	12	746	765	11	25	...	...	...	...	...	...	...	...
30—34 ...	435	417	17	10	410	367	8	40	622	680	10	8	597	606	15	66	...	...	...	...	...	...	...	...
35—39 ...	389	302	4	10	376	250	9	42	639	522	8	8	611	443	20	71	...	...	...	...	...	...	...	...
40—44 ...	323	299	3	10	311	209	9	80	502	519	5	4	467	355	30	160	...	...	...	...	...	...	...	...
45—49 ...	203	164	5	6	190	93	8	65	362	313	4	2	325	201	33	110	...	...	...	...	...	...	...	...
50—54 ...	200	189	2	5	192	64	6	120	312	322	3	1	257	141	52	180	...	...	...	...	...	...	...	...
55—59 ...	86	55	...	3	79	26	7	26	167	133	1	2	133	57	33	74	...	...	...	...	...	...	...	...
60 and over.	189	215	1	6	153	25	35	184	352	443	4	2	234	57	114	384	...	...	...	...	...	...	...	...
Not Stated.	7	3	7	1	...	...	...	2	...	1	...	...	...	...	...	1	...	...	...	...	...	...	...	...
All ages ...	5,972	5,780	3,331	2,642	2,545	2,533	96	605	8,816	8,842	4,241	4,206	4,264	4,203	311	1089	...	...	...	...	...	...	...	...

TABLE VIII.

Civil Condition by Religion and Age.—Chittur Taluq.

Age-period.	All Religions.												Hindu.							
	Total.			Unmarried.			Married.			Widowed.			Total.		Unmarried.		Married.		Widowed	
	Total.	Males.	Females.	Total.	Males.	Females.	Total.	Males.	Females.	Total.	Males.	Females.	Males.	Females.	Males.	Females.	Males.	Females.	Males.	Females.
1	2	3	4	5	6	7	8	9	10	11	12	13	14	15	16	17	18	19	20	21
0— 4 ...	**10,504**	**4,943**	**5,561**	10,495	4,943	5,552	8	...	8	1	...	1	**4,219**	**4,831**	4,219	4,822	...	8	...	1
5— 9 ...	**9,417**	**4,788**	**4,629**	9,383	4,787	4,596	34	1	33	...	...	...	**4,178**	**3,999**	4,177	3,969	1	30	...	...
10—14 ...	**8,778**	**4,536**	**4,242**	8,206	4,507	3,699	561	28	533	11	1	10	**3,916**	**3,696**	3,889	3,199	26	487	1	10
15—19 ...	**7,942**	**3,873**	**4,069**	4,800	3,493	1,307	3,079	378	2,701	63	2	61	**3,395**	**3,601**	3,062	1,148	331	2,394	2	59
20—24 ...	**7,645**	**3,568**	**4,077**	1,990	1,696	294	5,442	1,849	3,593	213	23	190	**3,136**	**3,569**	1,511	265	1,604	3,133	21	171
25—29 ...	**7,788**	**3,671**	**4,117**	622	496	126	6,755	3,118	3,637	411	57	354	**3,245**	**3,581**	440	116	2,752	3,163	53	302
30—34 ...	**6,629**	**3,114**	**3,515**	259	168	91	5,636	2,847	2,789	734	99	635	**2,718**	**3,092**	150	83	2,480	2,445	88	564
35—39 ...	**5,273**	**2,782**	**2,491**	126	71	55	4,343	2,608	1,735	804	103	701	**2,426**	**2,207**	64	50	2,269	1,549	93	609
40—44 ...	**4,981**	**2,531**	**2,450**	92	39	53	3,564	2,333	1,231	1,325	159	1,166	**2,239**	**2,137**	31	48	2,059	1,096	149	993
45—49 ...	**2,631**	**1,417**	**1,214**	47	22	25	1,825	1,294	531	759	101	658	**1,233**	**1,082**	16	24	1,123	474	94	584
50—54 ...	**2,934**	**1,338**	**1,596**	30	16	14	1,543	1,111	432	1,361	211	1,150	**1,183**	**1,395**	13	14	980	384	190	997
55—59 ...	**1,273**	**574**	**699**	15	7	8	662	466	196	596	101	495	**513**	**628**	7	8	411	175	95	445
60 and over.	**2,983**	**1,291**	**1,692**	28	7	21	1,114	896	218	1,841	388	1,453	**1,153**	**1,522**	5	16	787	192	361	1,314
Not Stated.	**6**	**3**	**3**	6	3	3	...	...	...	...	...	...	**1**	**2**	1	2	...	...	...	...
All ages ...	**78,784**	**38,429**	**40,355**	36,099	20,255	15,844	34,566	16,929	17,637	8,119	1,245	6,874	**33,555**	**35,342**	17,585	13,764	14,823	15,530	1147	6,049

TABLE VIII.—*Continued.*

Civil Condition by Religion and Age.—Chittur Taluq.

Age-period.	Mussalman.								Christian.								Jew.							
	Total.		Unmarried.		Married.		Widowed.		Total.		Unmarried.		Married.		Widowed		Total.		Unmarried.		Married.		Widowed	
	Males.	Females.	Males.	Females.	Males.	Females.	Males.	Females.	Males.	Females.	Males.	Females.	Males.	Females.	Males.	Females.	Males.	Females.	Males.	Females.	Males.	Females.	Males.	Females.
	22	23	24	25	26	27	28	29	30	31	32	33	34	35	36	37	38	39	40	41	42	43	44	45
0—4 ...	436	404	436	404	...	...	...	...	288	326	288	326	...	...	...	...	...	...	...	...	...	...	...	...
5—9 ...	382	402	382	399	...	3	...	...	228	228	228	228	...	...	...	...	...	...	...	...	...	...	...	...
10—14 ...	384	337	384	306	...	31	...	...	236	209	234	194	2	15	...	...	...	...	...	...	...	...	...	...
15—19 ...	270	287	250	98	20	187	...	2	208	181	181	61	27	120	...	...	...	...	...	...	...	...	...	...
20—24 ...	294	314	132	16	161	286	1	12	138	194	53	13	84	174	1	7	...	...	...	...	...	...	...	...
25—29 ...	257	317	39	6	215	278	3	33	169	219	17	4	151	196	1	19	...	...	...	...	...	...	...	...
30—34 ...	224	275	11	6	209	226	4	43	172	148	7	2	158	118	7	28	...	...	...	...	...	...	...	...
35—39 ...	221	191	5	4	213	120	3	67	135	92	2	1	126	66	7	25	...	...	...	...	...	...	...	...
40—44 ...	181	188	4	4	172	82	5	102	111	125	4	1	102	53	5	71	...	...	...	...	...	...	...	...
45—49 ...	116	81	4	...	109	35	3	46	68	51	2	1	62	22	4	28	...	...	...	...	...	...	...	...
50—54 ...	96	118	...	...	86	32	10	86	59	83	3	...	45	16	11	67	...	...	...	...	...	...	...	...
55—59 ...	33	47	...	...	30	17	3	30	28	24	...	...	25	4	3	20	...	...	...	...	...	...	...	...
60 and over...	92	109	1	4	72	16	19	89	46	61	1	1	37	10	8	50	...	...	...	...	...	...	...	...
Not Stated...	2	1	2	1	...	...	...	...	...	...	...	...	...	...	...	...	...	...	...	...	...	...	...	...
All ages ...	2,988	3,071	1,650	1,248	1287	1313	51	510	1,886	1,941	1,020	832	819	794	47	315	...	...	...	...	...	...	...	...

TABLE IX.

Education by Religion and Age.

In part (E) of this Table only those Taluqs are shown which contain Jews.

TABLE IX.

Education by Religion and Age. Part (A):—All Religior.

Taluq.	Total Population.			Total by Education.								Age Period.	
				Learning		Literate.		Illiterate.		Not Stated		0—9	
												Total.	
	Total.	Males.	Females.	Males.	Females.	Males.	Females.	Males.	Females.	Males.	Females.	Males.	Females.
1	2	3	4	5	6	7	8	9	10	11	12	13	14
1. Kanayannur ...	**102,033**	**52,454**	**49,579**	4,093	1,210	14,473	3,571	33,865	44,757	23	41	**14,125**	**13,864**
2. Cochin ...	**105,582**	**54,396**	**51,186**	3,960	1,394	16,113	2,378	34,307	47,139	16	275	**14,307**	**14,712**
3. Kotungallur ...	**27,965**	**14,111**	**13,854**	719	97	2,601	213	10,791	13,544	...	...	**4,398**	**4,238**
4. Mukundapuram ...	**145,690**	**72,814**	**72,876**	4,243	901	15,406	1,845	53,150	70,109	15	21	**20,616**	**21,346**
5. Trichur ...	**128,957**	**63,980**	**64,977**	4,623	1,400	16,891	2,872	42,436	60,690	30	15	**17,671**	**18,138**
6. Talappilli ...	**133,894**	**65,719**	**68,175**	4,308	943	14,191	1,928	47,206	65,285	14	19	**17,922**	**18,164**
7. Chittur ...	**78,785**	**38,430**	**40,355**	2,093	247	6,542	761	29,794	39,345	1	2	**9,731**	**10,190**
Total ...	**722,906**	**361,904**	**361,002**	24,039	6,192	86,217	13,568	251,549	340,869	99	373	**98,770**	**100,652**

TABLE IX.—*Continued.*

Education by Religion and Age. PART (A).—**All Religions.**

TALUQ.	Age Period—(*continued*). 0—9-(*continued*). Learning. Males.	Learning. Females.	Literate. Males.	Literate. Females.	Illiterate. Males.	Illiterate. Females.	Not Stated. Males.	Not Stated. Females.	10—14 Total. Males.	Total. Females.	Learning. Males.	Learning. Females.	Literate. Males.	Literate. Females.	Illiterate. Males.	Illiterate. Females.
	15	16	17	18	19	20	21	22	23	24	25	26	27	28	29	30
1. Kanayannur ...	1,822	645	14	7	12,289	13,212	...	...	**6,722**	**5,821**	1,726	461	756	278	4,240	5,082
2. Cochin ...	1,846	805	7	7	12,452	13,739	2	161	**6,645**	**5,937**	1,760	525	841	268	4,044	5,144
3. Kotungallur ...	297	53	...	...	4,101	4,185	...	...	**1,729**	**1,559**	341	36	70	11	1,318	1,512
4. Mukundapuram ...	1,916	516	121	28	18,579	20,802	...	...	**9,743**	**8,656**	1,934	304	779	170	7,030	8,182
5. Trichur ...	1,948	746	159	59	15,552	17,332	12	1	**8,428**	**7,846**	2,045	559	956	250	5,415	7,087
6 Talappilli ...	2,081	525	130	23	15,711	17,616	...	...	**8,084**	**7,364**	1,788	334	630	158	5,616	6,872
7. Chittur ...	959	142	10	2	8,762	10,046	...	...	**4,536**	**4,242**	886	92	246	86	3,404	4,064
Total ...	10,869	3,432	441	126	87,446	96,932	14	162	**45,887**	**41,425**	10,480	2,311	4,328	1,221	31,067	37,893

TABLE IX.—*Continued.*

Education by Religion and Age, PART (A):—**All Religions.**

Taluq.	Age Period—(*continued*).															
	10-14 (*cont*)		15—24										25 and over			
	Not Stated.		Total.		Learning.		Literate.		Illiterate.		Not stat.		Total.		Learning.	
	Males.	Females.	Males.	Females.	Males.	Females.	Males.	Females.	Males.	Females.	Males.	Females.	Males.	Females.	Males.	Females.
	31	32	33	34	35	36	37	38	39	40	41	42	43	44	45	46
1. Kanayannur ...	...	...	9,044	9,242	484	84	3,493	1,049	5,061	8,109	6	...	22,550	20,651	61	20
2. Cochin ...	...	...	9,685	96,94	342	47	4,160	850	5,171	8,734	12	63	23,756	20,841	12	17
3. Kotungallur ...	...	...	2,425	2,630	73	7	730	82	1,622	2,541	...	...	5,559	5,427	8	1
4. Mukundapuram ...	...	...	12,367	13,197	351	72	3,846	618	8,170	12,507	...	...	30,072	29,659	42	9
5. Trichur ...	12	...	11,750	12,311	566	77	4,305	892	6,879	11,341	...	1	26,126	26,672	64	18
6. Talappilli ...	...	...	11,287	12,805	420	64	3,367	636	7,500	12,105	...	...	28,393	29,810	19	20
7. Chittur ...	...	...	7,441	8,146	240	3	1,673	248	5,528	7,895	...	...	16,718	17,774	8	10
Total. ...	12	...	63,999	68,025	2,476	354	21,574	4,375	39,931	63,232	18	64	153,174	150,834	214	95

TABLE IX.—*Continued.*

Education by Religion and Age. PART (A).—**All Religions.**

TALUQ	Age-Period—(*continued*).															
	25—and over (*Continued*).						Not Stated.									
	Literate.		Illiterate.		Not Stated.		Total.		Learning.		Literate.		Illiterate.		Not Stated.	
	Males.	Females.	Males.	Females.	Males.	Females.	Males.	Females.	Males.	Females.	Males.	Females.	Males.	Females.	Males.	Females.
	47	48	49	50	51	52	53	54	55	56	57	58	59	60	61	62
1. Kanayannur ...	10,210	2,237	12,266	18,353	13	41	**13**	**1**	...	...	...	...	9	1	4	...
2. Cochin ...	11,105	1,253	12,638	19,521	1	50	**3**	**2**	...	...	...	...	2	1	1	1
3. Kotungallur ...	1,801	120	3,750	5,306	...	...	...	...	...	...	...	...	...	...	...	...
4. Mukundapuram ...	10,660	1,029	19,355	28,600	15	21	**16**	**18**	...	...	...	...	16	18	...	...
5. Trichur ...	11,471	1,671	14,585	24,970	6	13	**5**	**10**	...	...	...	...	5	10	...	...
6. Talappilli ...	10,014	1,111	18,346	28,660	14	19	**33**	**32**	...	...	...	...	33	32	...	...
7. Chittur ...	4,613	425	12,096	17,338	1	1	**4**	**3**	...	...	...	...	4	2	...	1
Total ...	59,874	7,846	93,036	142,748	50	145	**74**	**66**	...	...	...	...	69	64	5	2

TABLE IX.—*Continued.*

Education by Religion and Age. Part (B):—**Hindus.**

Taluq.	Total Hindus.			Total by Education.								Age-Period. 0—9			
				Learning.		Literate.		Illiterate.		Not Stated.		Total.		Learning.	
	Total.	Males.	Females.	Males.	Females.	Males.	Females.	Males.	Females.	Males.	Females.	Males.	Females.	Males.	Females.
1	2	3	4	5	6	7	8	9	10	11	12	13	14	15	16
1. Kanayannur ...	63,723	32,703	31,020	2,637	764	9,115	2,328	20,930	27,887	21	41	8,468	8,296	1,149	411
2. Cochin ...	52,238	26,973	25,265	1613	424	7,538	908	17,820	23,930	2	3	6,609	6,674	736	237
3. Kotungallur ...	20,056	10,064	9,992	591	96	1,962	202	7,511	9,694	...	...	3,121	3,013	252	52
4. Mukundapuram ...	98,995	49,312	49,683	2,604	498	10,209	1,318	36,491	47,859	8	8	13,597	14,129	1,207	303
5. Trichur ...	93,149	46,127	47,022	3,179	857	11,979	2,040	30,965	44,119	4	6	12,551	12,769	1,313	463
6. Talappilli ...	104,484	50,931	53,553	3,434	766	11,253	1,760	36,243	51,015	1	12	13,556	13,895	1,711	425
7. Chittur ...	68,899	33,556	35,343	1,860	231	5,634	724	26,061	34,387	1	1	8,397	8,830	859	137
Total. ...	501.544	249,666	251,878	15,918	3,636	57,690	9,280	176,021	238,891	37	71	66,299	67,606	7,227	2,028

TABLE IX.—*Continued.*

Education by Religion and Age PART (B):—**Hindus.**

Taluq.	Age-Period—(*continued*).															
	0—9—(*continued*).						10—14									
	Literate.		Illiterate.		Not Stated.		Total.		Learning.		Literate.		Illiterate.		Not Stated.	
	Males.	Females.	Males.	Females.	Males.	Females.	Males.	Females.	Males.	Females.	Males.	Females.	Males.	Females.	Males.	Females.
	17	18	19	20	21	22	23	24	25	26	27	28	29	30	31	32
1. Kanayannur ...	...	...	7,319	7,885	...	...	4,079	3,501	1,107	277	457	171	2,515	3,053	...	...
2. Cochin ...	...	...	5,873	6,437	...	...	3,106	2,720	698	158	356	73	2,052	2,489	...	...
3. Kotungallur ...	...	...	2,869	2,961	...	...	1,201	1,100	274	36	60	11	867	1,053	...	...
4. Mukundapuram ...	119	27	12,271	13,799	...	...	6,405	5,641	1,156	160	539	110	4,710	5,371	...	...
5. Trichur ...	155	48	11,083	12,258	...	...	5,923	5,583	1,403	334	674	170	3,846	5,079	...	...
6. Talappilli ...	129	23	11,716	13,447	...	...	6,209	5,619	1,402	272	564	139	4,243	5,208	...	...
7. Chittur ...	...	...	7,538	8,693	...	...	3,916	3,696	772	86	202	76	2,942	3,534	...	...
Total ...	403	98	58,669	65,480	...	...	30,839	27,860	6,812	1,323	2,852	750	21,175	25,787	...	...

TABLE IX.

Education by Religion and Age. Part (B):—**Hindus.**

Taluq.	Age-Period—(*continued*).													
	15—24										25 and over			
	Total.		Learning.		Literate.		Illiterate.		Not Stated.		Total.		Learning.	
	Males.	Females.	Males.	Females.	Males.	Females.	Males.	Females.	Males.	Females.	Males.	Females.	Males.	Females.
	33	34	35	36	37	38	39	40	41	42	43	44	45	46
1, Kanayannur ...	**5,657**	**5,860**	346	60	2,201	685	3,104	5,115	6	...	**14,495**	**13,362**	35	16
2. Cochin ...	**4,866**	**5,026**	172	18	1,895	348	2,797	4,659	2	1	**12,391**	**10,844**	7	11
3. Kotungallur ...	**1,718**	**1.906**	59	7	570	77	1,089	1,822	...	...	**4,024**	**3,973**	6	1
4. Mukundapuram ...	**8,368**	**9,030**	216	30	2,491	417	5,661	8,583	...	...	**20,932**	**20,875**	25	5
5. Trichur ...	**8,539**	**8,934**	425	50	3,056	633	5,058	8,251	...	...	**19,110**	**19,731**	38	10
6. Talappilli ...	**8,839**	**10,152**	306	49	2,679	587	5,854	9,516	...	...	**22,301**	**23,859**	15	20
7. Chittur ...	**6,531**	**7,170**	222	2	1,464	243	4,845	6,925	...	...	**14,710**	**15,645**	7	6
Total ...	**44,516**	**48,078**	1,746	216	14,356	2,990	28,408	44,871	8	1	**107,963**	**108,289**	133	69

TABLE IX.—*Continued.*

Education by Religion and Age. Part (B).—Hindus.

Taluq	Age-Period—(*continued*). 25—and over (*Continued*). Literate. Males.	Literate. Females.	Illiterate. Males.	Illiterate. Females.	Not Stated. Males.	Not Stated. Females.	Not Stated. Total. Males.	Total. Females.	Learning. Males.	Learning. Females.	Literate. Males.	Literate. Females.	Illiterate. Males.	Illiterate. Females.	Not Stated. Males.	Not Stated. Females.
	47	48	49	50	51	52	53	54	55	56	57	58	59	60	61	62
1. Kanayannur ...	6,457	1,472	7,990	11,833	13	41	4	1	...	...	...	...	2	1	2	...
2. Cochin ...	5,287	487	7,097	10,345	...	1	1	1	...	...	...	...	1	...	...	1
3. Kotungallur ...	1,332	114	2,686	3,858	...	...	...	...	...	...	...	...	...	...	...	...
4. Mukundapuram ...	7,060	764	13,839	20,098	8	8	10	8	...	...	...	...	10	8	...	...
5. Trichur ...	8,094	1,189	10,974	18,526	4	6	4	5	...	...	...	...	4	5	...	...
6. Talappilli ...	7,881	1,011	14,404	22,816	1	12	26	28	...	...	...	...	26	28	...	...
7. Chittur ...	3,968	405	10,734	15,233	1	1	2	2	...	...	...	...	2	2	...	...
Total ...	40,079	5,442	67,724	108,709	27	69	47	45	...	...	...	...	45	44	2	1

TABLE IX.—*Continued.*

Education by Religion and Age. PART (C):—**Musalmans.**

TALUQ.	Total Musalmans.			Total by Education.								Age-Period. 0—9							
				Learning		Literate.		Illiterate.		Not Stated.		Total.		Learning.		Literate.		Illiterate.	
	Total.	Males.	Females.	Males.	Females.	Males.	Females.	Males.	Females.	Males.	Females.	Males.	Females.	Males.	Females.	Males.	Females.	Males.	Females.
1	2	3	4	5	6	7	8	9	10	11	12	13	14	15	16	17	18	19	20
1. Kanayannur ...	5,082	2,656	2,426	178	24	657	59	1,819	2,343	2	...	727	680	69	14	12	4	646	662
2. Cochin ...	5,598	2,847	2,751	129	35	953	131	1,765	2,552	...	33	684	713	40	18	7	7	637	688
3. Kotungallur ...	6,483	3,288	3,195	99	1	454	...	2,735	3,194	...	...	1,070	1,002	34	1	...	...	1,036	1,001
4. Mukundapuram ...	7,041	3,581	3,460	151	16	499	28	2,930	3,415	1	1	1,127	1,159	63	9	2	1	1,062	1,149
5. Trichur ...	4,374	2,206	2,168	158	38	427	47	1,620	2,079	1	4	637	723	46	14	4	11	586	697
6. Talappilli ...	11,752	5,972	5,780	143	11	485	7	5,331	5,755	13	7	1,840	1,784	60	6	1	...	1,779	1,778
7. Chittur ...	6,059	2,988	3,071	127	1	462	14	2,399	3,055	...	1	818	806	55	...	10	2	753	804
Total ...	46,389	23,538	22,851	985	126	3,937	286	18,599	22,393	17	46	6,903	6,867	367	62	36	25	6,499	6,779

TABLE IX.—*Continued.*

Education by Religion and Age PART (C):—**Musalmans.**

TALUQ.	Age-Period—(*continued*).																			
	0—9-(*cont*)		10—14										15—24							
	Not Stated.		Total		Learning.		Literate.		Illiterate.		Not Stated.		Total.		Learning.		Literate.		Illiterate.	
	Males.	Females.	Males.	Females.	Males.	Females.	Males.	Females.	Males.	Females.	Males.	Females.	Males.	Females.	Males.	Females.	Males.	Females.	Males.	Females.
	21	22	23	24	25	26	27	28	29	30	31	32	33	34	35	36	37	38	39	40
1. Kanayannur ...	...	...	368	307	83	6	31	10	254	291	...	...	459	477	20	2	140	16	299	459
2. Cochin ...	...	...	276	282	69	10	38	9	169	263	...	...	540	604	20	5	229	34	291	532
3. Kotungallur ...	...	...	433	382	50	...	6	...	377	382	...	...	576	594	13	...	117	...	446	594
4. Mukundapuram ...	...	...	471	419	68	6	20	4	383	409	...	...	599	607	17	...	133	6	449	601
5. Trichur ...	1	1	306	253	69	15	13	...	224	238	...	...	382	381	31	8	89	18	262	354
6. Talappilli ...	...	...	805	669	64	3	16	...	725	666	...	...	967	1,107	19	2	105	1	843	1,104
7. Chittur ...	...	...	384	337	62	...	20	5	302	332	...	...	564	601	9	...	106	2	449	599
Total ...	1	1	3,043	2,649	465	40	144	28	2,434	2,581	...	...	4,087	4,371	129	17	919	77	3,039	4,243

TABLE IX. *Continued.*

Education by Religion and Age. PART (C):—**Musalmans.**

TALUQ.	Age-Period—(*continued*).																					
	15-24-(*Cont*)		25—and Over.										Not Stated.									
	Not Stated.		Total.		Learning.		Literate.		Illiterate.		Not Stated.		Total.		Learning.		Literate.		Illiterate.		Not Stated.	
	Males.	Females.	Males.	Females.	Males.	Females.	Males.	Females.	Males.	Females.	Males.	Females.	Males.	Females.	Males.	Females.	Males.	Females.	Males.	Females.	Males.	Females.
	41	42	43	44	45	46	47	48	49	50	51	52	53	54	55	56	57	58	59	60	61	62
1, Kanayannur ...	...	...	1,100	962	6	2	474	29	620	931	...	...	2	...	...	...	...	...	...	...	2	...
2. Cochin ...	...	33	1,347	1,152	...	2	679	81	668	1069	...	...	...	...	...	...	...	...	...	...	...	...
3. Kotungallur ...	...	...	1,209	1,217	2	...	331	...	876	1217	...	...	...	...	...	...	...	...	...	...	...	...
4. Mukundapuram ...	...	...	1,383	1,274	3	1	344	17	1,035	1255	1	1	1	1	...	...	...	...	1	1	...	...
5. Trichur ...	...	1	880	810	12	1	321	18	547	789	...	2	1	1	...	...	...	...	1	1	...	...
6. Talappilli ...	...	...	2,353	2,217	...	...	363	6	1,977	2204	13	7	7	3	...	...	...	...	7	3	...	...
7. Chittur ...	...	...	1,220	1,326	1	1	326	5	893	1320	...	...	2	1	...	...	...	...	2	...	...	1
Total ...	...	34	9,492	8,958	24	7	2,838	156	6,616	8785	14	10	13	6	...	...	...	...	11	5	2	1

TABLE IX.—*Continued.*

Education by Religion and Age. PART (D):—**Christians.**

TALUQ.	Total Christians.			Total by Education.								Age-Period. 0—9							
				Learning		Literate.		Illiterate.		Not Stated.		Total.		Learning.		Literate.		Illiterate.	
	Total.	Males.	Females.	Males.	Females.	Males.	Females.	Males.	Females.	Males.	Females.	Males.	Females.	Males.	Females.	Males.	Females.	Males.	Females.
1	2	3	4	5	6	7	8	9	10	11	12	13	14	15	16	17	18	19	20
1. Kanayannur ...	32,801	16,874	15,927	1259	416	4,661	1133	10,954	14,378	...	...	4,877	4,836	592	214	...	...	4,285	4,622
2. Cochin ...	47,121	24,280	22,841	2187	929	7,489	1307	14,590	20,366	14	239	6,953	7,246	1061	547	...	...	5,890	6,538
3. Kotungallur ...	1,426	759	667	29	...	185	11	545	656	...	...	207	223	11	...	...	...	196	223
4. Mukundapuram ...	39,564	19,872	19,692	1488	387	4,690	499	13,688	18,794	6	12	5,876	6,044	646	204	...	...	52,30	5,840
5. Trichur ...	31,434	15,647	15,787	1286	505	4,485	785	9,851	14,492	25	5	44,83	4,646	589	269	...	...	3,883	4,377
6. Talappilli ...	17,658	8,816	8,842	731	166	2,453	161	56,32	8,515	...	...	2,526	2,485	310	94	...	...	2,216	2,391
7. Chittur ...	3,827	1,886	1,941	106	15	446	23	1,334	1,903	...	...	516	554	45	5	...	...	471	549
Total. ...	173,831	88,134	85,697	7086	2418	24,409	3919	56,594	79,104	45	256	25,438	26,034	3254	1333	...	...	22,171	24,540

TABLE IX.—*Continued.*

Education by Religion and Age Part (D):—**Christians.**

Taluq.	Age-Period—(*continued*).																			
	0—9—(*cont*)		10—14										15—24							
	Not Stated.		Total		Learning.		Literate.		Illiterate.		Not Stated.		Total.		Learning.		Literate.		Illiterate.	
	Males.	Females.	Males.	Females.	Males.	Females.	Males.	Females.	Males.	Females.	Males.	Females.	Males.	Females.	Males.	Females.	Males.	Females.	Males.	Females.
	21	22	23	24	25	26	27	28	29	30	31	32	33	34	35	36	37	38	39	40
1. Kanayannur ...	...	...	**2,258**	**1,992**	531	178	265	94	1,462	1720	...	...	**2,879**	**2,870**	116	22	1143	333	1,620	2,515
2. Cochin ...	2	161	**3,225**	**2,915**	981	355	442	186	1,802	2374	...	...	**4,225**	**3,994**	141	23	2011	457	2,063	3,485
3. Kotungallur ...	...	...	**95**	**77**	17	...	4	...	74	77	...	...	**131**	**130**	1	...	43	5	87	125
4. Mukundapuram ...	...	...	**2,865**	**2,589**	710	138	220	56	1,935	2395	...	...	**3,387**	**3,552**	118	42	1219	195	2,050	3,315
5. Trichur ...	11	...	**2,199**	**2,010**	573	210	269	80	1,345	1720	12	...	**2,829**	**2,996**	110	19	1160	241	1,559	2,736
6. Talappilli ...	...	...	**1,070**	**1,076**	322	59	100	19	648	998	...	...	**1,481**	**1,546**	95	13	583	48	803	1,485
7. Chittur ...	...	...	**236**	**209**	52	6	24	5	160	198	...	...	**346**	**375**	9	1	103	3	234	371
Total ...	13	161	11,948	10,868	3,186	946	1324	440	7,426	9482	12	...	15,278	15,463	590	120	6262	1282	8,416	14,032

TABLE IX.—*Continued.*

Education by Religion and Age. PART (D):—**Christians.**

Taluq.	Age-Period—(continued). 15-24 (Cont) Not Stated.		25—and Over. Total.		Learning.		Literate.		Illiterate.		Not Stated.		Not Stated. Total.		Learning.		Literate.		Illiterate.		Not Stated.	
	Males.	Females.	Males.	Females.	Males.	Females.	Males.	Females.	Males.	Females.	Males.	Females.	Males.	Females.	Males.	Females.	Males.	Females.	Males.	Females.	Males.	Females.
	41	42	43	44	45	46	47	48	49	50	51	52	53	54	55	56	57	58	59	60	61	62
1. Kanayannur ...	...	...	**6,853**	**6,229**	20	2	3,253	706	3,580	5,521	...	...	**7**	...	...	...	...	...	7	...	...	...
2. Cochin ...	10	29	**9,875**	**8,685**	4	4	5,036	664	4,834	7,968	1	49	**2**	**1**	...	...	...	...	1	1	1	...
3. Kotungallur ...	...	...	**326**	**237**	...	...	138	6	188	231	...	...	...	...	...	...	...	...	...	...	...	...
4. Mukundapuram ...	...	...	**7,739**	**7,498**	14	3	3,251	248	4,468	7,235	6	12	**5**	**9**	...	...	...	...	5	9	...	...
5. Trichur ...	...	...	**6,136**	**6,131**	14	7	3,056	464	3,064	5,655	2	5	...	**4**	...	...	...	...	...	4	...	...
6. Talappilli ...	...	...	**3,739**	**3,734**	4	...	1,770	94	1,965	3,640	...	...	...	**1**	...	...	...	...	...	1	...	...
7. Chittur ...	...	...	**788**	**803**	...	3	319	15	469	785	...	...	...	...	...	...	...	...	...	...	...	...
Total ...	10	29	**35,456**	**33,317**	56	19	16,323	2197	18,568	31,035	9	66	**14**	**15**	...	...	...	...	13	15	1	...

TABLE IX.—*Continued.*

Education by Religion and Age. PART (E).—Jews.

Taluq	Total Jews.			Total by Education.						Age-Period.											
				Learning		Literate.		Illiterate.		0—9								10—14			
										Total.		Learning.		Literate.		Illiterate.		Total.		Learning.	
	Total.	Males.	Females.	Males.	Females.	Males.	Females.	Males.	Females.	Males.	Females.	Males.	Females.	Males.	Females.	Males.	Females.	Males.	Females.	Males.	Females.
I	2	3	4	5	6	7	8	9	10	11	12	13	14	15	16	17	18	19	20	21	22
1. Kanayannur ...	427	221	206	19	6	40	51	162	149	53	52	12	6	2	3	39	43	17	21	5	...
2. Cochin ...	625	296	329	31	6	133	32	132	291	61	79	9	3	...	...	52	76	38	20	12	2
4. Mukundapuram ...	90	49	41	...	...	8	...	41	41	16	14	...	...	...	...	16	14	2	7	...	...
Total. ...	1,142	566	576	50	12	181	83	335	481	130	145	21	9	2	3	107	133	57	48	17	2

Age-Period—(*Continued*).

Taluq.	10—14 (*Cont*)				15—24								25 and over								Not Stated							
	Literate.		Illiterate.		Total.		Learning.		Literate.		Illiterate.		Total.		Learning.		Literate.		Illiterate.		Total.		Learning.		Literate.		Illiterate.	
	Males.	Females.	Males.	Females.	Males.	Females.	Males.	Females.	Males.	Females.	Males.	Females.	Males.	Females.	Males.	Females.	Males.	Females.	Males.	Females.	Males.	Females.	Males.	Females.	Males.	Females.	Males.	Females.
	23	24	25	26	27	28	29	30	31	32	33	34	35	36	37	38	39	40	41	42	43	44	45	46	47	48	49	50
1. Kanayannur ...	3	3	9	18	49	35	2	...	9	15	38	20	102	98	...	...	26	30	76	68	...	...	...	...	...	...	...	...
2. Cochin ...	5	...	21	18	54	70	9	1	25	11	20	58	143	160	1	...	103	21	39	139	...	...	...	...	...	...	...	...
3. Mukundapuram ...	...	...	2	7	13	8	...	...	3	...	10	8	18	12	...	...	5	...	13	12	...	...	...	...	...	...	...	...
Total ...	8	3	32	43	116	113	11	1	37	26	68	86	263	270	1	...	134	51	128	219	...	...	...	...	...	...	...	...

TABLE X.

Parent Tongue.

TABLE X.

Parent Tongue.

Taluq.	Total Population.			A. Madras Languages														
				Malayalam.			Tamil.			Telugu.			Canarese.			Tulu,		
	Total.	Males.	Females.	Total.	Males.	Females.	Total.	Males.	Females.	Total.	Males.	Females.	Total.	Males.	Females.	Total.	Males.	Females.
1	2	3	4	5	6	7	8	9	10	11	12	13	14	15	16	17	18	19
1. Kanayannur ...	102,033	52,454	49,579	94,342	48,191	46,151	2,995	1,722	1,273	42	31	11	138	105	33	66	48	18
2. Cochin ...	105,582	54,396	51,186	93,569	47,805	45,764	1,311	748	563	45	23	22	336	293	43	53	44	9
3. Kotungallur ...	27,965	14,111	13,854	25,412	12,760	12,652	1,005	534	471	...	...	...	7	5	2	24	14	10
4. Mukundapuram.	145,690	72,814	72,876	139,927	69,743	70,184	3,457	1,810	1,647	416	237	179	48	43	5	20	16	4
5. Trichur ...	128,957	63,980	64,977	124,151	61,455	62,696	2,788	1,437	1,351	989	527	462	109	63	46	10	10	...
6. Talappilli ...	133,894	65,719	68,175	125,148	61,238	63,910	5,388	2,752	2,636	1,851	964	887	1,325	666	659	30	26	4
7. Chittur ...	78,785	38,430	40,355	39,189	19,105	20,084	27,833	13,564	14,269	8,744	4,227	4,517	1,951	978	973	94	60	34
Total ...	722,906	361,904	361,002	641,738	320,297	321,441	44,777	22,567	22,210	12,087	6,009	6,078	3,914	2,153	1,761	297	218	79

TABLE X.—*Continued.*

Parent Tongue.

Taluq.	A. Madras Languages—(*continued*).															B. Other Indian Languages.											
	Nagaram.			Konkani.			Hindustani.			Total, Group A.			Marathi.			Gujarati.			Kachhi.			Total, Group B.					
	Total.	Males.	Females.	Total.	Males.	Females.	Total.	Males.	Females.	Total.	Males.	Females.	Total.	Males.	Females.	Total.	Males.	Females.	Total.	Males.	Females.	Total.	Males.	Females.			
	20	21	22	23	24	25	26	27	28	29	30	31	32	33	34	35	36	37	38	39	40	41	42	43			
1. Kanayannur ...	1	1	...	2,544	1331	1213	244	144	100	100,372	51,573	48,799	1,378	749	629	1	1	...	...	...	...	1,379	750	629			
2. Cochin ...	30	21	9	4,392	2300	2092	190	110	80	99,926	51,344	48,582	4,391	2432	1959	366	262	104	214	...	214	4,971	2,694	2,277			
3. Kotungallur ...	...	...	...	...	...	...	18	16	2	26,466	13,329	13,137	1,499	782	717	...	...	...	...	...	...	1,499	782	717			
4. Mukundapuram ...	...	...	...	360	186	174	92	43	49	144,320	72,078	72,242	1,273	681	592	...	...	...	...	...	...	1,273	681	592			
5. Trichur ...	...	...	...	3	2	1	666	356	310	128,716	63,850	64,866	101	55	46	...	...	...	4	3	1	105	58	47			
6. Talappilli ...	...	...	...	...	...	...	78	40	38	133,820	65,686	68,134	19	9	10	...	...	...	...	...	...	19	9	10			
7. Chittur ...	...	...	...	31	13	18	785	386	399	78,627	38,333	40,294	71	40	31	...	...	...	...	...	...	71	40	31			
Total ...	31	22	9	7,330	3832	3498	2,073	1095	978	712,247	356,193	356,054	8,732	4748	3984	367	263	104	218	3	215	9,317	5,014	4,303			

TABLE X.—*Continued.*

Parent Tongue.

Taluq.	C. Asiatic Languages.												D. Non-Asiatic Languages.																		Not Stated.		
	Arabic.			Hebrew.			Syriac.			Total, Group C.			English.			Portuguese.			Dutch.			French.			German.			Total, Group D.					
	Total.	Males.	Females.	Total.	Males.	Females.	Total.	Males.	Females.	Total.	Males.	Females.	Total.	Males.	Femal es.	Total.	Males.	Females.	Total.	Males.	Females.	Total.	Males.	Females.	Total.	Males.	Females.	Total.	Males.	Females.	Total.	Males.	Females.
	44	45	46	47	48	49	50	51	52	53	54	55	56	57	58	59	60	61	62	63	64	65	66	67	68	69	70	71	72	73	74	75	76
1. Kanayannur ...	47	20	27	2	2	...	1	1	...	50	23	27	134	56	78	69	32	37	2	2	...	...	...	...	2	1	1	207	91	116	25	17	8
2. Cochin ...	34	23	11	261	127	134	...	...	...	295	150	145	12	8	4	349	182	167	...	...	...	...	...	...	3	2	1	364	192	172	26	16	10
3. Kotungallur ...	...	...	...	...	...	...	...	...	...	...	...	...	...	...	...	...	...	...	...	...	...	...	...	...	...	...	...	...	...	...	...	...	...
4. Mukundapuram ...	...	...	...	...	...	...	...	...	...	...	...	...	8	3	5	36	22	14	...	...	...	18	11	7	...	...	...	62	36	26	35	19	16
5. Trichur ...	32	15	17	...	...	...	1	1	...	33	16	17	71	42	29	6	2	4	...	...	...	...	...	...	4	1	3	81	45	36	22	11	11
6. Talappilli ...	38	17	21	...	...	...	...	...	...	38	17	21	...	...	...	4	2	2	...	...	...	...	...	...	...	...	...	4	2	2	13	5	8
7. Chittur ...	...	...	...	...	...	...	...	...	...	...	...	...	39	27	12	26	19	7	...	...	...	2	2	...	...	...	...	67	48	19	20	9	11
Total ...	151	75	76	263	129	134	2	2	...	416	206	210	264	136	128	490	259	231	2	2	...	20	13	7	9	4	5	785	414	371	141	77	64

TABLE XI.

Birth-Place.

Persons born in Cochin are not included in this Table. The following Statement gives their number, together with the total number of those born beyond the State.

Taluq.	Total Population.			Born in Cochin.			Born outside Cochin.			Birth-place not stated or not recognised.		
	Total.	Males.	Females.	Total.	Males.	Females.	Total.	Males.	Females.	Total.	Males.	Females.
1	2	3	4	5	6	7	8	9	10	11	12	13
1. Kanayannur.	102,033	52,454	49,579	99,256	51189	48067	2,763	1261	1507	9	4	5
2. Cochin.	105,582	54,396	51,186	102,380	52605	49775	3,063	1688	1375	139	103	36
3. Kotungallur.	27,965	14,111	13,854	26,750	13557	13193	1,215	554	661	...	...	...
4. Mukundapuram.	145,690	72,814	72,876	144,248	72061	72187	1,427	745	682	15	8	7
5. Trichur.	128,957	63,980	64,977	125,173	61977	63196	3,784	2003	1781	...	...	...
6. Talappilli.	133,894	65,719	68,175	131,666	64760	66906	2,216	953	1263	12	6	6
7. Chittur.	78,785	38,430	40,355	70,012	34735	35277	8,764	3691	5073	9	4	5
Total.	722,906	361,904	361,002	699,485	350884	348601	23,237	10895	12342	184	125	59

TABLE XI.

Birth-Place.

Group.	Birth-Place.	State-Total.			[illegible]: Distribution by Taluq.																					
					Kanayannur.			Cochin.			Kotungallur.			Mukundapuram.			Trichur.			Talappilli.			Chittur.			
		Total.	Males.	Females.	Total.	Males.	Females.	Total.	Males.	Females.	Total.	Males.	Females.	Total.	Males.	Females.	Total.	Males.	Females.	Total.	Males.	Females.	Total.	Males.	Females.	
1	2	3	4	5	6	7	8	9	10	11	12	13	14	15	16	17	18	19	20	21	22	23	24	25	26	
A. Districts or States within the Madras Presidency.	Travancore.	6,844	3,125	3,719	1,894	652	1242	1,745	788	957	600	304	296	572	323	244	1,934	1003	931	68	38	30	31	17	14	
	Malabar.	10,918	4,694	6,224	355	233	122	644	382	262	565	209	356	560	220	340	676	396	280	1,710	710	1000	6,408	2474	3934	
	South-Canara.	236	182	54	65	50	15	55	39	16	12	9	3	44	38	6	23	17	6	28	22	6	9	7	2	
	Nilagiris.	1	...	1	...	...	...	...	...	...	...	...	...	...	...	...	1	...	1	...	...	...	...	...	...	
	Coimbatore.	2,086	1,047	1,040	33	18	15	2	1	1	1	1	...	...	...	...	25	18	7	98	34	64	1,937	975	962	
	Salem.	18	11	7	...	...	...	1	1	...	...	...	...	...	...	...	3	1	2	...	...	...	14	9	5	
	Bellary.	6	3	3	...	...	...	...	...	...	...	...	...	...	...	...	6	3	3	...	...	...	...	...	...	
	Kurnool.	17	13	4	...	...	...	...	...	...	...	...	...	...	...	...	11	7	4	...	...	...	6	6	...	
	Cuddappah.	4	3	1	1	1	...	...	...	...	...	...	...	...	...	...	3	2	1	...	...	...	...	...	...	
	Tinnevelly.	607	446	161	134	115	19	131	106	25	29	24	5	80	60	20	146	87	59	66	38	28	21	16	5	
	Madura.	101	49	52	6	3	3	5	3	2	...	...	...	5	3	2	23	8	15	2	2	...	60	30	30	
	Tanjore.	118	73	45	13	9	4	16	10	6	3	3	...	9	7	2	60	32	28	...	...	...	17	12	5	

TABLE XI.

Birth-Place—*Continued.*

Group.	Birth-Place	State-Total.			Distribution by Taluq.																				
					Kanayannur.			Cochin.			Kotungallur.			Mukundapuram.			Trichur			Talappilli			Chittur.		
		Total.	Males.	Females.	Total.	Males.	Females.	Total.	Males.	Females.	Total.	Males.	Females.	Total.	Males.	Females.	Total.	Males.	Females.	Total.	Males.	Females.	Total.	Males.	Females.
1	2	3	4	5	6	7	8	9	10	11	12	13	14	15	16	17	18	19	20	21	22	23	24	25	26
A. Districts or States within the Madras Presidency (*cont*).	Trichinopoly	99	51	48	25	9	16	5	3	2	1	1	...	2	1	1	62	35	27	...	...	...	4	2	2
	South Arcot.	7	5	2	1	1	...	...	...	...	...	...	...	...	...	...	6	4	2	...	...	...	...	...	...
	North Arcot.	53	31	22	4	4	...	1	1	...	...	...	...	...	...	...	46	25	21	...	...	...	2	1	1
	Chingleput.	5	4	1	...	...	...	...	...	...	...	...	...	...	...	...	5	4	1	...	...	...	...	...	...
	Madras.	805	435	370	169	124	45	7	6	1	1	1	...	37	21	16	243	133	110	172	80	92	176	70	106
	Nellore.	5	3	2	...	...	...	...	...	...	...	...	...	...	...	...	3	2	1	...	...	...	2	1	1
	Kristna.	11	4	7	1	1	...	...	...	...	...	...	...	...	...	...	10	3	7	...	...	...	...	...	...
	Godavery.	19	13	6	5	4	1	...	...	...	...	...	...	...	...	...	14	9	5	...	...	...	...	...	...
	Visagapatam.	69	37	32	3	3	...	...	...	...	...	...	...	...	...	...	66	34	32	...	...	...	...	...	...
	Ganjam.	21	10	11	1	1	...	...	...	...	...	...	...	...	...	...	20	9	11	...	...	...	...	...	...
	Total, group A	22,060	10,169	11,891	2,710	1228	1482	2,612	1340	1272	1,212	552	660	1,309	673	636	3,386	1832	1554	2,144	924	1220	8,687	3620	5067

TABLE XI.

Birth-Place:—*Continued.*

Group.	Birth-Place.	State-Total.			Distribution by Taluq. Kanayannur.			Cochin.			Kotungallur.			Mukundapuram.			Trichur			Talappilli.			Chittur.		
		Total.	Males.	Females.	Total.	Males.	Females.	Total.	Males.	Females.	Total.	Males.	Females.	Total.	Males.	Females.	Total.	Males.	Females.	Total.	Males.	Females.	Total.	Males.	Females.
1	2	3	4	5	6	7	8	9	10	11	12	13	14	15	16	17	18	19	20	21	22	23	24	25	26
B. Provinces or States in India beyond the Madras Presidency.	I. British Territory.																								
	Bengal.	27	23	4	...	...	...	24	21	3	...	...	...	...	...	...	3	2	1	...	...	...	...	...	...
	Bombay.	181	121	60	3	1	2	151	101	50	...	...	...	3	1	2	24	18	6	...	...	...	...	...	...
	Burma.	3	2	1	...	...	...	3	2	1	...	...	...	...	...	...	...	...	...	...	...	...	...	...	...
	Central Provinces.	10	8	2	...	...	...	1	1	...	...	...	...	...	...	...	9	7	2	...	...	...	...	...	...
	Coorg.	8	7	1	...	...	...	1	1	...	...	...	...	...	...	...	...	...	...	...	...	...	7	6	1
	North West-Provinces	19	13	6	...	...	...	16	10	6	...	...	...	...	...	...	3	3	...	...	...	...	...	...	...
	Oudh.	15	14	1	...	...	...	15	14	1	...	...	...	...	...	...	...	...	...	...	...	...	...	...	...
	Panjab.	4	3	1	...	...	...	3	2	1	...	...	...	...	...	...	1	1	...	...	...	...	...	...	...
	India(Unspecified).	494	207	287	38	19	19	16	11	5	1	1	...	108	64	44	259	83	176	71	28	43	1	1	...
	Total I.	761	398	363	41	20	21	230	163	67	1	1	...	111	65	46	299	114	185	71	28	43	8	7	1

TABLE XI.

Birth-Place:—*Continued.*

Group.	Birth-Place.	State-Total.			Distribution by Taluq.																				
					Kanayannur.			Cochin.			Kotungallur.			Mukundapuram.			Trichur			Talappilli.			Chittur.		
		Total.	Males.	Females.	Total.	Males.	Females.	Total.	Males.	Females.	Total.	Males.	Females.	Total.	Males.	Females.	Total.	Males.	Females.	Total.	Males.	Females.	Total.	Males.	Females.
1	2	3	4	5	6	7	8	9	10	11	12	13	14	15	16	17	18	19	20	21	22	23	24	25	26
B. Provinces or States in India beyond the Madras Presidency (*continued*).	II. Feudatory States.																								
	Mysore.	90	74	16	3	3	...	2	2	...	2	1	1	1	1	...	29	18	11	...	...	...	53	49	4
	Hyderabad.	63	34	29	4	3	1	10	7	3	...	...	...	...	...	...	47	22	25	1	1	...	1	1	...
	Baroda.	14	9	5	7	5	2	5	3	2	...	...	...	...	...	...	2	1	1	...	...	...	...	...	...
	Bombay States.	128	113	15	1	1	...	127	112	15	...	...	...	...	...	...	...	...	...	...	...	...	...	...	...
	Central India States.	7	7	...	...	...	...	6	6	...	...	...	...	...	...	...	1	1	...	...	...	...	...	...	...
	Rajputana States.	7	2	5	...	...	...	7	2	5	...	...	...	...	...	...	...	...	...	...	...	...	...	...	...
	French Settlements.	2	1	1	...	...	...	2	1	1	...	...	...	...	...	...	...	...	...	...	...	...	...	...	...
	Portuguese-Settlements.	51	50	1	...	...	...	30	30	...	...	...	...	6	6	...	11	10	1	...	...	...	4	4	...
	Total II.	362	290	72	15	12	3	189	163	26	2	1	1	7	7	...	90	52	38	1	1	...	58	54	4
	Total, Group B.	1,123	688	435	56	32	24	419	326	93	3	2	1	118	72	46	389	166	223	72	29	43	66	61	5

TABLE XI.

Birth-Place:--*Continued.*

Group.	Birth-Place.	State-Total. Total.	State-Total. Males.	State-Total. Females.	Kanayannur. Total.	Kanayannur. Males.	Kanayannur. Females.	Cochin. Total.	Cochin. Males.	Cochin. Females.	Kotungallur. Total.	Kotungallur. Males.	Kotungallur. Females.	Mukunda-puram. Total.	Mukunda-puram. Males.	Mukunda-puram. Females.	Trichur Total.	Trichur Males.	Trichur Females.	Talappilli. Total.	Talappilli. Males.	Talappilli. Females.	Chittur. Total.	Chittur. Males.	Chittur. Females.
1	2	3	4	5	6	7	8	9	10	11	12	13	14	15	16	17	18	19	20	21	22	23	24	25	26
C. Countries in Asia beyond India.	Nipal.	13	5	8	...	...	...	13	5	8	...	...	...	...	...	...	...	...	...	...	...	...	...	...	...
	Ceylon.	7	4	3	...	...	...	5	3	2	...	...	...	...	...	...	2	1	1	...	...	...	...	...	...
	Turkey in Asia.	1	1	...	...	...	...	...	...	...	...	...	...	...	...	...	1	1	...	...	...	...	...	...	...
	Arabia.	11	11	...	...	...	...	11	11	...	...	...	...	...	...	...	...	...	...	...	...	...	...	...	...
	Total, Group **C.**	32	21	11	...	...	...	29	19	10	...	...	...	...	...	...	3	2	1	...	...	...	...	...	...
D. Countries in Europe.	England.	10	7	3	...	...	...	...	...	...	...	...	...	...	...	...	4	2	2	...	...	...	6	5	1
	Scotland.	1	1	...	1	1	...	...	...	...	...	...	...	...	...	...	...	...	...	...	...	...	...	...	...
	France.	6	6	...	...	...	...	2	2	...	...	...	...	...	...	...	...	...	...	...	...	...	...	...	...
	Italy.	1	...	1	1	...	1	...	...	...	...	...	...	...	...	...	...	...	...	...	...	...	4	4	...
	Switzerland.	1	1	...	...	...	...	1	1	...	...	...	...	...	...	...	...	...	...	...	...	...	...	...	...
	Europe (Unspecified).	3	2	1	...	...	...	...	...	...	...	...	...	...	...	...	2	1	1	...	...	...	1	1	...
	Total. Group **D.**	22	17	5	2	1	1	3	3	...	...	...	...	...	...	...	6	3	3	...	...	...	11	10	1
	Not Recognizable.	132	99	33	...	...	...	125	95	30	...	...	...	...	...	...	...	...	...	3	2	1	4	2	2
	Not Stated.	52	26	26	9	4	5	14	8	6	...	...	...	15	8	7	...	...	...	9	4	5	5	2	3
	Grand Total.	23421	11020	12401	2777	1265	1512	3202	1791	1411	1215	554	661	1442	753	689	3784	2003	1781	2228	959	1269	8,773	3695	5078

TABLES XII to XV.

Infirmities by Age.

TABLE XII.

Persons of Unsound mind by Age.

Age-Periods.	State-Total.			Distribution by Taluq.																				
				Kanayannur.			Cochin.			Kotungallur.			Mukundapuram.			Trichur.			Talappilli			Chittur.		
	Total.	Males.	Females.	Total.	Males.	Females.	Total	Males.	Females.	Total.	Males.	Females.	Total.	Males.	Females.	Total.	Males.	Females.	Total.	Males.	Females.	Total.	Males.	Females.
1	2	3	4	5	6	7	8	9	10	11	12	13	14	15	16	17	18	19	20	21	22	23	24	25
0—4 ...	...	...	...	...	...	...	...	...	...	...	...	...	...	...	...	...	...	...	...	...	...	...	...	...
5—9 ...	5	3	2	1	1	...	2	1	1	...	...	...	...	...	...	1	1	...	1	...	1	...	...	...
10—14 ...	5	3	2	1	1	...	...	...	...	...	...	...	3	1	2	...	...	...	1	1	...	...	...	...
15—19 ...	8	4	4	2	1	1	3	1	2	...	...	...	...	...	...	1	...	1	1	1	...	1	1	...
20—24 ...	17	7	10	2	1	1	...	...	...	2	2	...	3	1	2	4	1	3	4	2	2	2	...	2
25—29 ...	27	17	10	4	3	1	3	2	1	1	1	...	8	5	3	4	2	2	3	3	...	4	1	3
30—34 ...	39	22	17	6	3	3	5	2	3	4	1	3	5	2	3	10	6	4	4	4	...	5	4	1
35—39 ...	26	13	13	2	2	...	6	1	5	1	...	1	4	1	3	7	7	...	3	2	1	3	...	3
40—44 ...	34	17	17	1	...	1	5	3	2	3	2	1	6	2	4	9	3	6	6	4	2	4	3	1
45—49 ...	...	...	...	...	...	...	...	...	...	...	...	...	...	...	...	...	...	...	...	...	...	...	...	...
50—54 ...	27	14	13	5	1	4	1	1	...	1	...	1	9	6	3	5	4	1	2	...	2	4	2	2
55—59 ...	...	...	...	...	...	...	...	...	...	...	...	...	...	...	...	...	...	...	...	...	...	...	...	...
60 and over ...	16	8	8	1	1	...	6	5	1	...	...	...	...	...	...	3	...	3	2	1	1	4	1	3
Not Stated ...	9	9	...	9	9	...	...	...	...	...	...	...	...	...	...	...	...	...	...	...	...	...	...	...
Total ...	213	117	96	34	23	11	31	16	15	12	6	6	38	18	20	44	24	20	27	18	9	27	12	15

TABLE XIII.

Deaf-Mutes by Age.

Age-Periods.	State-Total.			Distribution by Taluq.																				
				Kanayannur.			Cochin.			Kotungallur.			Mukundapuram.			Trichur.			Talappilli			Chittur.		
	Total.	Males.	Females.	Total.	Males.	Females.	Total	Males.	Females.	Total.	Males.	Females.	Total.	Males.	Females.	Total.	Males.	Females.	Total.	Males.	Females.	Total.	Males.	Females.
1	2	3	4	5	6	7	8	9	10	11	12	13	14	15	16	17	18	19	20	21	22	23	24	25
0—4 ...	6	4	2	2	1	1	...	...	...	...	...	...	1	1	...	1	1	...	2	1	1	...	...	...
5—9 ...	39	24	15	5	5	...	3	2	1	...	...	...	9	6	3	6	3	3	12	5	7	4	3	1
10—14 ...	34	22	12	3	2	1	2	1	1	2	1	1	8	6	2	9	6	3	8	5	3	2	1	1
15—19 ...	63	35	28	6	2	4	5	4	1	1	...	1	17	8	9	13	11	2	17	8	9	4	2	2
20—24 ...	43	26	17	3	1	2	4	2	2	1	1	...	17	12	5	4	3	1	8	5	3	6	2	4
25—29 ...	40	21	19	7	4	3	8	5	3	...	...	...	8	4	4	5	3	2	10	4	6	2	1	1
30—34 ...	36	25	11	4	2	2	6	5	1	1	1	...	9	7	2	6	2	4	3	2	1	7	6	1
35—39 ...	27	17	10	2	2	...	6	4	2	...	...	...	6	6	...	7	2	5	2	...	2	4	3	1
40—44 ...	40	25	15	5	4	1	6	4	2	1	...	1	6	5	1	6	5	1	10	4	6	6	3	3
45—49 ...	...	...	...	...	...	...	...	...	...	...	...	...	...	...	...	...	...	...	...	...	...	...	...	...
50—54 ...	29	20	9	5	3	2	1	1	...	1	...	1	11	10	1	7	3	4	3	2	1	1	1	...
55—59 ...	...	...	...	...	...	...	...	...	...	...	...	...	...	...	...	...	...	...	...	...	...	...	...	...
60 and over ...	40	21	19	5	3	2	8	5	3	...	...	...	7	4	3	10	6	4	7	3	4	3	...	3
Not Stated ...	...	...	...	...	...	...	...	...	...	...	...	...	...	...	...	...	...	...	...	...	...	...	...	...
Total ...	397	240	157	47	29	18	49	33	16	7	3	4	99	69	30	74	45	29	82	39	43	39	22	17

TABLE XIV.

Blind by Age.

Age--Periods.	State-Total.			Distribution by Taluq.																				
				Kanayannur.			Cochin.			Kotungallur.			Mukundapuram.			Trichur.			Talappilli.			Chittur.		
	Total.	Males.	Females.	Total.	Males.	Females.	Total.	Males.	Females.	Total.	Males.	Females.	Total.	Males.	Females.	Total.	Males.	Females.	Total.	Males.	Females.	Total.	Males.	Females.
1	2	3	4	5	6	7	8	9	10	11	12	13	14	15	16	17	18	19	20	21	22	23	24	25
0— 4 ...	10	6	4	1	...	1	...	...	...	...	...	...	2	2	...	2	1	1	4	3	1	1	...	1
5— 9 ...	43	29	14	4	3	1	1	...	1	1	...	1	6	5	1	18	12		8	7	1	5	2	3
10—14 ...	59	38	21	10	6	4	3	2	1	1	1	...	7	6	1	12	7	5	16	12	4	10	4	6
15—19 ...	58	32	26	7	3	4	3	3	...	1	1	...	11	5	6	15	10	5	13	5	8	8	5	3
20—24 ...	80	47	33	5	3	2	4	4	...	1	...	1	25	18	7	23	12	11	15	7	8	7	3	4
25—29 ...	80	50	30	5	4	1	9	7	2	1	...	1	21	12	9	19	8	11	16	12	4	9	7	2
30—34 ...	75	41	34	8	5	3	1	...	1	3	1	2	21	10	11	19	13	6	19	10	9	4	2	2
35—39 ...	71	41	30	6	2	4	6	5	1	6	5	1	13	7	6	16	10	6	16	9	7	8	3	5
40—44 ...	103	67	36	11	9	2	9	7	2	3	2	1	16	8	8	26	15	11	26	19	7	12	7	5
45—49 ...	...	...	...	...	...	...	...	...	...	...	...	...	...	...	...	...	...	...	...	...	...	...	...	...
50—54 ...	105	52	53	8	3	5	15	11	4	7	2	5	19	8	11	23	11	12	23	13	10	10	4	6
55—59 ...	...	...	...	...	...	...	...	...	...	...	...	...	...	...	...	...	...	...	...	...	...	...	...	...
60 and over ...	179	80	99	15	8	7	18	9	9	6	4	2	28	10	18	46	23	23	46	19	27	20	7	13
Not Stated ...	...	...	...	...	...	...	...	...	...	...	...	...	...	...	...	...	...	...	...	...	...	...	...	...
Total ...	863	483	380	80	46	34	69	48	21	30	16	14	169	91	78	219	122	97	202	116	86	94	44	50

TABLE XV.

Lepers by Age.

Age--Periods.	State-Total.			Distribution by Taluq.																				
				Kanayannur.			Cochin.			Kotungallur.			Mukundapuram.			Trichur			Talappilli.			Chittur.		
	Total.	Males.	Females.	Total.	Males.	Females.	Total.	Males.	Females.	Total.	Males.	Females.	Total.	Males.	Females.	Total.	Males.	Females.	Total.	Males.	Females.	Total.	Males.	Females.
1	2	3	4	5	6	7	8	9	10	11	12	13	14	15	16	17	18	19	20	21	22	23	24	25
0— 4 ...	2	1	1	...	...	...	...	...	...	...	...	...	1	1	...	1	...	1	...	...	...	...	...	...
5— 9 ...	2	1	1	...	...	...	...	...	...	...	...	...	...	...	...	...	...	...	1	1	...	1	...	1
10—14 ...	14	9	5	1	...	1	3	3	...	...	...	...	7	5	2	1	1	...	1	...	1	1	...	1
15—19 ...	19	8	11	2	...	2	6	4	2	2	2	...	4	1	3	1	1	...	3	...	3	1	...	1
20—24 ...	23	17	6	8	7	1	4	4	...	...	...	...	7	5	2	3	...	3	1	1	...	...	...	...
25—29 ...	39	26	13	15	9	6	3	3	...	2	2	...	11	6	5	2	2	...	6	4	2	...	...	...
30—34 ...	43	30	13	10	9	1	6	6	...	2	2	...	10	5	5	6	3	3	9	5	4	...	...	...
35—39 ...	37	28	9	9	6	3	10	9	1	1	1	...	10	7	3	2	1	1	3	3	...	2	1	1
40—44 ...	83	57	26	21	15	6	13	10	3	7	5	2	18	13	5	10	6	4	7	4	3	7	4	3
45—49 ...	1	...	1	...	...	...	...	...	...	...	...	...	...	...	...	1	...	1	...	...	...	...	...	...
50—54 ...	42	31	11	8	8	...	7	6	1	6	5	1	8	3	5	2	1	1	10	7	3	1	1	...
55—59 ...	...	...	...	...	...	...	...	...	...	...	...	...	...	...	...	...	...	...	...	...	...	...	...	...
60 and over ...	45	31	14	11	10	1	5	4	1	1	1	...	12	8	4	6	3	3	5	1	4	5	4	1
Not Stated ...	...	...	...	...	...	...	...	...	...	...	...	...	...	...	...	...	...	...	...	...	...	...	...	...
Total ...	350	239	111	85	64	21	57	49	8	21	18	3	88	54	34	35	18	17	46	26	20	18	10	8

TABLES XII to XV.—*Combined.*

Infirmities.

Age-Periods.	Total Infirmities.			Infirmities.											
				Insanes.			Deaf-Mutes.			Blind.			Lepers.		
	Total.	Males.	Females.	Total.	Males.	Females.	Total.	Males.	Females.	Total.	Males.	Females.	Total.	Males.	Females.
1	2	3	4	5	6	7	8	9	10	11	12	13	14	15	16
0—4 ...	18	11	7	...	...	...	6	4	2	10	6	4	2	1	1
5—9 ...	89	57	32	5	3	2	39	24	15	43	29	14	2	1	1
10—14 ...	112	72	40	5	3	2	34	22	12	59	38	21	14	9	5
15—19 ...	148	79	69	8	4	4	63	35	28	58	32	26	19	8	11
20—24 ...	163	97	66	17	7	10	43	26	17	80	47	33	23	17	6
25—29 ...	186	114	72	27	17	10	40	21	19	80	50	30	39	26	13
30—34 ...	193	118	75	39	22	17	36	25	11	75	41	34	43	30	13
35—39 ...	161	99	62	26	13	13	27	17	10	71	41	30	37	28	9
40—44 ...	260	166	94	34	17	17	40	25	15	103	67	36	83	57	26
45—49 ...	1	...	1	...	...	...	...	...	...	—	...	...	1	...	1
50—54 ...	203	117	86	27	14	13	29	20	9	105	52	53	42	31	11
55—59 ...	...	...	...	...	...	...	...	...	...	...	...	...	...	...	...
60 and over ...	280	140	140	16	8	8	40	21	19	179	80	99	45	31	14
Not Stated ...	9	9	...	9	9	...	...	...	...	...	...	...	...	...	...
Total ...	1,823	1,079	744	213	117	96	397	240	157	863	483	380	350	239	111

TABLES XII—A to XV—A.

Infirmities by Caste.

TABLE XII— A.

Persons of Unsound Mind by Caste.

Class.	Group.	Caste Tribe &c.	Religion.	State-Total.			Distribution by Taluq.																				
							Kanayannur.			Cochin.			Kotungallur.			Mukunda-puram.			Trichur			Talappilli.			Chittur.		
				Total.	Males.	Females.	Total.	Males.	Females.	Total.	Males.	Females.	Total.	Males.	Females.	Total.	Males.	Females.	Total.	Males.	Females.	Total.	Males.	Females.	Total.	Males.	Females.
1	2	3	4	5	6	7	8	9	10	11	12	13	14	15	16	17	18	19	20	21	22	23	24	25	26	27	28
A	1	Nayar ...	Hindu.	38	24	14	4	3	1	2	2	...	1	1	...	7	4	3	13	6	7	8	5	3	3	3	...
„	2(a)	Muthaliar ...	„	2	...	2	...	...	...	...	...	...	...	...	...	...	...	...	...	...	...	...	...	...	2	...	2
„	2(a)	Manayar ...	„	2	1	1	...	...	...	...	...	...	...	...	...	...	...	...	...	...	...	...	...	...	2	1	1
„	2(a)	Vatukan ...	„	2	1	1	...	...	...	...	...	...	...	...	...	...	...	...	...	...	...	...	...	...	2	1	1
„	2(c)	Kanakkan ...	„	1	...	1	1	...	1	...	...	...	...	...	...	...	...	...	...	...	...	...	...	...	...	...	...
„	2(c)	Do	Christian.	7	7	...	5	5	...	2	2	...	...	...	...	...	...	...	...	...	...	...	...	...	...	...	...
„	2(c)	Parayan ...	Hindu.	1	1	...	...	...	...	...	...	...	...	...	...	...	...	...	...	...	...	1	1	...	...	...	...
„	2(c)	Pulayan ...	„	2	...	2	1	...	1	...	...	...	...	...	...	1	...	1	...	...	...	...	...	...	...	...	...
B	5	Brahmin- Empran.	„	1	1	...	1	1	...	...	...	...	...	...	...	...	...	...	...	...	...	...	...	...	...	...	...
„	5	Do Konkan ...	„	5	2	3	...	...	...	1	...	1	4	2	2	...	...	...	...	...	...	...	...	...	...	...	...
„	5	Do Mahratta ...	„	2	1	1	...	...	...	...	...	...	...	...	...	...	...	...	...	...	...	...	...	...	2	1	1
„	5	Do Nampuri ...	„	3	3	...	1	1	...	...	...	...	...	...	...	...	...	...	...	...	...	2	2	...	...	...	...
„	5	Do Pattar ...	„	3	3	...	...	...	...	...	...	...	...	...	...	1	1	...	...	...	...	1	1	...	1	1	...
„	6	Bairagi ...	„	1	1	...	1	1	...	...	...	...	...	...	...	...	...	...	...	...	...	...	...	...	...	...	...
„	7	Ampalavasi ...	„	5	2	3	2	1	1	...	...	...	...	...	...	1	...	1	1	...	1	1	1	...	...	...	...
„	10	Kaniyan ...	„	1	1	...	...	...	...	...	...	...	...	...	...	...	...	...	...	...	...	1	1	...	...	...	...
„	12	Panan ...	„	2	1	1	...	...	...	...	...	...	...	...	...	1	1	...	...	...	...	1	...	1	...	...	...
C	14	Chetti ...	„	3	2	1	...	...	...	1	1	...	...	...	...	...	...	...	1	1	...	...	...	...	1	...	1

TABLE XII. - A — *Continued.*

Persons of Unsound Mind by Caste.

Class.	Group.	Caste Tribe &c.	Religion.	State-Total. Total.	State-Total. Males.	State-Total. Females.	Kanayannur. Total.	Kanayannur. Males.	Kanayannur. Females.	Cochin. Total.	Cochin. Males.	Cochin. Females.	Kotungallur. Total.	Kotungallur. Males.	Kotungallur. Females.	Mukundapuram. Total.	Mukundapuram. Males.	Mukundapuram. Females.	Trichur. Total.	Trichur. Males.	Trichur. Females.	Talappilli. Total.	Talappilli. Males.	Talappilli. Females.	Chittur. Total.	Chittur. Males.	Chittur. Females.
1	2	3	4	5	6	7	8	9	10	11	12	13	14	15	16	17	18	19	20	21	22	23	24	25	26	27	28
C	14	Mappila ...	Mussalman.	15	8	7	3	3	...	3	2	1	4	1	3	1	...	1	1	2	1	3	2	1	...	...	...
,,	14	Ravuthan ...	,,	3	2	1	...	...	...	...	...	...	...	...	...	...	...	...	2	...	...	...	...	...	1	...	1
D	17	Thattan ...	Hindu.	1	...	1	...	...	...	...	...	...	...	...	...	1	...	1	...	1	...	...	...	...	...	...	...
,,	19	Karuvan ...	,,	2	1	1	...	...	...	...	...	...	...	...	...	...	...	...	2	...	1	...	...	...	...	...	...
,,	20	Asari ...	,,	5	3	2	...	...	...	1	1	...	...	...	...	2	1	1	...	...	...	1	1	...	1	...	1
,,	23	Chaliyan ...	,,	1	...	1	...	...	...	...	...	...	...	...	...	1	...	1	...	...	...	...	...	...	...	...	...
,,	23	Kaikolan ...	,,	1	1	...	...	...	...	...	...	...	...	...	...	...	...	...	...	...	...	...	...	...	1	1	...
,,	24	Mannan ...	,,	2	2	...	...	...	...	1	1	...	...	...	...	1	1	...	...	...	...	...	...	...	...	...	...
,,	24	Veluthetan ...	,,	1	1	...	...	...	...	...	...	...	...	...	...	...	...	...	...	...	...	1	1	...	...	...	...
,,	27	Vaniyan ...	,,	1	...	1	...	...	...	...	...	...	...	...	...	...	...	...	...	...	...	...	...	...	1	...	1
,,	30	Katuppattan ...	,,	1	...	1	...	...	...	...	...	...	...	...	...	...	...	...	...	...	...	...	...	...	1	...	1
,,	35	Katakkoti ...	Christian.	2	1	1	...	...	...	2	1	1	...	...	...	...	...	...	...	...	...	...	...	...	...	...	...
,,	35	Mukkuvan ...	Hindu.	2	1	1	...	...	...	2	1	1	...	...	...	...	...	...	...	...	...	...	...	...	...	...	...
,,	35	Valan ...	,,	1	...	1	1	...	1	...	...	...	...	...	...	...	...	...	...	...	...	...	...	...	...	...	...
,,	36	Iluvan ...	,,	49	26	23	7	2	5	5	1	4	3	2	1	8	6	2	15	9	6	3	2	1	8	4	4
,,	36	Do.	Christian.	1	1	...	...	...	...	1	1	...	...	...	...	...	...	...	...	...	...	...	...	...	...	...	...
,,	41	Ottar ...	Hindu.	1	...	1	...	...	...	...	...	...	...	...	...	...	...	...	...	...	...	...	...	...	1	...	1
,,	48	Pattan ...	Mussalman.	1	1	...	...	...	...	...	...	...	...	...	...	...	...	...	1	1	...	...	...	...	...	...	...
,,	52	Native Christians.	Christian.	42	18	24	7	6	1	10	3	7	...	...	...	13	4	9	8	4	4	4	1	3	...	...	...
		Total ...		213	117	96	34	23	11	31	16	15	12	6	6	38	18	20	44	24	20	27	18	9	27	12	15

TABLE XIII—A.

Deaf-Mutes by Caste.

Class.	Group.	Caste Tribe &c.	Religion.	State-Total. Total.	State-Total. Males.	State-Total. Females.	Kanayannur. Total.	Kanayannur. Males.	Kanayannur. Females.	Cochin. Total.	Cochin. Males.	Cochin. Females.	Kotungallur. Total	Kotungallur. Males.	Kotungallur. Females.	Mukundapuram Total.	Mukundapuram Males.	Mukundapuram Females.	Trichur. Total.	Trichur. Males.	Trichur. Females.	Talappilli Total.	Talappilli Males.	Talappilli Females.	Chittur. Total.	Chittur. Males.	Chittur. Females.
1	2	3	4	5	6	7	8	9	10	11	12	13	14	15	16	17	18	19	20	21	22	23	24	25	26	27	28
A	1	Kshatriya ...	Hindu.	2	1	1	...	...	...	1	1	...	...	...	...	1	...	1	...	...	...	...	...	...	...	...	...
"	1	Nayar ...	"	64	41	23	10	8	2	6	4	2	1	...	1	14	11	3	13	9	4	17	7	10	3	2	1
"	2(a)	Goundan ...	"	3	2	1	...	...	...	...	...	...	...	...	...	...	...	...	...	...	...	...	...	...	3	2	1
"	2(a)	Manayar ...	"	1	1	...	...	...	...	...	...	...	...	...	...	...	...	...	...	...	...	...	...	...	1	1	...
"	2(a)	Muthaliyar ...	"	3	3	...	...	...	...	...	...	...	...	...	...	...	...	...	...	...	...	...	...	...	3	3	...
"	2(a)	Vatukan ...	"	2	2	...	...	...	...	...	...	...	...	...	...	...	...	...	...	...	...	...	...	...	2	2	...
"	2(c)	Kanakkan ...	"	7	3	4	1	...	1	...	...	...	...	...	...	...	...	...	2	...	2	3	2	1	1	1	...
"	5(c)	Parayan ...	"	4	3	1	...	...	...	...	...	...	...	...	...	4	3	1	...	...	...	...	...	...	...	...	...
"	2(c)	Pulayan ...	"	15	6	9	2	...	2	1	1	...	...	...	...	7	3	4	...	...	...	4	2	2	1	...	1
"	2(c)	Do.	Christian.	2	1	1	...	...	...	2	1	1	...	...	...	...	...	...	...	...	...	...	...	...	...	...	...
"	4	Malayan ...	Hindu.	1	1	...	...	...	...	2	...	...	...	...	...	1	1	...	...	...	...	...	...	...	...	...	...
B	5	Brahmin-Elayathu.	"	1	1	...	1	1	...	...	...	...	...	...	...	...	...	...	...	...	...	...	...	...	...	...	...
"	5	Do Empran ...	"	1	1	...	...	...	...	...	...	...	1	1	...	...	...	...	...	...	...	...	...	...	...	...	...
"	5	Do Konkan ...	"	2	2	...	1	1	...	...	...	...	...	...	...	1	1	...	...	...	...	...	...	...	...	...	...
"	5	Do Nampuri ...	"	3	2	1	...	...	...	...	...	...	...	...	...	...	...	...	2	2	...	1	...	1	...	...	...
"	5	Do Pattar ...	"	10	5	5	...	...	...	...	...	...	...	...	...	1	1	...	2	2	...	5	2	3	2	...	2

Table XIII.— A

DEAF-MUTES BY CASTE.

TABLE XIII. - A — *Continued.*

Deaf-Mutes by Caste.

Class.	Group.	Caste Tribe &c.	Religion.	State-Total. Total.	State-Total. Males.	State-Total. Females.	Kanayannur. Total.	Kanayannur. Males.	Kanayannur. Females.	Cochin. Total.	Cochin. Males.	Cochin. Females.	Kotungallur. Total	Kotungallur. Males.	Kotungallur. Females.	Mukunda-puram. Total.	Mukunda-puram. Males.	Mukunda-puram. Females.	Trichur. Total.	Trichur. Males.	Trichur. Females.	Talappilli. Total.	Talappilli. Males.	Talappilli. Females.	Chittur. Total.	Chittur. Males.	Chittur. Females.
1	2	3	4	5	6	7	8	9	10	11	12	13	14	15	16	17	18	19	20	21	22	23	24	25	26	27	28
B	5	Pandaran ...	Hindu.	1	1	...	...	...	...	...	...	...	...	...	...	...	...	...	1	1	...	...	...	...	...	...	...
"	6	Ampalavasi ...	"	5	3	2	...	...	...	1	1	...	...	...	...	...	...	...	2	1	1	2	1	1	...	...	...
"	10	Kaniyan ...	"	2	1	1	...	...	...	...	...	...	...	...	...	...	...	...	1	1	...	1	...	1	...	...	...
"	12	Panan ...	"	2	2	...	1	1	...	...	...	...	...	...	...	...	...	...	1	1	...	...	...	...	...	...	...
C	14	Chetti ...	"	13	8	5	...	...	...	3	2	1	...	...	...	...	...	...	2	1	1	3	2	1	5	3	2
"	14	Mappila ...	Mussalman.	19	7	12	4	2	2	1	1	...	2	...	2	4	1	3	...	...	...	8	3	5	...	...	...
"	14	Revuthan ...	"	3	2	1	...	...	...	...	...	...	...	...	...	1	1	...	..	...	...	...	...	...	2	1	1
D	18	Ambittan ...	Hindu.	1	1	...	...	...	...	...	...	...	...	...	...	...	...	...	...	...	...	1	1	...	...	...	...
"	18	Velakkathalavan ...	"	3	1	2	...	...	...	...	...	...	...	...	...	1	...	1	...	...	...	2	1	1	..	...	...
"	19	Karuvan ...	"	5	4	1	...	...	...	...	...	...	...	...	...	4	3	1	1	1	...	...	...	...	...	...	...
"	19	Kollan ...	"	4	3	1	...	...	...	...	...	...	...	...	...	1	1	...	1	1	...	2	1	1	...	...	...
"	20	Asari ...	"	5	4	1	...	...	...	...	...	...	...	...	...	3	2	1	1	1	...	1	1	...	...	...	...
"	21	Musari ...	"	1	1	...	...	...	...	...	...	...	...	...	...	...	...	...	...	...	...	1	1	...	...	...	...
"	23	Chaliyan ...	"	6	5	1	4	3	1	1	1	...	...	...	...	...	...	...	...	...	...	...	...	...	1	1	...
"	24	Mannan ...	"	3	1	2	...	...	...	...	...	...	...	...	...	...	...	...	...	...	...	2	...	2	1	1	...
"	24	Velan ...	"	3	2	1	...	...	...	...	...	...	...	...	...	1	1	...	2	1	1	..	...	...	...	...	...

TABLE XIII. - A — *Continued.*

Deaf-Mutes by Caste.

Class.	Group.	Caste Tribe &c.	Religion.	State-Total.			Distribution by Taluq.																					
							Kanayannur.			Cochin.			Kotungallur.			Mukunda-puram.			Trichur.			Talappilli.			Chittur.		
				Total.	Males.	Females.	Total.	Males.	Females.	Total.	Males.	Females.	Total.	Males.	Females.	Total.	Males.	Females.	Total.	Males.	Females.	Total.	Males.	Females.	Total.	Males.	Females.
1	2	3	4	5	6	7	8	9	10	11	12	13	14	15	16	17	18	19	20	21	22	23	24	25	26	27	28
D	24	Veluthetan ...	Hindu.	3	2	1	1	1	...	...	...	...	...	...	...	...	...	...	1	...	1	1	1	...	...	...	...
„	27	Chakkan ...	„	2	1	1	...	...	...	...	...	...	...	...	...	...	...	...	...	...	...	...	...	...	2	1	1
„	28	Kusavan ...	„	1	...	1	...	...	...	...	...	...	...	...	...	...	...	...	...	...	...	1	...	1	...	...	...
„	28	Odan ...	„	1	1	...	...	...	...	...	...	...	...	...	...	...	...	...	1	1	...	...	...	...	...	...	...
„	30	Katuppattan ...	„	4	2	2	...	...	...	...	...	...	...	...	...	1	1	...	2	1	1	...	...	...	1	...	1
„	35	Aravan ...	„	3	2	1	...	...	...	1	1	...	2	1	1	...	...	...	...	...	...	...	...	...	...	...	...
„	35	Katakkoti ...	Christian.	2	1	1	2	1	1	...	...	...	...	...	...	...	...	...	...	...	...	...	...	...	...	...	...
„	35	Valan ...	Hindu.	2	...	2	1	...	1	1	1	...	...	...	...	...	...	...	...	...	...	...	...	...	...	...	...
„	36	Iluvan ...	„	95	58	37	7	4	3	12	8	4	1	1	...	26	22	4	24	12	12	19	9	10	6	2	4
E	41	Ottar ...	„	2	...	2	...	...	...	...	...	...	...	...	...	...	...	...	...	...	...	...	...	...	2	...	2
F	48	Jew ...	Jewish.	1	1	...	...	...	...	1	1	...	...	...	...	...	...	...	...	...	...	...	...	...	...	...	...
„	48	Pattan ...	Mussalman.	1	1	...	...	...	...	...	...	...	...	...	...	1	1	...	...	...	...	...	...	...	...	...	...
„	52	Native Christians.	Christian.	83	50	33	12	7	5	18	10	8	...	...	...	27	16	11	15	10	5	8	5	3	3	2	1
		Total ...		397	240	157	47	29	18	49	33	16	7	3	4	99	69	30	74	45	29	82	39	43	39	22	17

TABLE XIV.— A

Blind by Caste

Class.	Group.	Caste Tribe &c.	Religion.	State-Total. Total.	State-Total. Males.	State-Total. Females.	Kanayannur. Total.	Kanayannur. Males.	Kanayannur. Females.	Cochin. Total.	Cochin. Males.	Cochin. Females.	Kotungallur. Total.	Kotungallur. Males.	Kotungallur. Females.	Mukundapuram. Total.	Mukundapuram. Males.	Mukundapuram. Females.	Trichur Total.	Trichur Males.	Trichur Females.	Talappilli. Total.	Talappilli. Males.	Talappilli. Females.	Chittur. Total.	Chittur. Males.	Chittur. Females.
1	2	3	4	5	6	7	8	9	10	11	12	13	14	15	16	17	18	19	20	21	22	23	24	25	26	27	28
A	1	Mahratta Sudra ...	Hindu.	2	2	...	...	...	...	2	2	...	...	...	...	...	...	...	...	...	...	...	...	...	...	...	...
„	1	Nayar ...	„	192	95	97	17	7	10	5	4	1	4	3	1	34	18	16	59	34	25	61	25	36	12	4	8
„	2(a)	Agamudian ...	„	1	1	...	...	...	...	...	...	...	...	...	..	...	...	...	...	...	...	...	...	...	1	1	...
„	2(a)	Goundan ...	„	7	4	3	...	...	...	...	...	...	...	...	...	...	...	...	...	...	...	...	...	...	7	4	3
„	2(a)	Manayar ...	„	1	1	...	...	...	...	...	...	...	...	...	...	...	...	...	...	...	...	...	...	...	1	1	...
„	2(a)	Muthaliyar ...	„	1	...	1	...	...	...	...	...	...	...	...	...	...	...	...	...	...	...	...	...	...	1	...	1
„	2(a)	Pillai ...	„	4	3	1	...	...	...	...	...	...	...	...	...	...	...	...	4	3	1	...	...	...	...	...	...
„	2(a)	Vatukan ...	„	5	2	3	...	...	...	...	...	...	...	...	...	...	...	...	2	1	1	...	...	...	3	1	2
„	2(a)	Vellalan ...	„	6	4	2	...	...	...	...	...	...	...	...	...	...	...	...	...	...	...	...	...	...	6	4	2
„	2(c)	Kanakkan ...	„	15	7	8	...	...	...	...	...	...	2	2	...	...	...	...	4	2	2	7	2	5	2	1	1
„	2(c)	Parayan ...	„	10	5	5	1	1	...	...	...	...	...	...	...	...	...	...	1	...	1	6	3	3	2	1	1
„	2(c)	Pulayan ...	„	29	14	15	6	2	4	5	2	3	...	...	...	1	...	1	7	3	4	9	7	2	1	...	1
„	2(c)	Puluvan ...	„	1	...	1	...	...	...	...	...	...	...	...	...	...	...	...	...	...	...	...	...	...	1	...	1
B	5	Brahmin-Elayathu.	„	1	...	1	...	...	...	...	...	...	...	...	...	...	...	...	...	...	...	1	...	1	...	...	...

TABLE XIV.- A— *Continued.*

Blind by Caste.

Class.	Group.	Caste Tribe &c.	Religion.	State Total. Total.	State Total. Males.	State Total. Females.	Kanayannur. Total.	Kanayannur. Males.	Kanayannur. Females.	Cochin. Total.	Cochin. Males.	Cochin. Females.	Kotungallur. Total.	Kotungallur. Males.	Kotungallur. Females.	Mukundapuram. Total.	Mukundapuram. Males.	Mukundapuram. Females.	Trichur. Total.	Trichur. Males.	Trichur. Females.	Talappilli. Total.	Talappilli. Males.	Talappilli. Females.	Chittur. Total.	Chittur. Males.	Chittur. Females.
1	2	3	4	5	6	7	8	9	10	11	12	13	14	15	16	17	18	19	20	21	22	23	24	25	26	27	28
B	5	Brahmin,- Konkan.	Hindu.	5	4	1	1	1	...	3	2	1	...	...	...	1	1	...	...	...	...	...	...	...	...	...	...
,,	5	Do. Nampuri.	,,	13	10	3	...	...	...	...	...	...	1	1	...	4	2	2	4	3	1	4	4	...	...	...	...
,,	5	Do. Pattar	,,	13	5	8	1	1	...	...	...	...	...	...	...	2	...	2	4	1	3	2	2	...	4	1	3
,,	5	Pandaran ...	,,	6	2	4	...	...	...	...	...	...	...	...	...	2	1	1	3	...	3	...	...	...	1	1	...
,,	6	Andi ...	,,	2	1	1	...	...	...	...	...	...	...	...	...	...	...	...	...	...	...	...	...	...	2	1	1
,,	6	Bairagi ...	,,	1	1	...	...	...	...	...	...	...	...	...	...	...	...	...	...	...	...	1	1	...	...	...	...
,,	7	Ampalavasi ...	,,	11	7	4	...	...	...	1	1	...	...	...	...	2	1	1	5	2	3	3	3	...	...	...	...
,,	10	Kaniyan ...	,,	4	3	1	...	...	...	...	...	...	1	...	1	1	1	...	1	1	...	1	1	...	...	...	...
,,	12	Panan ...	,,	3	1	2	...	...	...	...	...	...	...	...	...	...	...	...	1	1	...	2	...	2	...	...	...
C	14	Chetti ...	,,	19	11	8	3	2	1	1	1	...	3	2	1	3	1	2	2	...	2	4	3	1	3	2	1
,,	14	Mappila ...	Mussalman.	31	18	13	1	1	...	5	3	2	7	4	3	4	3	1	5	2	3	9	5	4	...	...	...
,,	14	Ravuthan ...	,,	6	5	1	...	...	...	1	1	...	...	...	...	...	...	...	1	1	...	...	...	...	4	3	1
D	17	Thattan ...	Hindu.	3	3	...	...	...	...	...	...	...	...	...	...	...	...	...	1	1	...	2	2	...	...	...	...
,,	18	Ambattan ...	,,	1	...	1	...	...	...	...	...	...	...	...	...	...	...	...	...	...	...	1	...	1	...	...	...

TABLE XIV. A— *Continued.*

Blind by Caste.

Class.	Group.	Caste Tribe &c.	Religion.	State Total.			Distribution by Taluq.																				
							Kanayannur.			Cochin.			Kotungallur.			Mukundapuram.			Trichur.			Talappilli.			Chittur.		
				Total.	Males.	Females.	Total.	Males.	Females.	Total.	Males.	Females.	Total.	Males.	Females.	Total.	Males.	Females.	Total.	Males.	Females.	Total.	Males.	Females.	Total.	Males.	Females.
1	2	3	4	5	6	7	8	9	10	11	12	13	14	15	16	17	18	19	20	21	22	23	24	25	26	27	28
D	18	Velakkathalavan ...	Hindu.	4	...	4	...	...	...	...	...	...	...	...	...	...	...	...	...	...	...	4	...	4	...	...	...
„	19	Karuvan ...	„	5	5	...	...	...	...	...	...	...	...	...	...	1	1	...	3	3	...	1	1	...	...	...	...
„	19	Kollan ...	„	6	4	2	...	...	...	...	...	...	...	...	...	2	2	...	3	1	2	...	...	...	1	1	...
„	20	Asari ...	„	27	18	9	5	3	2	...	...	...	...	...	8	8	...	...	7	2	5	7	5	2	...	...	...
„	21	Musari ...	„	5	2	3	...	...	...	...	...	...	...	...	...	...	...	...	...	...	...	2	...	2	3	2	1
„	23	Kaikolan ...	„	4	2	2	...	...	...	...	...	...	...	...	...	...	...	...	...	...	...	...	...	...	4	2	2
„	24	Mannan ...	„	11	4	7	...	...	...	2	1	1	1	...	1	1	...	1	4	1	3	1	1	...	2	1	1
„	24	Velan ...	„	1	1	...	...	...	...	...	...	...	...	...	...	...	...	...	1	1	...	...	...	...	...	...	...
„	24	Veluthetan ...	„	4	3	1	...	...	...	...	...	...	...	...	...	...	...	...	3	2	1	1	1	...	...	...	...
„	26	Etayan ...	„	1	1	...	...	...	...	...	...	...	...	...	...	...	...	...	...	...	...	...	...	...	1	1	...
„	28	Kusavan ...	„	2	...	2	...	...	...	...	...	...	...	...	...	1	...	1	1	...	1	...	...	...	...	...	...
„	28	Odan ...	„	1	1	...	...	...	...	...	...	...	...	...	...	1	1	...	...	...	...	...	...	...	...	...	...
„	30	Katuppattan ...	„	19	12	7	...	...	...	...	...	...	...	...	...	...	...	...	10	4	6	8	8	...	1	...	1
„	35	Aravan ...	„	1	...	1	...	...	...	1	...	1	...	...	...	...	...	...	...	...	...	...	...	...	...	...	...

TABLE XIV. A — *Continued.*

Blind by Caste.

Class.	Group.	Caste Tribe &c.	Religion.	State-Total. Total.	State-Total. Males.	State-Total. Females.	Kanayannur. Total.	Kanayannur. Males.	Kanayannur. Females.	Cochin. Total.	Cochin. Males.	Cochin. Females.	Kotungallur. Total.	Kotungallur. Males.	Kotungallur. Females.	Mukundapuram. Total.	Mukundapuram. Males.	Mukundapuram. Females.	Trichur. Total.	Trichur. Males.	Trichur. Females.	Talappilli. Total.	Talappilli. Males.	Talappilli. Females.	Chittur. Total.	Chittur. Males.	Chittur. Females.
1	2	3	4	5	6	7	8	9	10	11	12	13	14	15	16	17	18	19	20	21	22	23	24	25	26	27	28
D	35	Katakkoti ...	Christian.	1	...	1	...	...	...	1	...	1	...	...	...	...	...	...	...	...	...	...	...	...	...	...	...
"	35	Mukkuvan ...	Hindu.	8	5	3	...	...	...	8	5	3	...	...	...	...	...	...	...	...	...	...	...	...	...	...	...
"	"	Valan ...	"	2	1	1	1	...	1	1	1	...	...	...	...	...	...	...	...	...	...	...	...	...	...	...	...
"	36	Iluvan ...	"	158	83	75	15	10	5	9	4	5	11	4	7	40	18	22	35	22	13	31	16	15	17	9	8
"	36	Thandan ...	"	5	2	3	...	...	...	...	...	...	...	...	...	...	...	...	2	1	1	3	1	2	...	...	...
E	41	Ottar ...	"	6	3	3	...	...	...	...	...	...	...	...	...	1	...	1	1	1	...	...	...	...	4	2	2
"	46	Kuruppu ...	"	2	2	...	...	...	...	...	...	...	...	...	...	2	2	...	...	...	...	...	...	...	...	...	...
"	47	Kuruvan ...	"	1	1	...	...	...	...	...	...	...	...	...	...	...	...	...	...	...	...	1	1	...	...	...	...
F	48	Jew ...	Jewish.	1	...	1	1	...	1	...	...	...	...	...	...	...	...	...	...	...	...	...	...	...	...	...	...
"	48	Pattan ...	Mussalman.	2	1	1	...	...	...	...	...	...	...	...	...	...	...	...	...	...	...	1	1	...	1	...	1
"	52	Native Christians.	Christian.	193	123	70	28	18	10	24	21	3	...	...	...	58	31	27	45	29	16	29	23	6	9	1	8
		Total ...		863	483	380	80	46	34	69	48	21	30	16	14	169	91	78	219	122	97	202	116	86	94	44	50

TABLE XV. — A

Lepers by Caste.

Class.	Group.	Caste Tribe &c.	Religion.	State-Total. Total.	State-Total. Males.	State-Total. Females.	Kanayannur. Total.	Kanayannur. Males.	Kanayannur. Females.	Cochin. Total.	Cochin. Males.	Cochin. Females.	Kotungallur. Total	Kotungallur. Males.	Kotungallur. Females.	Mukunda-puram Total.	Mukunda-puram Males.	Mukunda-puram Females.	Trichur. Total.	Trichur. Males.	Trichur. Females.	Talappilli. Total.	Talappilli. Males.	Talappilli. Females.	Chittur. Total.	Chittur. Males.	Chittur. Females.
1	2	3	4	5	6	7	8	9	10	11	12	13	14	15	16	17	18	19	20	21	22	23	24	25	26	27	28
A	1	Nayar ...	Hindu.	52	32	20	13	6	7	6	5	1	5	2	3	13	9	4	9	5	4	5	4	1	1	1	...
„	2(*a*)	Manayar ...	„	1	1	...	...	...	...	...	...	...	...	...	...	...	...	...	...	...	...	...	...	...	1	1	...
„	2(*c*)	Parayan ...	„	9	5	4	1	1	...	...	...	...	...	...	...	2	1	1	...	...	...	6	3	3	...	...	...
„	2(*c*)	Pulayan ...	„	42	25	17	11	8	3	8	6	2	...	...	...	10	5	5	1	1	...	11	4	7	1	1	...
„	4	Ullatan ...	„	1	1	...	...	...	...	...	...	...	...	...	...	1	1	...	...	...	...	...	...	...	...	...	...
B	5	Brahmin-Nampuri.	„	6	6	...	3	3	...	...	...	...	1	1	...	2	2	...	...	...	...	...	...	...	...	...	...
„	5	Do. Pattar ...	„	4	4	...	1	1	...	...	...	...	2	2	...	...	...	...	...	...	...	...	...	...	1	1	...
„	6	Andi ...	„	1	...	1	...	...	...	...	...	...	...	...	...	...	...	...	...	...	...	...	...	...	1	...	1
„	6	Bairagi ...	„	1	1	...	...	...	...	1	1	...	...	...	...	...	...	...	...	...	...	...	...	...	...	...	...
„	7	Ampalavasi ...	„	1	...	1	...	...	...	...	...	...	...	...	...	...	...	...	1	...	1	...	...	...	...	...	...
„	10	Kaniyan ...	„	3	1	2	...	...	...	...	...	...	...	...	...	...	...	...	...	...	...	...	...	...	3	1	2
„	12	Panan ...	„	4	2	2	1	1	...	...	...	...	...	...	...	3	1	2	...	...	...	...	...	...	...	...	...
C	14	Chetti ...	„	6	4	2	4	2	2	2	2	...	...	...	...	...	...	...	...	...	...	...	...	...	...	...	...
„	14	Mappila ...	Mussalman.	22	18	4	5	4	1	4	4	...	3	3	...	3	1	2	2	2	...	5	4	1	...	...	...
„	14	Ravuthan ...	„	3	2	1	1	1	...	...	...	...	...	...	...	...	...	...	...	...	...	...	...	...	2	1	1
D	18	Velakkathalan ...	Hindu,	1	...	1	...	...	...	...	...	...	...	...	...	...	...	...	1	...	1	...	...	...	...	...	...
„	19	Kollan ...	„	4	3	1	1	...	1	...	...	...	...	...	...	1	1	...	...	...	...	2	2	...	...	...	...

Table XV. — A

LEPERS BY CASTE

TABLE XV. A — *Continued.*

Lepers by Caste.

Class.	Group.	Caste Tribe &c.	Religion.	State-Total. Total.	State-Total. Males.	State-Total. Females.	Kanayannur. Total.	Kanayannur. Males.	Kanayannur. Females.	Cochin. Total.	Cochin. Males.	Cochin. Females.	Kotungallur. Total.	Kotungallur. Males.	Kotungallur. Females.	Mukundapuram. Total.	Mukundapuram. Males.	Mukundapuram. Females.	Trichur. Total.	Trichur. Males.	Trichur. Females.	Talappilli. Total.	Talappilli. Males.	Talappilli. Females.	Chittur. Total.	Chittur. Males.	Chittur. Females.
1	2	3	4	5	6	7	8	9	10	11	12	13	14	15	16	17	18	19	20	21	22	23	24	25	26	27	28
D	19	Asari ...	Hindu.	10	8	2	2	2	...	2	2	...	...	...	...	5	4	1	...	...	...	1	...	1	...	...	...
„	21	Kannan ...	„	1	...	1	...	...	...	...	...	...	...	...	...	...	...	...	...	...	...	...	...	...	1	...	1
„	21	Musari ...	„	2	1	1	1	1	...	...	...	...	...	...	...	1	...	1	...	...	...	...	...	...	...	...	...
„	23	Chaliyan ...	„	3	2	1	2	1	1	...	...	...	...	...	...	...	...	...	1	1	...	...	...	...	...	...	..
„	23	Kaikolan ...	„	1	1	...	...	...	...	...	...	...	...	...	...	...	...	...	...	...	...	...	...	...	1	1	...
„	24	Mannan ...	„	7	4	3	1	...	1	1	1	...	...	...	...	3	2	1	2	1	1	...	...	...	...	...	...
„	24	Veluthetan ...	„	3	3	...	1	1	...	...	...	...	...	...	...	...	...	...	1	1	...	1	1	...	...	...	...
„	30	Katuppattan ...	„	6	5	1	...	...	...	...	...	...	...	...	...	2	1	1	...	...	...	3	3	...	1	1	...
„	35	Aravan ...	„	2	1	1	...	...	...	2	1	1	...	...	...	...	...	...	...	...	...	...	...	...	...	...	...
„	„	Valan ...	„	2	2	...	2	2	...	...	...	...	...	...	...	...	...	...	...	...	...	...	...	...	...	...	...
„	36	Iluvan ...	„	78	54	24	15	13	2	13	10	3	8	8	...	21	13	8	8	4	4	9	4	5	4	2	2
E	41	Kallasari ...	„	1	...	1	...	...	...	...	...	...	...	...	...	1	...	1	...	...	...	...	...	...	...	...	...
„	41	Ottar ...	„	1	...	1	...	...	...	...	...	...	...	...	...	...	...	...	...	...	...	...	...	...	1	...	1
F	48	Pathan ...	Mussalman.	1	1	...	...	...	...	...	...	...	...	...	...	...	...	...	1	1	...	...	...	...	...	...	...
„	52	Native Christians.	Christian.	71	52	19	20	17	3	18	17	1	2	2	...	20	13	7	8	2	6	3	1	2	...	...	...
		Total ...		350	239	111	85	64	21	57	49	8	21	18	3	88	54	34	35	18	17	46	26	20	18	10	8

TABLE XVI.

Caste, Tribe, Race, &c.

Persons whose Caste is not returned are not included in this Table. The following Statement gives their Number and Religion.

Caste &c.	Religion.	Total.			Town.			Country.		
		Total.	Males.	Females.	Total.	Males.	Females.	Total.	Males.	Females.
Not Stated.	Hindu.	138	67	71	92	51	41	46	16	30
Do.	Mussalman.	70	70	...	...	...	...	70	70	...
Total.		208	137	71	92	51	41	116	86	30
Stated.		722,698	361,769	360,931	50,455	26,027	24,428	672,243	335,740	336,503
Grand Total.		722,906	361,904	361,002	50,547	26,078	24,469	672,359	335,826	336,533

TABLE XVI.

Caste, Tribe, Race &c.

Class.	Group.	Caste, Tribe, Race &c.	Religion.	No. of recorded sub-divisions.	Total.			Town.			Country.		
					Total.	Males.	Females.	Total.	Males.	Females.	Total.	Males.	Females.
1	2	3	4	5	6	7	8	9	10	11	12	13	14
A. Agriculture.	1. Military and Dominant.	1. Bhattiya ...	Hindu.	1	155	97	58	129	80	49	26	17	9
		2. Kshatriya ...	„	6	902	442	460	49	30	19	853	412	441
		3. Mahratta Sudra ...	„	1	75	71	4	41	37	4	34	34	...
		4. Maravar ...	„	1	57	24	33	...	...	...	57	24	33
		5. Naickar ...	„	2	147	74	73	67	34	33	80	40	40
		6. Nayar ...	„	55	101,691	48,930	52,761	6,497	3,401	3,096	95,194	45,529	49,665
		7. Rajput ...	„	1	64	55	9	59	53	6	5	2	3
		8. Raju ...	„	1	88	38	50	44	22	22	44	16	28
		9. Samanthan ...	„	4	274	131	143	58	35	23	216	96	120
		Total, group 1 — 9	„	72	103,453	49,862	53,591	6,944	3,692	3,252	96,509	46,170	50,339
	2(a). Cultivators.	1. Agamudiyan ...	Hindu.	2	265	127	138	63	25	38	202	102	100
		2. Augani ...	„	1	2	...	2	2	...	2	...	...	...
		3. Arasu ...	„	3	314	154	160	26	13	13	288	141	147
		4. Goundan ...	„	8	3,080	1,488	1,592	71	33	38	3,009	1,455	1,554
		5. Do. ...	Christian.	1	7	4	3	...	...	...	7	4	3

TABLE XVI.

Caste, Tribe, Race &c.

Class.	Group.	Caste, Tribe, Race &c.	Religion.	No. of recorded sub-divisions.	Total.			Town.			Country.		
					Total.	Males.	Females.	Total.	Males.	Females.	Total.	Males.	Females.
1	2	3	4	5	6	7	8	9	10	11	12	13	14
A. Agriculture—(Continued.)	2(a). Cultivators—(Continued.)	6. Kallar ...	Hindu.	1	32	14	18	...	...	...	32	14	18
		7. Kapu ...	„	2	19	8	11	7	3	4	12	5	7
		8. Kotikar ...	„	1	30	17	13	17	10	7	13	7	6
		9. Manayar ...	„	2	91	38	53	21	11	10	70	27	43
		10. Mathiya ...	„	1	7	4	3	7	4	3	...	...	...
		11. Mupanar ...	„	1	1	1	...	1	1	...	...	...	...
		12. Mupan ...	„	1	1	...	1	1	...	1	...	...	...
		13. Muthaliyar ...	„	1	137	72	65	27	15	12	110	57	53
		14. Do. ...	Christian.	1	5	3	2	...	...	...	5	3	2
		15. Nayadu ...	Hindu.	1	126	61	65	101	50	51	25	11	14
		16. Okkiliyan ...	„	2	81	46	35	...	...	...	81	46	35
		17. Pillai ...	„	4	1,305	655	650	553	301	252	752	354	398
		18. Reddi ...	„	3	40	17	23	9	4	5	31	13	18
		19. Sathan ...	„	1	1	1	...	1	1	...	...	...	...
		20. Sami ...	„	1	7	3	4	7	3	4	...	...	...
		21. Thelinga ...	„	2	6	3	3	6	3	3	...	...	...

TABLE XVI.

Caste, Tribe, Race &c.

Class.	Group.	Caste, Tribe, Race &c.	Religion.	No. of recorded subdivisions.	Total.			Town.			Country.		
					Total.	Males.	Females.	Total.	Males.	Females.	Total.	Males.	Females.
1	2	3	4	5	6	7	8	9	10	11	12	13	14
A. Agriculture—(*Continued.*)	2(*a*). Cultivators—(*Continued.*)	22. Thottiyar ...	Hindu.	2	318	147	171	67	37	30	251	110	141
		23. Utayar ...	"	1	53	26	27	12	6	6	41	20	21
		24. Vanniar ...	"	1	5	4	1	...	...	...	5	4	1
		25. Vatukar ...	"	3	988	472	516	106	51	55	882	421	461
		26. Velambar ...	"	1	21	11	10	...	...	...	21	11	10
		27. Vellalar ...	"	5	2,868	1,402	1,466	750	389	361	2,118	1,013	1,105
		28. Do. ...	Christian.	1	183	97	86	17	7	10	166	90	76
		Total, group, 2 (*a*) 28.		53	9,993	4,875	5,118	1,872	967	905	8,121	3,908	4,213
	2(*b*). Cattle-Breeders and Graziers.	1. Kammatiyar ...	Hindu.	1	56	33	23	...	...	...	56	33	23
		Total, group, 2 (*b*)— 1.		1	56	33	23	...	...	...	56	33	23
	2(*c*). Field Labourers.	1. Cherumar ...	Hindu.	3	14,696	7,070	7,626	17	9	8	14,679	7,061	7,618
		2. Kanakkan ...	"	5	9,926	4,981	4,945	176	93	83	9,750	4,888	4,862
		3. Kuttan ...	"	1	520	259	261	...	...	...	520	259	261
		4. Parayan ...	"	3	6,245	3,193	3,052	36	18	18	6,209	3,175	3,034

TABLE XVI.

Caste, Tribe, Race &c.

Class.	Group.	Caste, Tribe, Race &c.	Religion.	No. of recorded sub-divisions.	Total.			Town.			Country.		
					Total.	Males.	Females.	Total.	Males.	Females.	Total.	Males.	Females.
1	2	3	4	5	6	7	8	9	10	11	12	13	14
A. Agriculture—(Continued.)	2(c) Field Labourers. (Continued.)	7. Pulayan ...	Hindu.	4	36,555	18,092	18,463	255	137	118	36,300	17,955	18,345
		8. Paluvan ...	„	2	61	28	33	8	6	2	53	22	31
		9. Sakalli ...	„	1	4	3	1	4	3	1	...	...	...
		10. Thevar ...	„	1	17	13	4	8	4	4	9	9	...
		11. Uppiliyan ...	„	1	15	9	6	...	...	...	15	9	6
		12. Vettuwan ...	„	1	747	367	380	68	29	39	679	338	341
		Total Group 2(c)— 12	„	22	68,786	34,015	34,771	572	299	273	68,214	33,716	34,498
	4. Forest and Hill Tribes	1. Katar ...	Hindu.	1	221	94	127	...	...	...	221	94	127
		2. Kurumbar ...	„	1	150	73	77	6	2	4	144	71	73
		3. Malayar ...	„	4	3,094	1,543	1,551	2	2	...	3,092	1,541	1,551
		4. Nayati ...	„	1	123	61	62	...	...	...	123	61	62
		5. Ullatan ...	„	1	439	208	231	...	...	...	439	208	231
		Total Group 4— 5	„	8	4,027	1,979	2,048	8	4	4	4,019	1,975	2,044
		Total, Class A. 50		156	186,315	90,764	95,551	9,396	4,962	4,434	176,919	85,802	91,117

TABLE XVI.

Caste, Tribe, Race &c.

Class.	Group.	Caste, Tribe, Race &c.	Religion.	No. of recorded subdivisions.	Total.			Town.			Country.		
					Total.	Males.	Females.	Total.	Males.	Females.	Total.	Males.	Females.
1	2	3	4	5	6	7	8	9	10	11	12	13	14
B. Professional.	5. Priests.	1. Brahmin,- Aiyenkar...	Hindu.	1	50	26	24	31	18	13	19	8	11
		2. Do. Elayathu ...	„	2	845	430	405	65	38	27	770	392	378
		3. Do. Empranthiri.	„	1	495	390	105	43	33	10	452	357	95
		4. Do. Gauda ...	„	2	1,256	651	605	103	50	53	1,153	601	552
		5. Do. Konkan ...	„	6	6,086	3,208	2,878	2,071	1,058	1,013	4,015	2,150	1,865
		6. Do. Madhwa ...	„	2	. 103	62	41	54	36	18	49	26	23
		7. Do. Nampuri ...	„	5	5,002	2,647	2,355	412	251	161	4,590	2,396	2,194
		8. Do. Pattar ...	„	4	12,151	6,235	5,916	4,104	2,173	1,931	8,047	4,062	3,985
		9. Do. Others ...	„	6	245	138	107	154	96	58	91	42	49
		10. Pandaram ...	„	3	341	166	175	45	25	20	296	141	155
		11. Saiad ...	Mussalman.	1	18	12	6	8	5	3	10	7	3
		12. Valluvan ...	Hindu.	1	565	262	303	...	...	...	565	262	303
		Total, Group 5— 12		34	27,147	14,227	12,920	7,090	3,783	3,307	20,057	10,444	9,613

TABLE XVI.

Caste, Tribe, Race &c.

Class.	Group.	Caste, Tribe, Race &c.	Religion.	No. of recorded sub-divisions.	Total. Total.	Total. Males.	Total. Females.	Town. Total.	Town. Males.	Town. Females.	Country. Total.	Country. Males.	Country. Females.
1	2	3	4	5	6	7	8	9	10	11	12	13	14
B. Professional—(Continued.)	6. Devotees.	1. Andi ...	Hindu.	5	432	191	241	60	18	42	372	173	199
		2. Bairagi ...	"	1	98	80	18	62	51	11	36	29	7
		3. Dasar ...	"	1	16	10	6	16	10	6	...	...	...
		Total, Group, 6 — 3		7	546	281	265	138	79	59	408	202	206
	7. Temple Servants.	1. Ampalavasi ...	Hindu.	17	7,096	3,520	3,576	794	393	401	6,302	3,127	3,175
		2. Ampalavanavar ...	"	1	13	9	4	...	...	...	13	9	4
		3. Malakaran ...	"	1	70	38	32	22	11	11	48	27	21
		Total, Group, 7— 3		19	7,179	3,567	3,612	816	404	412	6,363	3,163	3,200
	10. Astrologers.	1. Kaniyan ...	Hindu.	6	2,522	1,261	1,261	68	32	36	2,454	1,229	1,225
		Total, Group, 10 — 1		6	2,522	1,261	1,261	68	32	36	2,454	1,229	1,225
	12. Dancers and Singers.	1. Panan ...	Hindu.	3	2,398	1,201	1,197	101	54	47	2,297	1,147	1,150
		Total, Group, 12 — 1		3	2,398	1,201	1,197	101	54	47	2,297	1,147	1,150
	13. Actors and Mimes.	1. Chakiyar ...	Hindu.	1	8	8	...	2	2	...	6	6	...
		2. Nampiyar ...	"	1	39	14	25	11	5	6	28	9	19
		Total, Group, 13 — 2		2	47	22	25	13	7	6	34	15	19
		Total, Class, B. 22		71	39,839	20,559	19,280	8,226	4,359	3,867	31,613	16,200	15,413

TABLE XVI.

Caste, Tribe, Race &c.

Class.	Group.	Caste, Tribe, Race &c.	Religion.	No. of recorded subdivisions.	Total.			Town.			Country.		
					Total.	Males.	Females.	Total.	Males.	Females.	Total.	Males.	Females.
1	2	3	4	5	6	7	8	9	10	11	12	13	14
C. Commerce.	14. Traders.	1. Bahja ...	Hindu.	5	40	25	15	29	19	10	11	6	5
		2. Baniya ...	"	1	147	88	59	127	79	48	20	9	11
		3. Chetty. ...	"	22	20,218	10,522	9,696	1,760	915	845	18,458	9,607	8,851
		4. Mappila ...	Mussalman.	1	36,393	18,510	17,883	3,701	18,43	1,858	32,692	16,667	16,025
		5. Ravuthan ...	"	1	6,486	3,215	3,271	746	419	327	5,740	2,796	2,944
		6. Tharakan ...	Hindu.	2	593	278	315	187	82	105	406	196	210
		7. Vaisya ...	"	3	61	34	27	42	22	20	19	12	7
		Total, Group, 14 — 7		35	63,938	32,672	31,266	6,592	3,379	3,213	57,346	29,293	28,053
		Total, Class, C. 7		35	63,938	32,672	31,266	6,592	3,379	3,213	57,346	29,293	28,053

TABLE XVI.

Caste, Tribe, Race &c.

Class.	Group.	Caste, Tribe, Race &c.	Religion.	No. of recorded sub-divisions.	Total. Total.	Total. Males.	Total. Females.	Town. Total.	Town. Males.	Town. Females.	Country. Total.	Country. Males.	Country. Females.
1	2	3	4	5	6	7	8	9	10	11	12	13	14
D. Artisan and Village Menial.	17. Goldsmiths.	1. Thattan ...	Hindu.	4	5,173	2,634	2,539	711	360	351	4,462	2,274	2,188
		Total, Group, 17 — 1		4	5,173	2,634	2,539	711	360	351	4,462	2,274	2,188
	18. Barbers.	1. Ambattan ...	Hindu.	3	1,354	709	645	256	133	123	1,098	576	522
		2. Do. ...	Christian.	1	8	5	3	8	5	3	...	...	...
		3. Kavuthiyan ...	Hindu.	1	10	6	4	...	...	....	10	6	4
		4. Mangala ...	"	2	6	5	1	6	5	1	...	...	...
		5. Pittilan ...	"	1	11	4	7	...	...	...	11	4	7
		6. Vathi ...	"	2	692	355	337	...	...	...	692	355	337
		7. Velakkathalavan ...	"	1	2,299	1,083	1,216	158	79	79	2,141	1,004	1,137
		Total, Group, 18 — 7		11	4,380	2,167	2,213	428	222	206	3,952	1,945	2,007
	19. Blacksmiths.	1. Karuvan ...	Hindu.	1	2,741	1,356	1,385	65	27	38	2,676	1,329	1,347
		2. Kollan ...	"	6	3,804	1,867	1,937	188	94	94	3,616	1,773	1,843
		Total, Group, 19 — 2		7	6,545	3,223	3,322	253	121	132	6,292	3,102	3,190
	20. Carpenters and Turners.	1. Aasari ...	Hindu.	2	14,618	7,230	7,388	528	269	259	14,090	6,961	7,129
		2. Do. ...	Christian.	1	5	3	2	5	3	2	...	...	...
		Total, Group, 20 — 2		3	14,623	7,233	7,390	533	272	261	14,090	6,961	7,129

TABLE XVI.

Caste, Tribe, Race &c.

Class.	Group.	Caste, Tribe, Race &c.	Religion.	No. of recorded sub-divisions.	Total.			Town.			Country.		
					Total.	Males.	Females.	Total.	Males.	Females.	Total.	Males.	Females.
1	2	3	4	5	6	7	8	9	10	11	12	13	14
D. Artisan and Village Menial—(*Continued.*)	21. Brass and Copper Smiths.	1. Kannan ...	Hindu.	1	243	127	116	90	47	43	153	80	73
		2. Musari ...	„	1	786	378	408	74	38	36	712	340	372
		Total, Group, 21 — 2		2	1,029	505	524	164	85	79	865	420	445
	23. Weavers.	1. Chaliyan ...	Hindu.	1	1,586	806	780	140	79	61	1,446	727	719
		2. Chetan. ...	„	3	2,033	994	1,039	346	176	170	1,687	818	869
		3. Do. ...	Christian.	1	17	9	8	...	...	...	17	9	8
		4. Kaikolan ...	Hindu.	2	3,645	1,782	1,863	771	403	368	2,874	1,379	1,495
		5. Do. ...	Christian.	1	36	19	17	5	3	2	31	16	15
		Total, Group, 23 — 5		8	7,317	3,610	3,707	1,262	661	601	6,055	2,949	3,106
	24. Washermen.	1. Mannan ...	Hindu.	2	4,978	2,431	2,547	163	77	86	4,815	2,354	2,461
		2. Do. ...	Christian.	1	14	7	7	14	7	7	...	...	...
		3. Velan ...	Hindu.	1	2,524	1,269	1,255	235	118	117	2,289	1,151	1,138
		4. Veluthetan ...	„	1	2,989	1,390	1,599	120	58	62	2,869	1,332	1,537
		Total, Group, 24 — 4		5	10,505	5,097	5,408	532	260	272	9,973	4,837	5,136

TABLE XVI.

Caste, Tribe, Race &c.

Class.	Group.	Caste, Tribe, Race &c.	Religion.	No. of recorded sub-divisions.	Total.			Town.			Country.		
					Total.	Males.	Females.	Total.	Males.	Females.	Total.	Males.	Females.
1	2	3	4	5	6	7	8	9	10	11	12	13	14
D. Artisan and Village Menial—(Continued.)	26. Shepherds and Wool-weavers.	1. Etayan ...	Hindu.	2	116	72	44	40	23	17	76	49	27
		2. Golla ...	"	2	5	3	2	5	3	2	...	...	...
		3. Konan ...	"	2	223	106	117	76	52	24	147	54	93
		4. Yedagulu ...	"	1	1	1	...	1	1	...	...	...	...
		Total, Group, 26 — 4		7	345	182	163	122	79	43	223	103	120
	27. Oil-Pressers.	1. Chakkan ...	Hindu.	2	1,068	507	561	155	73	82	913	434	479
		2. Vaniyan ...	"	1	683	360	323	79	36	43	604	324	280
		3. Do. ...	Christian.	1	2,570	1,264	1,306	263	129	134	2,307	1,135	1,172
		Total, Group, 27 — 3		4	4,321	2,131	2,190	497	238	259	3,824	1,893	1,931
	28. Potters.	1. Kusavan ...	Hindu.	3	2,168	1,143	1,025	162	82	80	2,006	1,061	945
		2. Otan ...	"	1	657	342	315	28	15	13	629	327	302
		Total, Group, 28 — 2		4	2,825	1,485	1,340	190	97	93	2,635	1,388	1,247
	30. Salt &c. Workers.	1. Katuppattan ...	Hindu.	3	11,796	5,866	5,930	60	26	34	11,736	5,840	5,896
		Total, Group, 30 — 1		3	11,796	5,866	5,630	60	26	34	11,736	5,840	5,896
	35. Fishermen, Boatmen &c.	1. Aravan ...	Hindu.	1	3,093	1,568	1,525	60	32	28	3,033	1,536	1,497
		2. Katakkoti ...	Christian.	1	1,815	931	884	77	41	36	1,738	890	848
		3. Marakkan ...	Hindu.	1	37	24	13	7	7	...	30	17	13

TABLE XVI.

Caste, Tribe, Race &c.

Class.	Group.	Caste, Tribe, Race &c.	Religion.	No. of recorded sub-divisions.	Total. Total.	Total. Males.	Total. Females.	Town. Total.	Town. Males.	Town. Females.	Country. Total.	Country. Males.	Country. Females.
1	2	3	4	5	6	7	8	9	10	11	12	13	14
D. Artisan and Village Menial—(Continued.)	35. Fishermen, Boatmen, Palki-bearers, Cooks &c.	4. Mukkuvan ...	Hindu.	1	1,436	753	683	10	7	3	1,426	746	680
		5. Do. ...	Christian.	1	5	2	3	5	2	3	...	...	...
		6. Paravan ...	Hindu.	1	28	10	18	...	...	...	28	10	18
		7. Pondan ...	„	1	155	82	73	17	14	3	138	68	70
		8. Valan ...	„	1	6,157	3,177	2,980	417	219	198	5,740	2,958	2,782
		Total, Group, 35 — 8		8	12,726	6,547	6,179	593	322	271	12,133	6,225	5,908
	36. Distillers, and Toddy-Drawers.	1. Chanan ...	Hindu.	1	101	45	56	8	5	3	93	40	53
		2. Iluvan ...	„	3	167,467	84,151	83,316	4,414	2,227	2,187	163,053	81,924	81,129
		3. Thandan ...	„	1	1,690	820	870	19	12	7	1,671	808	863
		4. Thiyyan ...	„	1	111	48	63	...	...	...	111	48	63
		Total, Group, 36 — 4		6	169,369	85,064	84,305	4,441	2,244	2,197	164,928	82,820	82,108
	38. Leather Workers.	1. Chakkiliyan ...	Hindu.	1	696	364	332	46	24	22	650	340	310
		2. Do. ...	Christian.	1	37	19	18	37	19	18	...	...	...
		3. Tholkollan ...	Hindu.	1	698	360	338	7	5	2	691	355	336
		Total, Group, 38 — 3		3	1,431	743	688	90	48	42	1,341	695	646
		Total, Class, D.		76	252,385	126,487	125,898	9,876	5,035	4,841	242,509	121,452	121,057

TABLE XVI.

Caste, Tribe, Race &c.

Class.	Group.	Caste, Tribe, Race &c.	Religion.	No. of recorded sub-divisions.	Total.			Town.			Country.		
					Total.	Males.	Females.	Total.	Males.	Females.	Total.	Males.	Females.
1	2	3	4	5	6	7	8	9	10	11	12	13	14
E. Miscellaneous and Disreputable Livers.	40. Grind stone makers and Quarriers.	1. Kallandi ...	Hindu.	1	138	53	85	...	...	...	138	53	85
		2. Mannottan ...	"	1	145	71	74	19	9	10	126	62	64
		Total, Group, 40 — 2		2	283	124	159	19	9	10	264	115	149
	41. Earth-Workers and Stone-Dressers.	1. Kallan ...	Hindu.	1	254	133	121	27	15	12	227	118	109
		2. Kallassri ...	"	1	1,210	574	636	91	52	39	1,119	522	597
		3. Otta-Naickan ...	"	6	2,719	1,386	1,333	202	109	93	2,517	1,277	1,240
		Total, Group, 41 — 3		8	4,183	2,093	2,090	320	176	144	3,863	1,917	1,946
	45. Miscellaneous Disreputable Livers.	1. Dasi ...	Hindu.	4	252	86	166	63	20	43	189	66	123
		Total, Group, 45 — 1		4	252	86	166	63	20	43	189	66	123
	46. Tumblers and Acrobats.	1. Kotanki ...	Hindu.	1	57	26	31	...	...	...	57	26	31
		2. Kuruppu ...	"	3	1,087	535	552	52	34	18	1,035	501	534
		Total, Group, 46 — 2		4	1,144	561	583	52	34	18	1,092	527	565
	47. Jugglers, Snake-Charmers &c. and Animal-Exhibitors.	1. Kuravan ...	Hindu.	5	555	300	255	34	18	16	521	282	239
		2. Pulluvan ...	"	1	111	53	58	...	...	...	111	53	58
		Total, Group, 47 — 2		6	666	353	313	34	18	16	632	335	297
		Total, Class, E		24	6,528	3,217	3,311	488	257	231	6,040	2,960	3,080

TABLE XVI.

Caste, Tribe, Race &c.

Class.	Group.	Caste, Tribe, Race &c.	Religion.	No. of recorded subdivisions.	Total.			Town.			Country.		
					Total.	Males.	Females.	Total.	Males	Females.	Total.	Males.	Females.
1	2	3	4	5	6	7	8	9	10	11	12	13	14
F. Non-Indian Races and Christian Converts.	48. Non-Indian Asiatic Races.	1. Arab ...	Mussalman.	1	433	189	244	73	35	38	360	154	206
		2. Hussian ...	"	1	2	2	...	2	2	...	...	...	...
		3. Jew ...	Judaism.	1	1,142	566	576	895	427	468	247	139	108
		4. Mughal ...	Mussalman.	1	423	213	210	211	109	102	212	104	108
		5. Pathan ...	"	1	2,291	1,163	1,128	390	193	197	1,901	970	931
		6. Shaik ...	"	1	273	164	109	124	73	51	149	91	58
		Total, Group, 48 — 6		6	4,564	2,297	2,267	1,695	839	856	2,869	1,458	1,411
	50. Non-Asiatic Races.	1. Europeans ...	Christian.	7	38	27	11	22	14	8	16	13	3
		Total, Group, 50 — 1		7	38	27	11	22	14	8	16	13	3
	51. Eurasians.	1. Eurasians ...	Christian.	1	270	155	115	118	69	49	152	86	66
		Total, Group, 51 — 1		1	270	155	115	118	69	49	152	86	66
	52. Christian converts.	Native Christians ...	Christian.	1	168,821	85,589	83,232	14,042	7,113	6,929	154,779	78,476	76,303
		Total, Group, 52 — 1		1	168,821	85,589	83,232	14,042	7,113	6,929	154,779	78,476	76,303
		Total, Class F, 9		15	173,693	88,068	85,625	15,877	8,035	7,842	157,816	80,033	77,783
		Grand, Total ...		379	722,698	361,767	360,931	50,455	26,027	24,428	672,243	335,740	336,503

TABLE XVII.

Occupation.

For Reasons explained in the body of the Report, the returns of the British Military Limits in the State cannot be incorporated with this Table. They are therefore given in a Supplement at the end of the Table.

TABLE XVII.

Occupation.

Class.	Order.	Sub-order and Group.	Number in Census Commissioner's List.	Serial Number.	Occupation.	State Total. Workers. Males. 0–4	5–14	15 and over.	Total.	Workers. Females. 0–4	5–14	15 and over.	Total.	Dependents. Males.	Females.	Total. Males.	Females.	Total.
1	2	3	4	5	6	7	8	9	10	11	12	13	14	15	16	17	18	19
A. Government.	I. Administration.	1. Service of the Imperial and Provincial Governments.	3	1	Clerical Establishment ...	...	...	6	6	...	...	...	...	12	11	18	11	29
			4	2	Constables and Bailiffs ...	...	...	4	4	...	...	...	...	2	3	6	3	9
					Total, Sub-order 1	...	...	10	10	...	...	...	...	14	14	24	14	38
					Total, Order I.	...	...	10	10	...	...	...	...	14	14	24	14	38
	III. Foreign and Feudatory Service	6. Administrative Service	19	3	Chiefs and Officers ...	8	11	273	292	9	11	19	39	604	688	896	727	1,623
			20	4	Clerical Establishments ...	...	7	736	743	...	...	...	...	632	818	1,375	818	2,193
			21	5	Menials ...	...	4	1,660	1,664	...	...	10	10	1,377	1,868	3,041	1,878	4,919
					Total, Sub-order 6	8	22	2,669	2,699	9	11	29	49	2,613	3,374	5,312	3,423	8,735
		7. Army and Marine.	22	6	Officers ...	...	...	16	16	...	...	...	...	9	20	25	20	45
			23	7	Privates ...	...	...	409	409	...	...	...	...	80	150	489	150	639
					Total, Sub-order 7	...	...	425	425	...	...	...	...	89	170	514	170	684
					Total, Order III.	8	22	3,094	3,124	9	11	29	49	2,702	3,544	5,826	3,593	9,419
					Total, Class A.	8	22	3,104	3,134	9	11	29	49	2,716	3,558	5,850	3,607	9,457

TABLE XVII.

Occupation:—*Continued.*

Serial Number.	Town.													Country.												
	Workers.								Dependents.		Total.			Workers.								Dependents.		Total.		
	Males.				Females.									Males.				Females.								
	0–4	5–14	15 and over.	Total.	0–4	5–14	15 and over.	Total.	Males.	Females.	Males.	Females.	Total.	0–4	5–14	15 and over.	Total.	0–4	5–14	15 and over.	Total.	Males.	Females.	Males.	Females.	Total.
	20	21	22	23	24	25	26	27	28	29	30	31	32	33	34	35	36	37	38	39	40	41	42	43	44	45
1	...	...	6	6	...	...	...	...	12	11	18	11	29	...	...	...	...	...	...	...	...	...	...	...	...	...
2	...	...	4	4	...	...	...	...	2	3	6	3	9	...	...	...	...	...	...	...	...	...	...	...	...	...
	...	...	10	10	...	...	...	...	14	14	24	14	38	...	...	...	...	...	...	...	...	...	...	...	...	...
	...	...	10	10	...	...	...	...	14	14	24	14	38	...	...	...	...	...	...	...	...	...	...	...	...	...
3	...	...	147	147	...	...	...	...	296	348	443	348	791	8	11	126	145	9	11	19	39	308	340	453	379	832
4	...	...	374	374	...	...	...	...	375	432	749	432	1,181	...	7	362	369	...	...	...	...	257	386	626	386	1,012
5	...	4	480	484	...	...	4	4	517	729	1,001	733	1,734	...	...	1,180	1,130	...	...	6	6	860	1,139	2,040	1,145	3,185
	...	4	1,001	1,005	...	...	4	4	1,188	1,509	2,193	1.513	3,706	8	18	1,668	1,694	9	11	25	45	1,425	1,865	3,119	1,910	5,029
6	...	...	10	10	...	...	...	...	2	5	12	5	17	...	...	6	6	...	...	...	...	7	15	13	15	28
7	...	...	136	136	...	...	...	...	26	49	162	49	211	...	...	273	273	...	...	...	...	54	101	327	101	428
	...	...	146	146	...	...	...	...	28	54	174	54	228	...	...	279	279	...	...	...	...	61	116	340	116	456
	...	4	1,147	11,51	...	...	4	4	1,216	1,563	2,367	1,567	3,934	8	18	1,947	1,973	9	11	25	45	1.486	1,981	3,459	2,026	5,485
	...	4	1,157	1,161	...	...	4	4	1,230	1,577	2.391	1,581	3,972	8	18	1,947	1,973	9	11	25	45	1.486	1,981	3,459	2,026	5,485

TABLE XVII.

Occupation:-*Continued.*

Class.	Order.	Sub-Order and Group.	Number in Census Commissioner's List.	Serial Number.	Occupation.	State-Total. Workers. Males. 0–4	5–14	15 and over.	Total.	Females. 0–4	5–14	15 and over.	Total.	Dependents. Males.	Females.	Total. Males.	Females.	Total.
1	2	3	4	5	6	7	8	9	10	11	12	13	14	15	16	17	18	19
B. Pasture and Agriculture.	IV. Live—Stock.	8. Stock-Breeding and Dealing.	24	8	Horse Breeders and Dealers	...	...	12	12	...	...	...	...	21	25	33	25	58
			25	9	Cattle Breeders and Dealers	...	...	150	150	...	...	...	...	86	126	236	126	362
			26	10	Herdsmen	...	50	154	204	...	8	50	58	66	97	270	155	425
			28	11	Elephant Catchers and Breeders	...	...	17	17	...	...	...	...	11	17	28	17	45
			31	12	Sheep & Goat Breeders and Dealers	...	...	32	32	...	...	...	...	14	29	46	29	75
			31 (a)	13	Shepherds	...	2	47	49	...	1	9	10	24	63	73	73	146
			32	14	Pig Breeders and Dealers	...	1	11	12	...	...	4	4	16	23	28	27	55
					Total, Sub-order 8	...	53	423	476	...	9	63	72	238	380	714	452	1166
		9. Subsidiary Services to Stock.	33	15	Veterinary Surgeons	...	...	8	8	...	...	...	...	16	20	24	20	44
			36	16	Vermin Destroyers	...	...	12	12	...	...	4	4	13	14	25	18	43
					Total, Sub-order 9	...	...	20	20	...	...	4	4	29	34	49	38	87
					Total, Order IV.	...	53	443	496	...	9	67	76	267	414	763	490	1253
	V. Agriculture.	10. Interest in Land.	37	17	Land Occupants, not cultivating	6	24	390	420	5	20	60	85	356	378	776	463	1239
			38	18	Land Occupants, cultivating	...	117	2893	3010	...	29	191	220	5324	7864	8334	8084	16418
			39	19	Tenants, not cultivating	7	94	5082	5183	4	38	428	470	8203	14620	13386	15090	28476
			41	20	Tenants and Sharers, cultivating	...	555	7408	7963	...	247	1743	1990	8485	15014	16448	17004	33452
			41 (a)	21	Agriculture (Unspecified)	...	987	18815	19802	...	191	1431	1622	20062	35031	39864	36653	76517
					Total, Sub-order 10	13	1777	34588	36378	9	525	3853	4387	42430	72907	78808	77294	156102

TABLE XVII.

Occupation:—*Continued.*

Serial Number.	Town.													Country.												
	Workers.								Dependents.		Total.			Workers.								Dependents.		Total.		
	Males.				Females.									Males.				Females.								
	0–4	5–14	15 and over.	Total.	0–4	5–14	15 and over.	Total.	Males.	Females.	Males.	Females.	Total.	0–4	5–15	15 and over.	Total.	0–4	5–14	15 and over.	Total.	Males.	Females.	Males.	Females.	Total.
	20	21	22	23	24	25	26	27	28	29	30	31	32	33	34	35	36	37	38	39	40	41	42	43	44	45
8	...	...	2	2	...	...	...	...	2	3	4	3	7	...	...	10	10	...	...	...	...	19	22	29	22	51
9	...	...	17	17	...	...	...	...	9	21	26	21	47	...	...	133	133	...	...	..	...	77	105	210	105	315
10	...	2	15	17	...	2	2	4	3	9	20	13	33	...	48	139	187	...	6	48	54	63	88	250	142	392
11	...	...	...	...	...	...	...	...	...	...	...	...	...	...	...	17	17	...	...	...	...	11	17	28	17	45
12	...	...	...	...	...	...	...	...	...	...	...	...	...	...	...	32	32	...	...	...	...	14	29	46	29	75
13	...	...	2	2	...	...	...	...	1	2	3	2	5	...	2	45	47	...	1	9	10	23	61	70	71	141
14	...	...	...	...	...	...	...	...	...	...	...	...	...	...	1	11	12	...	...	4	4	16	23	28	27	55
	...	2	36	38	...	2	2	4	15	35	53	39	92	...	51	387	438	...	7	61	68	223	345	661	413	1074
15	...	...	...	...	...	...	...	...	...	...	...	...	...	...	...	8	8	...	...	...	...	10	20	24	20	44
16	...	...	...	...	...	...	...	...	...	...	...	...	...	...	...	12	12	...	...	4	4	13	14	25	18	43
	...	...	...	...	...	...	...	...	...	...	...	...	...	...	...	20	20	...	...	4	4	29	34	49	38	87
	...	2	36	38	...	2	2	4	15	35	53	39	92	...	51	407	458	...	7	65	72	252	379	710	451	1161
17	1	4	188	193	...	1	36	37	224	232	417	269	686	5	20	202	227	5	19	24	48	132	146	359	194	553
18	...	2	164	166	...	...	6	6	224	410	390	416	806	...	115	2729	2844	...	29	185	214	5100	7454	7944	7668	15612
19	2	10	202	214	...	2	32	34	352	452	566	486	1052	5	84	4880	4969	4	36	396	436	7851	14168	12820	14604	27424
20	...	...	140	140	...	...	7	7	42	135	182	142	324	...	555	7268	7823	...	247	1736	1983	8413	14879	16266	16862	33128
21	...	26	553	579	...	3	62	65	631	1284	1210	1349	2559	...	961	18362	19323	...	188	1369	1557	19431	33747	38754	35304	74058
	3	42	1147	1292	...	6	143	149	1473	2513	2765	2662	5427	10	1735	33441	35186	9	519	3710	4238	40957	70394	76143	74632	150775

TABLE XVII.

Occupation:—*Continued.*

Class.	Order.	Sub-order and Group.	Number in Census Commissioner's List.	Serial Number.	Occupation.	State Total. Workers. Males. 0–4	5–14	15 and over.	Total.	Females. 0–4	5–14	15 and over.	Total.	Dependents. Males.	Females.	Total. Males.	Females.	Total.
1	2	3	4	5	6	7	8	9	10	11	12	13	14	15	16	17	18	19
B. Pasture and Agriculture—(*Continued.*)	V. Agriculture—(*Continued.*)	11. Agricultural Labourers.	42	22	Farm Servants	...	12	240	**252**	...	13	96	**109**	103	200	**355**	**309**	**664**
			43	23	Field Labourers and Crop Watchers	...	1436	23967	**25403**	...	553	5321	**5874**	25241	45045	**50644**	**50919**	**101563**
					Total, Sub-order 11	...	1448	24207	**25655**	...	566	5417	**5983**	25344	45245	**50999**	**51228**	**102227**
		12. Growers of special products and trees.	44	24	Coffee Planters, Managers and Assistants	...	...	41	**41**	...	...	...	...	23	30	**64**	**30**	**94**
			45	25	Cocoanut Growers	...	35	844	**879**	...	1	25	**26**	479	1336	**1358**	**1362**	**2720**
			46	26	Betel-vine and Areca-nut Growers	...	1	24	**25**	...	...	7	**7**	6	28	**31**	**35**	**66**
			48	27	Cardamom and Pepper Growers	...	2	31	**33**	...	1	10	**11**	5	29	**38**	**40**	**78**
			51	28	Market Gardeners (Vegetable Growers.)	...	7	54	**61**	...	7	25	**32**	67	74	**128**	**106**	**234**
			52	29	Gardeners, Seedsmen &c.	...	5	106	**111**	...	...	4	**4**	59	119	**170**	**123**	**293**
			53	30	Manure Preparers and Sellers	...	4	15	**19**	...	15	117	**132**	72	60	**91**	**192**	**283**
			54	31	Forest Officers	...	...	2	**2**	...	...	...	...	11	12	**13**	**12**	**25**
			55	32	Forest Rangers, Guards, Peons &c.	...	...	60	**60**	...	...	...	...	19	96	**79**	**96**	**175**
					Total, Sub-order 12	...	54	1177	**1231**	...	24	188	**212**	741	1784	**1972**	**1996**	**3968**
		13. Agricultural training and Supervision	58	33	Agents and Managers of landed Estates.	...	...	42	**42**	...	...	...	...	26	33	**68**	**33**	**101**
					Total, Sub-order 13	...	...	42	**42**	...	...	...	...	26	33	**68**	**33**	**101**
					Total, Order **V**.	13	3279	60014	**63306**	9	1115	9458	**10582**	68541	119969	**131847**	**130551**	**262398**
					Total, Class **B**.	13	3332	60457	**63802**	9	1124	9525	**10658**	68808	120383	**132610**	**131041**	**263651**

TABLE XVII.

Occupation—*Continued.*

Serial Number.	Town.													Country.												
	Workers.								Dependents.		Total.			Workers.								Dependents.		Total.		
	Males.				Females.									Males.				Females.								
	0–4	5–14	15 and over.	Total.	0–4	5–14	15 and over.	Total.	Males.	Females.	Males.	Females.	Total.	0–4	5–15	15 and over.	Total.	0–4	5–14	15 and over.	Total.	Males.	Females.	Males.	Females.	Total.
	20	21	22	23	24	25	26	27	28	29	30	31	32	33	34	35	36	37	38	39	40	41	42	43	44	45
22	...	...	3	**3**	...	...	1	**1**	3	3	**6**	**4**	**10**	...	12	237	**249**	...	13	95	**108**	100	197	**349**	**305**	**654**
23	...	6	52	**58**	...	3	33	**36**	45	57	**103**	**93**	**196**	...	1430	23915	**25345**	...	550	5288	**5838**	25196	44988	**50541**	**50826**	**101367**
	...	6	55	**61**	...	3	34	**37**	48	60	**109**	**97**	**206**	...	1442	24152	**25594**	...	563	5383	**5946**	25296	45185	**50890**	**51131**	**102021**
24	...	...	...	...	...	...	...	...	...	...	...	...	...	...	...	41	**41**	...	...	...	...	23	30	**64**	**30**	**94**
25	...	4	93	**97**	...	...	3	**3**	67	119	**164**	**122**	**286**	...	31	751	**782**	...	1	22	**23**	412	1217	**1194**	**1240**	**2434**
26	...	...	...	...	...	...	...	...	...	...	...	...	...	...	1	24	**25**	...	...	7	**7**	6	28	**31**	**35**	**66**
27	...	...	...	...	...	...	...	...	...	...	...	...	...	...	2	31	**33**	...	1	10	**11**	5	29	**38**	**40**	**78**
28	...	...	...	...	...	...	...	...	...	...	...	...	...	...	7	54	**61**	...	7	25	**32**	67	74	**128**	**106**	**234**
29	...	1	17	**18**	...	...	...	...	12	16	**30**	**16**	**46**	...	4	89	**93**	...	...	4	**4**	47	103	**140**	**107**	**247**
30	...	...	...	...	...	...	...	...	...	...	...	...	...	...	4	15	**19**	...	15	117	**132**	72	60	**91**	**192**	**283**
31	...	...	2	**2**	...	...	...	...	11	12	**13**	**12**	**25**	...	...	...	...	...	...	...	...	...	...	...	...	...
32	...	...	29	**29**	...	...	...	...	8	39	**37**	**39**	**76**	...	...	31	**31**	...	...	...	...	11	57	**42**	**57**	**99**
	...	5	141	**146**	...	...	3	**3**	98	186	...	...	...	...	49	1036	**1085**	...	24	185	**209**	643	1598	**1728**	**1807**	**3535**
33	...	...	7	**7**	...	...	...	...	3	7	**10**	**7**	**17**	...	...	35	**35**	...	...	...	...	23	26	**58**	**26**	**84**
	...	...	7	**7**	...	...	...	...	3	7	**10**	**7**	**17**	...	...	35	**35**	...	...	...	...	23	26	**58**	**26**	**84**
V.	3	53	1350	**1406**	...	9	180	**189**	1622	2766	**3028**	**2955**	**5983**	10	3226	58664	**61900**	9	1100	9278	**10393**	66919	11723	**128819**	**22116**	**150935**
B.	3	55	1386	**1444**	...	11	182	**193**	1637	2801	**3081**	**2994**	**6075**	10	3277	59071	**62358**	9	1113	9343	**10465**	67171	117582	**129529**	**128047**	**257576**

TABLE XVII.

Occupation:-*Continued.*

Class.	Order.	Sub-Order and Group.	Number in Census Commissioner's List.	Serial Number.	Occupation.	State-Total. Workers. Males. 0–4	5–14	15 and over.	Total.	Females. 0–4	5–14	15 and over.	Total.	Dependents. Males.	Females.	Total. Males.	Females.	Total.
1	2	3	4	5	6	7	8	9	10	11	12	13	14	15	16	17	18	19
C. Personal Services.	VI. Personal and Domestic Services.	14. Personal and Domestic Services.	59	34	Barbers	...	139	1057	**1,196**	...	45	448	**493**	730	1,414	**1,926**	**1,907**	**3,833**
			59 (a)	35	Shampooing	...	...	29	**29**	...	...	...	...	27	41	**56**	**41**	**97**
			60	36	Ear-Pickers	...	1	5	**6**	...	1	10	**11**	12	10	**18**	**21**	**39**
			63	37	Washermen	...	168	1418	**1,586**	...	220	2,008	**2,228**	1,058	1,887	**2,644**	**4,115**	**6,759**
			64	38	Water-Carriers	...	1	15	**16**	...	...	4	**4**	8	9	**24**	**13**	**37**
			65	39	Cooks	...	22	339	**361**	...	8	66	**74**	171	319	**532**	**393**	**925**
			66	40	Indoor-Servants	...	47	441	**488**	...	95	730	**825**	195	375	**683**	**1,200**	**1,883**
			67	41	Grooms, Coachmen, Dog boys &c.	...	...	38	**38**	...	...	...	...	30	28	**68**	**28**	**96**
			68	42	Door-Keepers &c.	...	26	576	**602**	...	69	706	**775**	494	1,022	**1,096**	**1,797**	**2,893**
					Total, Sub-order 14	...	404	3918	**4,322**	...	438	3,972	**4,410**	2,725	5,105	**7,047**	**9,515**	**16,562**
		15. Non-Domestic Establishment.	69	43	Hotel, Lodging and Boarding House--Keepers	...	3	68	**71**	...	4	45	**49**	60	100	**131**	**149**	**280**
			70	44	Rest-House, Serai, Owners and Managers	...	1	22	**23**	...	...	1	**1**	11	14	**34**	**15**	**49**
					Total, Sub--order 15	...	4	90	**94**	...	4	46	**50**	71	114	**165**	**164**	**329**
		16. Sanitation.	74	45	Sweepers and Scavengers	...	11	55	**66**	...	34	567	**601**	138	365	**204**	**966**	**1,170**
					Total, Sub-order 16	...	11	55	**66**	...	34	567	**601**	138	365	**204**	**966**	**1,170**
					Total, Order VI.	...	419	4063	**4,482**	...	476	4,585	**5,061**	2,934	5,584	**7,416**	**10,645**	**18,061**
					Total, Class C.	...	419	4063	**4,482**	...	476	4,585	**5,061**	2,934	5,584	**7.416**	**10,645**	**18,061**

TABLE XVII.

Occupation—*Continued.*

Serial Number.	Town.													Country.												
	Workers.								Dependents.		Total.			Workers.								Dependents.		Total.		
	Males.				Females.									Males.				Females.								
	0–4	5–14	15 and over.	Total.	0–4	5–14	15 and over.	Total.	Males.	Females.	Males.	Females.	Total.	0–4	5–14	15 and over.	Total.	0–4	5–14	15 and over.	Total.	Males.	Females.	Males.	Females.	Total.
	20	21	22	23	24	25	26	27	28	29	30	31	32	33	34	35	36	37	38	39	40	41	42	43	44	45
34	...	11	102	113	...	...	32	32	75	139	188	171	359	...	128	955	1083	...	45	416	461	655	1275	1738	1736	3474
35	...	...	3	3	...	...	...	...	2	3	5	3	8	...	...	26	26	...	...	...	...	25	38	51	38	89
36	...	...	1	1	...	...	2	2	2	1	3	3	6	...	1	4	5	...	1	8	9	10	9	15	18	33
37	...	14	67	81	...	10	110	120	56	60	137	180	317	...	154	1351	1505	...	210	1898	2108	1002	1827	2507	3935	6442
38	...	...	12	12	...	...	1	1	4	6	16	7	23	...	1	3	4	...	...	3	3	4	3	8	6	14
39	...	9	169	178	...	2	10	12	20	35	198	47	245	...	13	170	183	...	6	56	62	151	284	334	346	680
40	...	18	259	277	...	5	142	147	161	174	438	321	759	...	29	182	211	...	90	558	678	34	201	245	879	1124
41	...	...	10	10	...	...	...	...	2	8	12	8	20	...	...	28	28	...	...	...	...	28	20	56	20	76
42	...	9	78	87	...	12	69	81	60	61	147	142	289	...	17	498	515	...	57	637	694	434	961	949	1655	2604
	...	61	701	762	...	29	366	395	382	487	1144	882	2026	...	343	3217	3560	...	409	3606	4015	2343	4618	5903	8633	14536
43	...	...	26	26	...	4	18	22	21	28	47	50	97	...	3	42	45	...	...	27	27	39	72	84	99	183
44	...	...	7	7	...	...	...	...	5	7	12	7	19	...	1	15	16	...	...	1	1	6	7	22	8	30
	...	...	33	33	...	4	18	22	26	35	59	57	116	...	4	57	61	...	...	28	28	45	79	106	107	213
45	...	1	9	10	...	5	151	156	63	31	73	187	260	...	10	46	56	...	29	416	445	75	334	131	779	910
	...	1	9	10	...	5	151	156	63	31	73	187	260	...	10	46	56	...	29	416	445	75	334	131	779	910
VI.	...	62	743	805	...	38	535	573	471	553	1276	1126	2402	...	357	3320	3677	...	438	4050	4488	2463	5031	6140	9519	15659
C.	...	62	743	805	...	38	535	573	471	553	1276	1126	2402	...	357	3320	3677	...	438	4050	4488	2463	5031	6140	9519	15659

TABLE XVII.

Occupation:—*Continued.*

Class.	Order.	Sub-order and Group.	Number in Census Commissioner's List.	Serial Number.	Occupation.	State Total. Workers. Males. 0–4	5–14	15 and over.	Total.	Females. 0–4	5–14	15 and over.	Total.	Dependents. Males.	Females.	Total. Males.	Females.	Total.
1	2	3	4	5	6	7	8	9	10	11	12	13	14	15	16	17	18	19
D. Preparation and Supply of Material Substances.	VII. Food and Drink.	17. Animal Food.	76	46	Cow and Buffalo-Keepers, and Milk and Butter Sellers	...	8	139	147	...	12	177	189	104	185	251	374	625
			77	47	Ghee Preparers and Sellers	...	10	170	180	...	12	275	287	160	145	340	432	772
			79	48	Butchers	...	2	26	28	...	3	30	33	26	30	54	63	117
			80	49	Fowl and Egg Dealers	...	12	70	82	...	9	15	24	132	158	214	182	396
			81	50	Fishermen and Fish Curers	...	136	2,142	2,278	...	13	125	138	1,463	2,151	3,741	2,289	6,030
			82	51	Fish Dealers	...	30	841	871	...	11	159	170	665	1,238	1,536	1,408	2,944
					Total, Sub-order 17	...	198	3,388	3,586	...	60	781	841	2,550	3,907	6,136	4,748	10,884
		18. Vegetable Food.	83	52	Grain Dealers	...	52	1,337	1,389	...	24	462	486	1,315	2,224	2,704	2,710	5,414
			84	53	Grain Parchers	...	23	541	564	...	31	360	391	365	664	929	1,055	1,984
			85	54	Pulse & Flour Preparers and Sellers	...	59	483	542	...	64	338	402	322	483	864	885	1,749
			87	55	Bakers	...	...	40	40	...	...	35	35	44	57	84	92	176
			88	56	Bran Sellers	...	...	24	24	...	...	41	41	36	51	60	92	152
			89	57	Vegetable Sellers	...	11	120	131	...	8	60	68	108	166	239	234	473
			90	58	Fruit Sellers	...	...	41	41	...	...	8	8	50	76	91	84	175
			91	59	Cocoa-nut Dealers	...	22	270	292	...	...	25	25	492	449	784	474	1,258
			92	60	Confectioners and Sweetmeat Makers and Sellers and Cooks	...	42	454	496	...	33	524	557	434	704	930	1,261	2,191
					Total, Sub-order 18	...	209	3,310	3,519	...	160	1,853	2,013	3,166	4,874	6,685	6,887	13,572

TABLE XVII.

Occupation:—*Continued.*

Serial Number.	Town.													Country.												
	Workers.								Dependents.		Total.			Workers.								Dependents.		Total.		
	Males.				Females.									Males.				Females.								
	0–4	5–14	15 and over.	Total.	0–4	5–14	15 and over.	Total.	Males.	Females.	Males.	Females.	Total.	0–4	5–14	15 and over.	Total.	0–4	5–14	15 and over.	Total.	Males.	Females.	Males.	Females.	Total.
	20	21	22	23	24	25	26	27	28	29	30	31	32	33	34	35	36	37	38	39	40	41	42	43	44	45
46	...	1	20	**21**	...	2	32	**34**	22	30	**43**	**64**	**107**	...	7	119	**126**	...	10	145	**155**	82	155	**208**	**310**	**518**
47	...	...	20	**20**	...	...	27	**27**	16	12	**36**	**39**	**75**	...	10	150	**160**	...	12	248	**260**	144	133	**304**	**393**	**697**
48	...	...	11	**11**	...	...	17	**17**	8	8	**19**	**25**	**44**	...	2	15	**17**	...	3	13	**16**	18	22	**35**	**38**	**73**
49	...	...	14	**14**	...	...	4	**4**	12	21	**26**	**25**	**51**	...	12	56	**68**	...	9	11	**20**	120	137	**188**	**157**	**345**
50	...	10	198	**208**	...	4	84	**88**	212	322	**420**	**410**	**830**	...	126	1944	**2070**	...	9	41	**50**	1251	1829	**3321**	**1879**	**5200**
51	...	4	82	**86**	...	1	73	**74**	181	217	**267**	**291**	**558**	...	26	759	**785**	...	10	86	**96**	484	1021	**1269**	**1117**	**2386**
	...	15	345	**360**	...	7	237	**244**	451	610	**811**	**854**	**1665**	...	183	3043	**3226**	...	53	544	**597**	2099	3297	**5325**	**3894**	**9219**
52	...	4	311	**315**	...	2	90	**92**	383	784	**698**	**876**	**1574**	...	48	1026	**1074**	...	22	372	**394**	932	1440	**2006**	**1834**	**3840**
53	...	...	55	**55**	...	...	42	**42**	76	131	**131**	**173**	**304**	...	23	486	**509**	...	31	318	**349**	289	533	**798**	**882**	**1680**
54	...	...	7	**7**	...	...	2	**2**	6	9	**13**	**11**	**24**	...	59	476	**535**	...	64	336	**400**	316	474	**851**	**874**	**1725**
55	...	...	8	**8**	...	...	5	**5**	13	29	**21**	**34**	**55**	...	...	32	**32**	...	...	30	**30**	31	28	**63**	**58**	**121**
56	...	...	2	**2**	...	...	3	**3**	1	1	**3**	**4**	**7**	...	...	22	**22**	...	...	38	**38**	35	50	**57**	**88**	**145**
57	...	3	16	**19**	...	...	2	**2**	4	8	**23**	**10**	**33**	...	8	104	**112**	...	8	58	**66**	101	158	**216**	**224**	**440**
58	...	...	9	**9**	...	...	3	**3**	17	34	**26**	**37**	**63**	...	...	32	**32**	...	...	5	**5**	33	42	**65**	**47**	**112**
59	...	...	15	**15**	...	...	...	...	10	18	**25**	**18**	**43**	...	22	255	**277**	...	...	25	**25**	482	431	**759**	**456**	**1215**
60	...	8	110	**118**	...	4	168	**172**	121	245	**239**	**417**	**656**	...	34	344	**378**	...	29	356	**385**	313	459	**691**	**844**	**1535**
	...	15	533	**548**	...	6	315	**321**	631	1259	**1179**	**1530**	**2759**	...	194	2777	**2971**	...	154	1538	**1692**	2535	3615	**5506**	**5307**	**10813**

TABLE XVII.

Occupation:—*Continued.*

Class.	Order.	Sub-order and Group.	Number in Census Commissioner's List.	Serial Number.	Occupation.	State Total. Workers. Males. 0–4	5–14	15 and over.	Total.	Females. 0–4	5–14	15 and over.	Total.	Dependents. Males.	Females.	Total. Males.	Females.	Total.
1	2	3	4	5	6	7	8	9	10	11	12	13	14	15	16	17	18	19
D. Preparation and Supply of Material Substances—(*Continued.*)	VII. Food and Drink—(*Continued.*)	19. Drink, Condiments and Narcotics.	95 (a)	61	Ginger-Driers ...	...	...	9	**9**	...	...	6	**6**	7	15	**16**	**21**	**37**
			96	62	Sharbat Preparers and Sellers ...	...	...	12	**12**	...	1	8	**9**	14	28	**26**	**37**	**63**
			97	63	Country Spirits Distillers and Sellers ...	...	8	310	**318**	...	6	60	**66**	447	645	**765**	**711**	**1476**
			98	64	Toddy-Drawers and Sellers ...	...	552	13025	**13577**	...	178	2104	**2282**	10979	19078	**24556**	**21360**	**45916**
			99	65	Foreign Wine and Spirit Dealers ...	...	...	4	**4**	...	...	...	...	5	11	**9**	**11**	**20**
			101	66	Tea-Sellers ...	...	...	1	**1**	...	...	...	...	...	3	**1**	**3**	**4**
			102	67	Coffee Preparers and Sellers ...	...	...	4	**4**	...	...	...	...	11	6	**15**	**6**	**21**
			103	68	Sugar Manufacturers and Sellers ...	...	...	14	**14**	...	...	...	...	10	16	**24**	**16**	**40**
			103 (a)	69	Sugar-Cane Sellers ...	...	...	8	**8**	...	...	6	**6**	6	13	**14**	**19**	**33**
			104	70	Molasses (Jaggery, Gur &c.) Makers and Sellers ...	...	4	75	**79**	...	7	74	**81**	73	163	**152**	**244**	**396**
			105	71	Salt Preparers and Sellers ...	...	5	264	**269**	...	4	86	**90**	210	281	**479**	**371**	**850**
			106	72	Assafœtida, Turmeric &c. Sellers ...	...	2	29	**31**	...	...	10	**10**	51	43	**82**	**53**	**135**
			109	73	Grocers and General Condiment Dealers.	...	104	2126	**2230**	...	22	436	**458**	2128	3937	**4358**	**4395**	**8753**
			111	74	Betel-leaf and Areca-nut Sellers ...	...	54	1118	**1172**	...	19	119	**138**	923	1817	**2095**	**1955**	**4050**
			112	75	Tobacco & Snuff Manufacturers & Sellers	...	18	245	**263**	...	14	32	**46**	211	429	**474**	**475**	**949**
			113	76	Prepared Hookah Sellers ...	...	...	3	**3**	...	...	1	**1**	7	4	**10**	**5**	**15**
			114	77	Opium Sellers ...	...	...	14	**14**	...	...	...	...	13	22	**27**	**22**	**49**
			115	78	Bhang, Ganja &c. Preparers & Sellers...	...	...	4	**4**	...	...	...	...	5	12	**9**	**12**	**21**
					Total, Sub-order 19	...	747	17265	**18012**	...	251	2912	**3193**	15100	26523	**33112**	**29716**	**62828**
					Total, Order **VII**.	...	1154	23963	**25117**	...	471	5576	**6047**	20816	35304	**45933**	**41351**	**87284**

Table XVII.

OCCUPATON.

TABLE XVII.

Occupation:—*Continued.*

Serial Number.	Town.													Country.												
	Workers.								Dependents		Total.			Workers.								Dependents.		Total.		
	Males.				Females.									Males.				Females.								
	0–4	5–14	15 and over.	Total.	0–4	5–14	15 and over.	Total.	Males.	Females.	Males.	Females.	Total.	0–4	5–14	15 and over.	Total.	0–4	5–14	15 and over.	Total.	Males.	Females.	Males.	Females.	Total.
	20	21	22	23	24	25	26	27	28	29	30	31	32	33	34	35	36	37	38	39	40	41	42	43	44	45
61	...	...	...	...	...	...	...	...	...	...	...	...	...	...	...	9	9	...	...	6	6	7	15	16	21	37
62	...	...	6	6	...	1	5	6	2	3	8	9	17	...	...	6	6	...	...	3	3	12	25	18	28	46
63	...	2	34	36	...	1	13	14	59	116	95	130	225	...	6	276	282	...	5	47	52	388	529	670	581	1251
64	...	10	473	483	...	3	62	65	390	748	873	813	1686	...	542	12552	13094	...	175	2042	2217	10589	18330	23683	20547	44230
65	...	...	2	2	...	...	...	...	2	5	4	5	9	...	...	2	2	...	...	...	...	3	6	5	6	11
66	...	...	1	1	...	...	...	...	...	3	1	3	4	...	...	...	...	...	...	...	...	...	...	...	...	...
67	...	...	1	1	...	...	...	...	...	...	1	...	1	...	...	3	3	...	...	...	...	11	6	14	6	20
68	...	...	5	5	...	...	...	...	4	8	9	8	17	...	...	9	9	...	...	...	...	6	8	15	8	23
69	...	...	2	2	...	...	1	1	2	2	4	3	7	...	...	6	6	...	...	5	5	4	11	10	16	26
70	...	...	11	11	...	2	12	14	14	33	25	47	72	...	4	64	68	...	5	62	67	59	130	127	197	324
71	...	...	22	22	...	...	5	5	15	29	37	34	71	...	5	242	247	...	4	81	85	195	252	442	337	779
72	...	2	10	12	...	...	4	4	17	29	29	33	62	...	...	19	19	...	...	6	6	34	14	53	20	73
73	...	19	846	865	...	3	73	76	1023	1948	1888	2024	3912	...	85	1280	1365	...	19	363	382	1105	1989	2470	2371	4841
74	...	4	71	75	...	...	8	8	45	88	120	96	216	...	50	1047	1097	...	19	111	130	878	1729	1975	1859	3834
75	...	13	86	99	...	8	21	29	74	147	173	176	349	...	5	159	164	...	6	11	17	137	282	301	299	600
76	...	...	3	3	...	...	1	1	7	4	10	5	15	...	...	...	...	...	...	...	...	...	...	...	...	...
77	...	...	4	4	...	...	...	...	3	6	7	6	13	...	...	10	10	...	...	...	...	10	16	20	16	36
78	...	...	2	2	...	...	...	...	3	6	5	6	11	...	...	2	2	...	...	...	...	2	6	4	6	10
	...	50	1579	1629	...	18	205	223	1660	3175	3289	3398	6687	...	697	15686	16383	...	233	2737	2970	13440	23318	29823	26318	56141
I.	...	80	2457	2537	...	31	757	788	2742	5044	5279	5832	11111	...	1074	21506	22580	...	440	4819	5259	18074	30260	40654	35519	76173

TABLE XVII.

Occupation:–*Continued.*

Class.	Order.	Sub-Order and Group.	Number in Census Commissioner's List.	Serial Number.	Occupation.	State-Total. Workers. Males. 0–4	5–14	15 and over.	Total.	Females. 0–4	5–14	15 and over.	Total.	Dependents. Males.	Females.	Total. Males.	Females.	Total.
1	2	3	4	5	6	7	8	9	10	11	12	13	14	15	16	17	18	19
D. Preparation and Supply of Material Substances–(*Continued.*)	VIII. Light, Firing and Forage.	20. Lighting.	116	79	Oil Pressers and Sellers	...	389	5464	5853	...	73	921	994	6038	8595	11891	9589	21480
			118	80	Oil Cake Dealers	...	...	141	141	...	...	52	52	222	217	363	299	662
			119	81	Candle Makers and Sellers	...	...	1	1	...	...	...	...	2	2	3	2	5
			120	82	Torch Makers and Sellers	...	...	20	20	...	...	5	5	30	35	50	40	90
			123	83	Lamp & Lantern Makers & Sellers.	...	1	19	20	...	1	2	3	17	29	37	32	69
					Total, Sub-order 20	...	390	5645	6035	...	74	980	1054	6309	8908	12344	9962	22306
		21. Fuel and Forage.	125	84	Firewood & Grass Gatherers & Sellers	...	23	578	601	...	12	579	591	564	692	1165	1283	2448
			126	85	Firewood Contractors and Dealers	...	...	25	25	...	...	...	...	30	45	55	45	100
			129	86	Charcoal Burners and Dealers	...	...	6	6	...	...	2	2	5	10	11	12	23
			130	87	Cowdung Fuel Preparers & Sellers	...	...	15	15	...	...	34	34	25	36	40	70	110
			131	88	Hay &c. Contractors and Dealers	...	1	15	16	...	...	...	...	14	29	30	29	59
					Total, Sub-order 21	...	29	634	663	...	12	615	627	638	812	1301	1439	2740
					Total, Order VIII	...	419	6279	6698	...	86	1595	1681	6947	9720	13645	11401	25046

TABLE XVII.

Occupation:—*Continued.*

Serial Number.	Town. Workers. Males. 0–4	5–14	15 and over.	Total.	Females. 0–4	5–14	15 and over.	Total.	Dependents. Males.	Females.	Total. Males.	Females.	Total.	Country. Workers. Males. 0–4	5–14	15 and over.	Total.	Females. 0–4	5–14	15 and over.	Total.	Dependents. Males.	Females.	Total. Males.	Females.	Total.
	20	21	22	23	24	25	26	27	28	29	30	31	32	33	34	35	36	37	38	39	40	41	42	43	44	45
79	...	9	363	372	...	3	95	98	286	404	658	582	1,250	...	380	5,101	5,481	...	70	826	896	5,752	8,101	11,233	8,997	20,230
80	...	...	13	13	...	...	4	4	4	8	17	12	29	...	...	128	128	...	...	48	48	218	239	346	287	633
81	...	...	...	...	...	...	...	...	...	...	...	...	...	...	...	1	1	...	...	...	...	2	2	3	2	5
82	...	...	4	4	...	...	2	2	2	6	6	8	14	...	...	16	16	...	...	3	3	28	29	44	32	76
83	...	1	9	10	...	1	1	2	9	10	19	12	31	...	...	10	10	...	...	1	1	8	19	18	20	38
	...	10	389	399	...	4	102	106	301	518	700	624	1,324	...	380	5,256	5,636	...	70	878	948	6,008	8,390	11,644	9,338	20,982
84	...	...	20	20	...	...	27	27	59	66	79	93	172	...	28	553	581	...	12	552	564	505	626	1,086	11,90	2,276
85	...	...	2	2	...	...	...	...	...	...	2	...	2	...	...	23	23	...	...	...	...	30	45	53	45	98
86	...	...	...	...	...	...	...	...	...	...	...	...	...	...	...	6	6	...	...	2	2	5	10	11	12	23
87	...	...	...	...	...	...	2	2	...	...	...	2	2	...	...	15	15	...	...	32	32	25	36	40	68	108
88	...	...	...	...	...	...	...	...	...	...	...	...	...	...	1	15	16	...	...	...	...	14	29	30	29	59
	...	...	22	22	...	...	29	29	59	66	81	95	176	...	29	612	641	...	12	586	598	579	746	1,220	13,44	2,564
	...	10	410	471	...	4	131	135	360	584	831	719	1,550	...	409	5,868	6,277	...	82	1,464	1,546	6,587	9,136	12,864	10,682	23,546

TABLE XVII.

Occupation:—*Continued.*

Class.	Order.	Sub-order and Group.	Number in Census Commissioner's List.	Serial Number.	OCCUPATION.	State Total.													
						Workers.								Dependents.		Total.		
						Males.				Females.								
						0–4	5–14	15 and over.	Total.	0–4	5–14	15 and over.	Total.	Males.	Females.	Males.	Females.	Total.
1	2	3	4	5	6	7	8	9	10	11	12	13	14	15	16	17	18	19
D. Preparation and Supply of Material Substances—(*Continued.*)	IX. Buildings.	22. Building Materials.	132	89	Brick and Tile Burners and Sellers	...	5	188	**193**	...	6	91	**97**	192	272	**385**	**369**	**754**
			133	90	Lime, Chunnam and Shell Burners and Sellers	...	7	189	**196**	...	11	121	**132**	145	229	**341**	**361**	**702**
			134	91	Stone quarry Owners, Contractors &c.	...	5	256	**261**	...	...	8	**8**	239	429	**500**	**437**	**937**
			135	92	Thatch Dealers and Thatchers	...	14	243	**257**	...	27	340	**367**	175	280	**432**	**647**	**1,079**
					Total, Sub-order 22	...	31	876	**907**	...	44	560	**604**	751	1,210	**1,658**	**1,814**	**3,472**
		23. Artificers in building.	136	93	Building Contractors	...	...	136	**136**	...	...	...	...	120	151	**256**	**151**	**407**
			137	94	Stone Workers	...	7	66	**73**	...	...	36	**36**	54	124	**127**	**160**	**287**
			138	95	Masons	...	77	1,021	**1,098**	...	10	57	**67**	754	1,611	**1,852**	**1,678**	**3,530**
			139	96	Builders and Joiners	...	...	3	**3**	...	...	...	...	4	8	**7**	**8**	**15**
			140	97	Plasterers and House Painters	...	...	73	**73**	...	...	50	**50**	87	95	**160**	**145**	**305**
			141	98	Mud wall and Roof Builders	...	...	17	**17**	...	...	...	...	14	32	**31**	**32**	**63**
			143	99	Tilers and Tile-Turners	...	1	47	**48**	...	...	...	...	40	64	**88**	**64**	**152**
					Total, Sub-order 23	...	85	1,363	**1,448**	...	10	143	**153**	1,073	2,085	**2,521**	**2,238**	**4,759**
					Total, Order IX.	...	116	2,239	**2,355**	...	54	703	**757**	1,824	3,295	**4,179**	**4,052**	**8,231**

TABLE XVII.

Occupation:—*Continued.*

Serial Number.	Town.													Country.												
	Workers.								Dependents.		Total.			Workers.								Dependents.		Total.		
	Males.				Females.									Males.				Females.								
	0–4	5–14	15 and over.	Total.	0–4	5–14	15 and over.	Total.	Males.	Females.	Males.	Females.	Total.	0–4	5–14	15 and over.	Total.	0–4	5–14	15 and over.	Total.	Males.	Females.	Males.	Females.	Total.
	20	21	22	23	24	25	26	27	28	29	30	31	32	33	34	35	36	37	38	39	40	41	42	43	44	45
89	...	...	4	4	...	...	3	3	3	7	7	10	17	...	5	184	189	...	6	88	94	189	265	378	359	737
90	...	...	19	19	...	...	2	2	21	29	40	31	71	...	7	170	177	...	11	119	130	124	200	301	330	681
91	...	...	11	11	...	...	...	...	20	35	31	35	66	...	5	245	250	...	...	8	8	219	394	469	402	871
92	...	1	13	14	...	...	19	19	12	16	26	35	61	...	13	230	243	...	27	321	348	163	264	406	612	1,018
	...	1	47	48	...	...	24	24	56	87	104	111	215	...	30	829	859	...	44	536	580	695	1,123	1,554	1,703	3,257
93	...	...	4	4	...	...	...	...	2	5	6	5	11	...	...	132	132	...	...	...	...	118	146	250	146	396
94	...	2	15	17	...	...	4	4	22	30	39	34	73	...	5	51	56	...	...	32	32	32	94	88	126	214
95	...	7	88	95	...	...	11	11	71	163	166	174	340	...	70	933	1,003	...	10	46	56	683	1,448	1,686	1,504	3,190
96	...	...	...	...	...	...	...	...	...	...	...	...	...	...	...	3	3	...	...	...	...	4	8	7	8	15
97	...	...	16	16	...	...	14	14	19	21	35	35	70	...	...	57	57	...	...	36	36	68	74	125	110	235
98	...	...	1	1	...	...	...	...	...	...	1	...	1	...	...	16	16	...	...	...	...	14	32	30	32	62
99	...	...	10	10	...	...	...	...	7	14	17	14	31	...	1	37	38	...	...	...	...	33	50	71	50	121
	...	9	134	143	...	...	29	29	121	233	264	262	526	...	76	1229	1,305	...	10	114	124	952	1,852	2,257	1,976	4,233
IX	...	10	181	191	...	...	53	53	177	320	368	373	741	...	106	2058	2,164	...	54	650	704	1,647	2,975	3,811	3,679	7,490

TABLE XVII.

Occupation:-*Continued.*

Class.	Order.	Sub-Order and Group.	Number in Census Commissioner's List.	Serial Number.	OCCUPATION.	State-Total. Workers. Males. 0–4	5–14	15 and over.	Total.	Females. 0–4	5–14	15 and over.	Total.	Dependents. Males.	Females.	Total. Males.	Females.	Total.
1	2	3	4	5	6	7	8	9	10	11	12	13	14	15	16	17	18	19
D. Preparation and Supply of Material Substances—(*Continued.*)	X. Vehicles and Vessels.	26. Ships and Boats.	148	100	Ship-wrights and Boat-builders	...	...	13	13	...	...	...	...	15	18	28	18	46
					Total, Sub-order 26	...	...	13	13	...	...	...	...	15	18	28	18	46
					Total, Order X	...	...	13	13	...	...	...	..	15	18	28	18	46
	XI. Supplementary Requirements.	27. Paper.	153	101	Paper Makers and Sellers and Palmleaf Binders	...	...	27	27	...	...	3	3	20	43	47	46	93
			155	102	Waste Paper and Rag Dealers	...	...	3	3	...	...	1	1	2	8	5	9	14
					Total, Sub-order 27	...	...	30	30	...	...	4	4	22	51	52	55	107
		28. Books & Prints &c.	157	103	Press Proprietors and Printers	...	...	20	20	...	...	...	...	31	42	51	42	93
			158	104	Book-Binders	...	...	13	13	...	...	2	2	13	15	26	17	43
			159	105	Book Sellers and Publishers	...	...	25	25	...	...	...	...	18	32	43	32	75
					Total, Sub-order 28	...	...	58	58	...	...	2	2	62	89	120	91	211
		29. Watches, Clocks & Scientific Instruments.	163	106	Watch and Clock Repairers	...	...	7	7	...	...	...	...	7	15	14	15	29
					Total, Sub-order 29	...	...	7	7	...	...	...	...	7	15	14	15	29
		30. Carving, Engraving &c.	169	107	Wood and Ebony Carvers	...	1	4	5	...	...	...	...	6	13	11	13	24
			170	108	Ivory Carvers	...	...	3	3	...	...	...	...	3	6	6	6	12
			172	109	Turners and Lacquerers	...	1	42	43	...	...	...	...	36	52	79	52	131
			174	110	Type Founders	...	...	2	2	...	...	...	...	3	4	5	4	9
			176	111	Mosaic Workers and Sellers	...	...	2	2	...	...	...	...	3	4	5	4	9
					Total, Sub-order 30	...	2	53	55	...	...	...	...	51	79	106	79	185

TABLE XVII.

Occupation:—*Continued.*

Serial Number.	Town. Workers. Males. 0–4	5–14	15 and over.	Total.	Females. 0–4	5–14	15 and over.	Total.	Dependents. Males.	Females.	Total. Males.	Females.	Total.	Country. Workers. Males. 0–4	5–14	15 and over.	Total.	Females. 0–4	5–14	15 and over.	Total.	Dependents. Males.	Females.	Total. Males.	Females.	Total.
	20	21	22	23	24	25	26	27	28	29	30	31	32	33	34	35	36	37	38	39	40	41	42	43	44	45
100	...	...	3	3	...	...	...	...	4	6	7	6	13	...	...	10	10	...	...	...	...	11	12	21	12	33
	...	...	3	**3**	...	...	...	...	4	6	**7**	**6**	**13**	...	...	10	**10**	...	...	...	...	11	12	**21**	**12**	**33**
X	...	...	3	3	...	...	...	...	4	6	7	6	13	...	...	10	10	...	...	...	...	11	12	21	12	33
101	...	...	11	11	...	...	1	1	1	4	12	5	17	...	...	16	16	...	...	2	2	19	39	35	41	76
102	...	...	3	3	...	...	1	1	2	8	5	9	14	...	...	...	...	...	...	...	...	...	...	...	...	...
	...	...	14	**14**	...	...	2	**2**	3	12	**17**	**14**	**31**	...	...	16	**16**	...	...	2	**2**	19	39	**35**	**41**	**76**
103	...	...	5	5	...	...	...	...	8	11	13	11	24	...	...	15	15	...	...	...	...	23	31	38	31	69
104	...	...	3	3	...	...	1	1	3	4	6	5	11	...	...	10	10	...	...	1	1	10	11	20	12	32
105	...	...	12	12	...	...	...	...	7	15	19	15	34	...	...	13	13	...	...	...	...	11	17	24	17	41
	...	...	20	**20**	...	...	1	**1**	18	30	**38**	**31**	**69**	...	...	38	**38**	...	...	1	**1**	44	59	**82**	**60**	**142**
106	...	...	2	2	...	...	...	...	1	3	3	3	6	...	...	5	5	...	...	...	...	6	12	11	12	23
	...	...	2	**2**	...	...	...	...	1	3	**3**	**3**	**6**	...	...	5	**5**	...	...	...	...	6	12	**11**	**12**	**23**
107	...	...	...	...	...	...	...	...	...	...	...	...	...	...	1	4	5	...	...	...	...	6	13	11	13	24
108	...	...	2	2	...	...	...	...	1	3	3	3	6	...	...	1	1	...	...	...	...	2	3	3	3	6
109	...	...	17	17	...	...	...	...	11	17	28	17	45	...	1	25	26	...	...	...	...	25	35	51	35	86
110	...	...	2	2	...	...	...	...	3	4	5	4	9	...	...	...	...	...	...	...	...	...	...	...	...	...
111	...	...	...	...	...	...	...	...	...	...	...	...	...	...	...	2	2	...	...	...	...	3	4	5	4	9
	...	...	21	**21**	...	...	...	...	15	24	**36**	**24**	**60**	...	2	32	**34**	...	...	...	...	36	55	**70**	**55**	**125**

TABLE XVII.

Occupation:-*Continued.*

Class.	Order.	Sub-Order and Group.	Number in Census Commissioner's List.	Serial Number.	OCCUPATION.	State-Total. Workers. Males. 0–4	5–14	15 and over.	Total.	Females. 0–4	5–14	15 and over.	Total.	Dependents. Males.	Females.	Total. Males.	Females.	Total.
1	2	3	4	5	6	7	8	9	10	11	12	13	14	15	16	17	18	19
D. Preparation and Supply of Material Substances-(*Continued.*)	XI. Supplementary Requirements.	31. Toys, Curiosities &c.	177	112	Toy, Kite & Cage Makers & Sellers.	...	...	15	**15**	...	...	5	**5**	20	32	**35**	**37**	**72**
					Total, Sub-order 31	...	...	15	**15**	...	...	5	**5**	20	32	**35**	**37**	**72**
		33. Necklaces, Bracelets, Beads, Sacred Threads &c.	185	113	Bangle Makers and Sellers in Lac.	...	1	8	**9**	...	...	8	**8**	7	19	**16**	**27**	**43**
			188	114	Bangle Makers and Sellers in Clay.	...	...	7	**7**	...	...	6	**6**	7	19	**14**	**25**	**39**
			194	115	Flower Garland Makers and Sellers.	...	5	25	**30**	...	1	12	**13**	7	20	**37**	**33**	**70**
					Total, Sub-order 33	...	6	40	**46**	...	1	26	**27**	21	58	**67**	**85**	**152**
		34. Furniture.	198	116	Furniture Makers	...	...	6	**6**	...	...	...	...	7	14	**13**	**14**	**27**
					Total, Sub-order 34	...	...	6	**6**	...	...	...	...	7	14	**13**	**14**	**27**
		36. Tools and Machinery.	204	117	Knife & Tool Makers & Sellers	...	2	14	**16**	...	...	4	**4**	13	24	**29**	**28**	**57**
			207	118	Machanics (*Not Railway.*)	...	...	2	**2**	...	...	...	...	1	6	**3**	**6**	**9**
					Total, Sub-order 36	...	2	16	**18**	...	...	4	**4**	14	30	**32**	**34**	**66**
		37. Arms and Ammunition.	210	119	Ammunition and Cap Dealers	...	...	5	**5**	...	...	...	...	10	21	**15**	**21**	**36**
			211	120	Gunpowder Makers and Sellers	...	...	8	**8**	...	...	...	...	9	16	**17**	**16**	**33**
			212	121	Fire-Work Makers and Sellers	...	...	17	**17**	...	...	...	...	19	41	**36**	**41**	**77**
			215	121	Bow & Arrow Makers & Sellers	...	...	13	**13**	...	...	4	**4**	16	21	**29**	**25**	**54**
					Total, Sub-order 37	...	...	43	**43**	...	...	4	**4**	54	99	**97**	**103**	**200**
					Total, Order XI.	...	10	268	**278**	...	1	45	**46**	258	467	**536**	**513**	**1,049**

TABLE XVII.

Occupation:—*Continued.*

Serial Number.	Town.													Country.												
	Workers.								Dependents.		Total.			Workers.								Dependents.		Total.		
	Males.				Females.									Males.				Females.								
	0–4	5–14	15 and over.	Total.	0–4	5–14	15 and over.	Total.	Males.	Females.	Males.	Females.	Total.	0–4	5–14	15 and over.	Total.	0–4	5–14	15 and over.	Total.	Males.	Females.	Males.	Females.	Total.
	20	21	22	23	24	25	26	27	28	29	30	31	32	33	34	35	36	37	38	39	40	41	42	43	44	45
112	...	...	7	**7**	...	...	2	**2**	9	15	**16**	**17**	**33**	...	...	8	**8**	...	...	3	**3**	11	17	**19**	**20**	**39**
	...	...	7	**7**	...	...	2	**2**	9	15	**16**	**17**	**33**	...	...	8	**8**	...	...	3	**3**	11	17	**19**	**20**	**39**
113	...	1	3	**4**	...	...	4	**4**	4	9	**8**	**13**	**21**	...	...	5	**5**	...	...	4	**4**	3	10	**8**	**14**	**22**
114	...	...	1	**1**	...	...	2	**2**	2	10	**3**	**12**	**15**	...	...	6	**6**	...	...	4	**4**	5	9	**11**	**13**	**24**
115	...	3	10	**13**	...	1	3	**4**	3	10	**16**	**14**	**30**	...	2	15	**17**	...	...	9	**9**	4	10	**21**	**19**	**40**
	...	4	14	**18**	...	1	9	**10**	9	29	**27**	**39**	**66**	...	2	26	**28**	...	...	17	**17**	12	29	**40**	**46**	**86**
116	...	...	2	**2**	...	...	...	...	2	5	**4**	**5**	**9**	...	...	4	**4**	...	...	...	...	5	9	**9**	**9**	**18**
	...	...	2	**2**	...	...	...	...	2	5	**4**	**5**	**9**	...	...	4	**4**	...	...	...	...	5	9	**9**	**9**	**18**
117	...	...	2	**2**	...	...	...	...	3	5	**5**	**5**	**10**	...	2	12	**14**	...	...	4	**4**	10	19	**24**	**23**	**47**
118	...	...	2	**2**	...	...	...	...	1	6	**3**	**6**	**9**	...	...	...	...	...	...	...	...	...	...	...	...	...
	...	...	4	**4**	...	...	...	...	4	11	**8**	**11**	**19**	...	2	12	**14**	...	...	4	**4**	10	19	**24**	**23**	**47**
119	...	...	2	**2**	...	...	...	...	4	7	**6**	**7**	**13**	...	...	3	**3**	...	...	...	...	6	14	**9**	**14**	**23**
120	...	...	3	**3**	...	...	...	...	2	5	**5**	**5**	**10**	...	...	5	**5**	...	...	...	...	7	11	**12**	**11**	**23**
{121	...	...	5	**5**	...	...	...	...	9	17	**14**	**17**	**31**	...	...	12	**12**	...	...	...	...	10	24	**22**	**24**	**46**
{121	...	...	...	...	...	...	...	...	...	...	...	...	...	...	...	13	**13**	...	...	4	**4**	16	21	**29**	**25**	**54**
	...	...	10	**10**	...	...	...	...	15	29	**25**	**29**	**54**	...	...	33	**33**	...	...	4	**4**	39	70	**72**	**74**	**146**
XI	...	4	94	**98**	...	1	14	**15**	76	158	**174**	**173**	**347**	...	6	174	**180**	...	...	31	**31**	182	309	**362**	**340**	**702**

TABLE XVII.

Occupation:—*Continued.*

Class.	Order.	Sub-order and Group.	Number in Census Commissioner's List.	Serial Number.	Occupation.	State Total. Workers. Males. 0-4	5-14	15 and over.	Total.	Females. 0-4	5-14	15 and over.	Total.	Dependents. Males.	Females.	Total. Males.	Females.	Total.
1	2	3	4	5	6	7	8	9	10	11	12	13	14	15	16	17	18	19
D. Preparation and Supply of Material Substances—(*Continued.*)	XII. Textile Fabrics and Dress.	40. Cotton.	233	122	Cotton Spinners &c.	...	2	23	25	...	8	59	67	20	53	45	120	165
			234	123	Cotton Weavers &c.	...	140	1921	2061	...	48	486	534	1199	2577	3260	3111	6371
					Total, Sub-order 40	...	142	1944	2086	...	56	545	601	1219	2630	3305	3231	6536
		41. Jute, Flax, Coir &c.	240	124	Flax-Spinners, Weavers and Sellers	...	...	6	6	...	...	1	1	1	6	7	7	14
			241	125	Hemp Rope Makers and Sellers	...	...	31	31	...	...	10	10	8	25	39	35	74
			242	126	Jute Manufacturers &c. (*Packers*)	...	...	13	13	...	...	...	...	6	19	19	19	38
			244	127	Net Makers and Sellers	...	3	47	50	...	1	6	7	27	70	77	77	154
			246	128	Coir Preparers, Manufacturers and Sellers	...	687	4393	5080	...	1374	8127	9501	3959	6655	9039	16156	25195
					Total, Sub-order 41	...	690	4490	5180	...	1375	8144	9519	4001	6775	9181	16294	25475
		42. Dress.	247	129	Tailors and Darners	...	32	903	935	...	25	340	365	623	794	1558	1159	2717
			248	130	Milliners and Dress Makers	...	3	17	20	...	2	24	26	25	39	45	65	110
			249	131	Out-Fitters Clothes and Quilt Dealers	...	...	293	293	...	...	6	6	184	228	477	234	711
			251	132	Cap and Turban Makers and Sellers	...	...	7	7	...	...	2	2	8	14	15	16	31
			252	133	Turban Binders	...	...	3	3	...	...	...	...	4	8	7	8	15
			253	134	Umbrella Makers and Sellers	...	57	447	504	...	33	204	237	278	361	782	598	1380
					Total, Sub-order 42	...	92	1670	1762	...	60	576	636	1122	1444	2884	2080	4964
					Total, Order XII	...	924	8104	9028	...	1491	9265	10756	6348	10849	15376	21605	36981

TABLE XVII.

Occupation:—*Continued.*

Serial Number.	Town. Workers. Males. 0–4	Town. Workers. Males. 5–14	Town. Workers. Males. 15 and over.	Town. Workers. Males. Total.	Town. Workers. Females. 0–4	Town. Workers. Females. 5–14	Town. Workers. Females. 15 and over.	Town. Workers. Females. Total.	Town. Dependents. Males.	Town. Dependents. Females.	Town. Total. Males.	Town. Total. Females.	Town. Total. Total.	Country. Workers. Males. 0–4	Country. Workers. Males. 5–14	Country. Workers. Males. 15 and over.	Country. Workers. Males. Total.	Country. Workers. Females. 0–4	Country. Workers. Females. 5–14	Country. Workers. Females. 15 and over.	Country. Workers. Females. Total.	Country. Dependents. Males.	Country. Dependents. Females.	Country. Total. Males.	Country. Total. Females.	Country. Total. Total.
	20	21	22	23	24	25	26	27	28	29	30	31	32	33	34	35	36	37	38	39	40	41	42	43	44	45
122	...	...	4	4	...	1	6	7	4	7	8	14	22	...	2	19	21	...	7	53	60	16	46	37	106	413
123	...	12	137	149	...	2	29	31	136	362	285	393	678	...	128	1784	1912	...	46	457	503	1063	2215	2975	2718	5693
	...	12	141	153	...	3	35	38	140	369	293	407	700	...	130	1803	1933	...	53	510	563	1079	2261	3012	2824	5836
124	...	...	...	...	...	...	...	...	...	...	...	...	...	...	...	6	6	...	...	1	1	1	6	7	7	14
125	...	...	6	6	...	...	3	3	5	8	11	11	22	...	...	25	25	...	...	7	7	3	17	28	24	52
126	...	...	4	4	...	...	...	...	1	4	5	4	9	...	...	9	9	...	...	...	...	5	15	14	15	29
127	...	...	5	5	...	...	1	1	2	4	7	5	12	...	3	42	45	...	1	5	6	25	66	70	72	142
128	...	20	221	241	...	23	127	150	204	413	445	563	1,008	...	667	4172	4839	...	1351	8000	9351	3755	6242	8594	15593	24187
	...	20	236	256	...	23	131	154	212	429	468	583	1,051	...	670	4254	4924	...	1352	8013	9365	3789	6346	8713	15711	24424
129	...	2	65	67	...	2	67	69	68	96	135	165	300	...	30	838	868	...	23	273	296	555	698	1423	994	2417
130	...	2	9	11	...	2	13	15	12	14	23	29	52	...	1	8	9	...	...	11	11	13	25	22	36	58
131	...	...	171	171	...	...	2	2	108	201	279	203	482	...	...	122	122	...	...	4	4	76	27	198	31	229
132	...	...	3	3	...	...	2	2	2	4	5	6	11	...	...	4	4	...	...	...	...	6	10	10	10	20
133	...	...	2	2	...	...	...	...	2	5	4	5	9	...	...	1	1	...	...	...	...	2	3	3	3	6
134	...	1	11	12	...	...	2	2	8	17	20	19	39	...	56	436	492	...	33	202	235	270	344	762	579	1341
	...	5	261	266	...	4	86	90	200	337	466	427	893	...	87	1409	1496	...	56	490	546	922	1107	2418	1653	4071
XII.	...	37	638	675	...	30	252	282	552	1,135	1,227	1,427	2,654	...	887	7466	8353	...	1461	9013	10474	5790	9714	14143	20188	34331

TABLE XVII.

Occupation:—*Continued.*

Class.	Order.	Sub-order and Group.	Number in Census Commissioner's List.	Serial Number.	Occupation.	State Total. Workers. Males. 0–4	5–14	15 and over.	Total.	Females. 0–4	5–14	15 and over.	Total.	Dependents. Males.	Females.	Total. Males.	Females.	Total.
1	2	3	4	5	6	7	8	9	10	11	12	13	14	15	16	17	18	19
II. Preparation and Supply of Material Substances—(Continued.)	XIII. Metals and Precious Stones.	43. Gold, Silver and Precious Stones.	258	135	Gold and Silver Dealers	...	...	46	46	...	...	...	...	45	67	91	67	158
			260	136	Gold and Silver Workers	...	100	1,308	1,408	...	3	39	42	978	2,294	23,86	2,336	4722
			265	137	Gilders	...	...	20	20	...	...	...	...	25	33	45	33	78
			268	138	Diamond Sellers	...	...	2	2	...	...	...	...	2	5	4	5	9
			271	139	Ruby and Emerald &c. Sellers	...	...	2	2	...	...	...	...	2	3	4	3	7
			273	140	Pearl & Other Precious Stone Dealers	...	...	9	9	...	...	1	1	6	10	15	11	26
			273(a)	141	Mother of Pearl Dealers	...	...	3	3	...	...	...	...	1	4	4	4	8
			274	142	Coral Dealers	...	...	11	11	...	...	...	...	7	14	18	14	32
					Total, Sub-order 43	...	100	1,401	1,501	...	3	40	43	1,066	2,430	2,567	2,473	5,040
		44. Brass, Copper and Bell-Metal.	277	143	Brass Pot Makers and Sellers	...	2	18	20	...	...	5	5	24	48	44	53	97
			278	144	Brass Image Casters and Sellers	...	...	2	2	...	...	...	...	4	7	6	7	13
			279	145	Copper Workers and Sellers	...	107	1,014	1,121	...	...	332	332	763	2,004	1,884	2,336	4,220
			281	146	Bell-Metal Workers and Sellers	...	24	327	351	...	2	28	30	211	477	592	507	1,099
			283	147	Brass and Copper Dealers	...	...	132	132	...	...	...	...	104	213	236	213	449
					Total, Sub-order 44	...	133	1,493	1,626	...	2	365	367	1,136	2,749	2,762	3,116	5,878

TABLE XVII.

Occupation:—*Continued.*

Serial No.	Town. Workers. Males. 0–4	5–14	15 and over.	Total.	Females. 0–4	5–14	15 and over.	Total.	Dependents. Males.	Females.	Total. Males.	Females.	Total.	Country. Workers. Males. 0–4	5–14	15 and over.	Total.	Females. 0–4	5–14	15 and over.	Total.	Dependents. Males.	Females.	Total. Males.	Females.	Total.
	20	21	22	23	24	25	26	27	28	29	30	31	32	33	34	35	36	37	38	39	40	41	42	43	44	45
[illegible]	...	...	31	31	...	...	...	...	25	51	56	51	107	...	...	15	15	...	...	...	...	20	16	35	16	51
136	...	14	203	217	...	...	5	5	136	382	353	387	740	...	86	1,105	1,191	...	3	34	37	842	1,912	2,033	1,949	3,982
[illegible]	...	...	11	11	...	...	...	...	10	15	21	15	36	...	...	9	9	...	...	...	...	15	18	24	18	42
[illegible]	...	...	2	2	...	...	...	...	2	5	4	5	9	...	...	...	...	...	...	...	...	...	...	...	...	...
[illegible]	...	...	2	2	...	...	...	...	2	3	4	3	7	...	...	...	...	...	...	...	...	...	...	...	...	...
140	...	...	6	6	...	...	1	1	4	7	10	8	18	...	...	3	3	...	...	...	...	2	3	5	3	8
[illegible]	...	...	3	3	...	...	...	...	1	4	4	4	8	...	...	...	...	...	...	...	...	...	...	...	...	...
[illegible]	...	...	4	4	...	...	...	...	2	4	6	4	10	...	...	7	7	...	...	...	...	5	10	12	10	22
	...	14	262	276	...	...	6	6	182	471	458	477	935	...	86	1,139	1,225	...	3	34	37	884	1,959	2,109	1,996	4,105
[illegible]	...	...	4	4	...	...	1	1	4	5	8	6	14	...	2	14	16	...	...	4	4	20	43	36	47	83
[illegible]	...	...	...	...	...	...	...	...	...	...	...	...	...	...	...	2	2	...	...	...	...	4	7	6	7	13
[illegible]	...	4	41	45	...	...	2	2	4	36	49	38	87	...	103	973	1,076	...	...	330	330	759	1,968	1,835	2,298	4,133
[illegible]	...	1	30	31	...	...	...	...	21	54	52	54	106	...	23	297	320	...	2	28	30	220	423	540	453	993
[illegible]	...	...	15	15	...	...	...	...	4	20	19	20	39	...	...	117	117	...	...	...	...	100	193	217	193	410
	...	5	90	95	...	...	3	3	33	115	128	118	246	...	128	1,403	1,531	...	2	362	364	1,103	2,634	2,634	2,998	5,632

TABLE XVII.

Occupation.—*Continued.*

Class.	Order.	Sub-Order and Group.	Number in Census Commissioner's List.	Serial Number.	Occupation.	State-Total. Workers. Males. 0–4	5–14	15 and over.	Total.	Females. 0–4	5–14	15 and over.	Total.	Dependents. Males.	Females.	Total. Males.	Females.	Total.
1	2	3	4	5	6	7	8	9	10	11	12	13	14	15	16	17	18	19
D. Preparation and Supply of Material Substances—(*Continued.*)	XIII. Metals and Precious Stones (*Continued.*)	45. Tin, Zinc, Mercury and Lead.	284	148	Tin Workers and Sellers	...	...	17	17	...	...	...	...	14	34	31	34	65
			286	149	Zinc Workers and Sellers	...	...	9	9	...	...	1	1	4	12	13	12	25
			287	150	Lead and Quick Silver Workers and Sellers	...	...	3	3	...	...	...	...	1	3	4	3	7
					Total, Sub-order 45	...	...	29	29	...	...	1	1	19	49	48	49	97
		46. Iron and Steel.	290	151	Blacksmiths	...	104	1203	1,307	...	40	161	201	873	1,922	2,180	2,123	4,303
			291	152	Iron and Hardware Dealers	...	51	508	559	...	4	57	61	394	750	953	811	1,764
					Total, Sub-order 46	...	155	1711	1,866	...	44	218	262	1,267	2,672	3,133	2,934	6,067
					Total, Order XIII.	...	388	4634	5,022	...	49	624	673	3,488	7,900	8,510	8,573	17,083
	XIV. Glass, Pottery and Stone Ware.	47. Glass and Chinaware.	296	153	Bottle Dealers	...	...	6	6	...	...	...	...	5	10	11	10	21
			297	154	Glass and Chinaware Dealers	...	...	10	10	...	...	...	...	11	18	21	18	39
					Total, Sub-order 47	...	...	16	16	...	...	...	...	16	28	32	28	60
		48. Earthen and Stone Ware.	298	155	Potters and Pot and Pipe-Bowl Makers and Sellers	...	111	700	811	...	76	491	567	484	686	1,295	1,253	2,548
			300	156	Pestle & Mortar Makers & Sellers	...	...	17	17	...	...	...	...	17	29	34	29	63
					Total, Sub-order 48	...	111	717	828	...	76	491	567	501	715	1,329	1,282	2,611
					Total, Order XIV.	...	111	733	844	...	76	491	567	517	743	1,361	1,310	2,671

TABLE XVII.

Occupation—*Continued.*

Serial Number.	Town.													Country.												
	Workers.								Dependents.		Total.			Workers.								Dependents.		Total.		
	Males.				Females.									Males.				Females.								
	0–4	5–14	15 and over.	Total.	0–4	5–14	15 and over.	Total.	Males.	Females.	Males.	Females.	Total.	0–4	5–14	15 and over.	Total.	0–4	5–14	15 and over.	Total.	Males.	Females.	Males.	Females.	Total.
	20	21	22	23	24	25	26	27	28	29	30	31	32	33	34	35	36	37	38	39	40	41	42	43	44	45
148	...	...	6	6	...	...	...	...	3	8	9	8	17	...	...	11	11	...	...	...	...	11	26	22	26	48
149	...	...	7	7	...	...	1	1	2	6	9	7	16	...	...	2	2	...	...	...	...	2	6	4	6	10
150	...	...	3	3	...	...	...	...	1	3	4	3	7	...	...	...	...	...	...	...	...	...	...	...	...	...
	...	...	16	16	...	...	1	1	6	17	22	18	40	...	...	13	13	...	...	...	...	13	32	26	32	58
151	...	4	106	110	...	2	9	11	78	172	188	183	371	...	100	1097	1197	...	38	152	190	795	1750	1992	1940	3932
152	...	2	36	38	...	...	4	4	25	61	63	65	128	...	49	472	521	...	4	53	57	369	689	890	746	1636
	...	6	142	148	...	2	13	15	103	233	251	248	499	...	149	1569	1718	...	42	205	247	1164	2439	2882	2686	5568
XIII.	...	25	510	535	...	2	23	25	324	836	859	861	1720	...	363	4124	4487	...	47	601	648	3164	7064	7651	7712	15363
153	...	...	6	6	...	...	...	...	5	10	11	10	21	...	...	...	...	...	...	...	...	...	...	...	...	...
154	...	...	4	4	...	...	...	...	4	9	8	9	17	...	...	6	6	...	...	...	...	7	9	13	9	22
	...	...	10	10	...	...	...	...	9	19	19	19	38	...	...	6	6	...	...	...	...	7	9	13	9	22
155	...	10	85	95	...	10	49	59	78	129	173	188	361	...	101	615	716	...	66	442	508	406	557	1122	1065	2187
156	...	...	...	...	...	...	...	...	...	...	...	...	...	...	...	17	17	...	...	...	...	17	29	34	29	63
	...	10	85	95	...	10	49	59	78	129	173	188	361	...	101	632	733	...	66	442	508	423	586	1156	1094	2250
XIV.	...	10	95	105	...	10	49	59	87	148	192	207	399	...	101	638	739	...	66	442	508	430	595	1169	1103	2272

TABLE XVII.

Occupation:—*Continued.*

Class.	Order.	Sub-order and Group.	Number in Census Commissioner's List.	Serial Number.	Occupation.	State Total. Workers. Males. 0–4	5–14	15 and over.	Total.	Females. 0–4	5–14	15 and over.	Total.	Dependents. Males.	Females.	Total. Males.	Females.	Total.
1	2	3	4	5	6	7	8	9	10	11	12	13	14	15	16	17	18	19
D. Preparation and Supply of Material Substances—(*Continued.*)	XV. Wood, Cane and Leaves &c.	49. Timberand Wood.	302	157	Timber and Bamboo Agents & Dealers	...	...	299	**299**	...	...	74	**74**	298	525	**597**	**599**	**1196**
			303	158	Wood Cutters and Sawyers	...	56	1290	**1346**	...	...	37	**37**	1213	2138	**2559**	**2175**	**4734**
			304	159	Carpenters	...	262	3806	**4068**	...	15	89	**104**	3222	6350	**7290**	**6454**	**13744**
			305	160	Coopers and Box Makers	...	36	688	**724**	...	...	11	**11**	508	1018	**1232**	**1029**	**2261**
					Total, Sub-order 49	...	354	6083	**6437**	...	15	211	**226**	5241	10031	**11678**	**10257**	**21935**
		50. Canework, Matting and Leaves &c.	306	161	Bamboo and Rattan Splitters, Workers and Sellers	...	1	88	**89**	...	...	6	**6**	66	168	**155**	**174**	**329**
			307	162	Basket Weavers and Sellers	...	133	1025	**1158**	...	100	1010	**1110**	743	1177	**1901**	**2287**	**4188**
			308	163	Mat Makers and Sellers	...	25	213	**238**	...	76	920	**996**	309	746	**547**	**1742**	**2289**
			310	164	Leaf-Plate Makers and Sellers	...	1	19	**20**	...	...	15	**15**	8	28	**28**	**43**	**71**
			312	165	Leaf-Fan Makers and Sellers	...	...	17	**17**	...	...	6	**6**	20	29	**37**	**35**	**72**
			313	166	Comb Makers and Sellers	...	...	4	**4**	...	...	...	...	...	4	**4**	**4**	**8**
			315	167	Pith and Bark Collectors, Workers and Sellers	...	2	64	**66**	...	...	11	**11**	39	67	**105**	**78**	**183**
					Total, Sub-order 50	...	162	1430	**1592**	...	176	1968	**2144**	1185	2219	**2777**	**4363**	**7140**
					Total, Order **XV**.	...	516	7513	**8029**	...	191	2179	**2370**	6426	12250	**14455**	**14620**	**29075**

TABLE XVII.

Occupation—*Continued.*

Serial Number.	Town.													Country.												
	Workers.								Dependents.		Total.			Workers.								Dependents.		Total.		
	Males.				Females.									Males.				Females.								
	0–4	5–14	15 and over.	Total.	0–4	5–14	15 and over.	Total.	Males.	Females.	Males.	Females.	Total.	0–4	5–14	15 and over.	Total.	0–4	5–14	15 and over.	Total.	Males.	Females.	Males.	Females.	Total.
	20	21	22	23	24	25	26	27	28	29	30	31	32	33	34	35	36	37	38	39	40	41	42	43	44	45
157	...	...	91	91	...	...	9	9	114	181	205	190	395	...	...	208	208	...	...	65	65	184	344	392	409	801
158	...	2	262	264	...	...	13	13	253	306	517	319	836	...	54	1028	1082	...	...	24	24	1060	1832	2142	1856	3998
159	...	20	343	363	...	...	27	27	280	562	643	589	1232	...	242	3463	3705	...	15	62	77	2942	5788	6647	5865	12512
160	...	6	105	111	...	...	3	3	68	157	179	160	339	...	30	583	613	...	...	8	8	440	861	1053	869	1922
	...	28	801	829	...	...	52	52	715	1206	1544	1258	2802	...	326	5282	5608	...	15	159	174	4626	8825	10234	8999	19233
161	...	...	2	2	...	...	...	...	2	3	4	3	7	...	1	86	87	...	...	6	6	64	165	151	171	322
162	...	3	14	17	...	4	17	21	13	10	30	31	61	...	130	1011	1141	...	96	993	1089	730	1167	1871	2256	4127
163	...	...	11	11	...	...	9	9	8	22	19	31	50	...	25	202	227	...	76	911	987	301	724	528	1711	2239
164	...	...	3	3	...	...	2	2	1	4	4	6	10	...	1	16	17	...	...	13	13	7	24	24	37	61
165	...	...	...	...	...	...	...	...	...	...	...	...	...	...	...	17	17	...	...	6	6	20	29	37	35	72
166	...	...	4	4	...	...	...	...	...	4	4	4	8	...	...	...	...	...	...	...	...	...	...	...	...	...
167	...	...	3	3	...	...	1	1	3	4	6	5	11	...	2	61	63	...	...	10	10	36	63	99	73	172
	...	3	37	40	...	4	29	33	27	47	67	80	147	...	159	1393	1552	...	172	[illegible]	2111	1158	2172	2710	4283	6993
XV.	...	31	838	869	...	4	81	85	642	1253	1511	1338	2349	...	485	6675	7160	...	187	2096	2283	5784	10997	12944	13282	26226

TABLE XVII.

Occupation:-*Continued.*

Class.	Order.	Sub-Order and Group.	Number in Census Commissioner's List.	Serial Number.	OCCUPATION.	State-Total.												
						Workers.								Dependents.		Total.		
						Males.				Females.								
						0-4	5-14	15 and over.	Total.	0-4	5-14	15 and over.	Total.	Males.	Females.	Males.	Females.	Total.
1	2	3	4	5	6	7	8	9	10	11	12	13	14	15	16	17	18	19
D. Preparation and Supply of Material Substances—(*Continued.*)	XVI. Drugs, Gums Dyes &c.	51. Gums, Wax and Similar Forest Produce.	323	168	Wax, Honey &c. Collectors & Sellers	...	12	433	445	...	...	21	21	428	789	873	810	1683
					Total, Sub-order 51	...	12	433	445	...	...	21	21	428	789	873	810	1683
		52. Drugs, Dyes, Pigments &c.	324	169	Chemists and Druggists	...	11	202	213	...	...	16	16	179	283	392	299	691
			326	170	Saltpetre Workers and Sellers	...	...	8	8	...	...	...	...	1	5	9	5	14
			328	171	Soap Makers and Sellers	...	...	18	18	...	...	11	11	11	25	29	36	65
			329	172	Sulphur Workers and Sellers	...	...	2	2	...	...	...	...	2	3	4	3	7
			330	173	Indigo Workers and Dealers	...	...	2	2	...	...	...	...	2	4	4	4	8
			332	174	Ink Makers and Sellers	...	...	2	2	...	...	...	...	6	3	8	3	11
			337	175	Perfume Preparers and Sellers	...	...	14	14	...	...	...	...	...	...	14	...	14
					Total, Sub-order 52	...	11	248	259	...	...	27	27	201	323	460	350	810
					Total, Order XVI.	...	23	681	704	...	...	48	48	629	1112	1333	1160	2493
	XVII. Leather, Horns, Bones and Grease.	53. Leather &c.	338	176	Tanners, Curriers and Hide Sellers	...	30	334	364	...	3	44	47	346	510	710	557	1267
			339	177	Shoe, Sandals, Boot, Makers & Sellers	...	1	40	41	...	...	...	...	24	57	65	57	122
			342	178	Hide, Horns and Bone Dealers	...	2	9	11	...	...	8	8	16	19	27	27	54
					Total, Sub-order 53	...	33	383	416	...	3	52	55	386	586	802	641	1443
					Total, Order XVII.	...	33	383	416	...	3	52	55	386	586	802	641	1443
					Total, Class D.	...	36910	54810	58504	...	2422	20578	23000	47648	82244	106152	105244	211396

TABLE XVII.

Occupation:—*Continued.*

Serial Number.	Town. Workers. Males. 0–4	5–14	15 and over.	Total.	Females. 0–4	5–14	15 and over.	Total.	Dependents. Males.	Females.	Total. Males.	Females.	Total.	Country. Workers. Males. 0–4	5–14	15 and over.	Total.	Females. 0–4	5–14	15 and over.	Total.	Dependents. Males.	Females.	Total. Males.	Females.	Total.
	20	21	22	23	24	25	26	27	28	29	30	31	32	33	34	35	36	37	38	39	40	41	42	43	44	45
168	...	...	7	7	...	...	...	...	8	12	15	12	27	...	12	426	438	...	...	21	21	420	777	858	798	1656
	...	...	7	7	...	...	...	...	8	12	15	12	27	...	12	426	438	...	...	21	21	420	777	858	798	1656
169	...	...	82	82	...	...	...	...	63	148	145	148	293	...	11	120	131	...	...	16	16	116	135	247	151	398
170	...	...	6	6	...	...	...	...	...	4	6	4	10	...	...	2	2	...	...	...	...	1	1	3	1	4
171	...	...	...	...	...	...	...	...	...	...	...	...	...	...	...	18	18	...	...	11	11	11	25	29	36	65
172	...	...	2	2	...	...	...	...	2	3	4	3	7	...	...	...	...	...	...	...	...	...	...	...	...	...
173	...	...	1	1	...	...	...	...	...	...	1	...	1	...	...	1	1	...	...	...	...	2	4	3	4	7
174	...	...	2	2	...	...	...	...	6	3	8	3	11	...	...	...	...	...	...	...	...	...	...	...	...	...
175	...	...	9	9	...	...	...	...	...	...	9	...	9	...	...	5	5	...	...	...	...	...	...	5	...	5
	...	...	102	102	...	...	...	...	71	158	173	158	331	...	11	146	157	...	...	27	27	130	165	287	192	479
XVI.	...	...	109	109	...	...	...	...	79	170	188	170	358	...	23	572	592	...	...	48	48	550	942	1142	990	2132
176	...	...	15	15	...	...	...	...	20	37	35	37	72	...	30	319	349	...	3	44	47	326	473	675	520	1205
177	...	...	7	7	...	...	...	...	4	9	11	9	20	...	1	33	34	...	...	...	...	20	48	54	48	102
178	...	...	3	3	...	...	...	...	6	10	9	10	19	...	2	6	8	...	...	8	8	10	9	18	17	35
	...	...	25	25	...	...	...	...	30	56	55	56	111	...	33	358	391	...	3	52	55	356	530	747	585	1332
XVII.	...	...	25	25	...	...	...	...	30	56	55	56	111	...	33	358	391	...	3	52	55	356	530	747	585	1332
Cl. D.	...	207	5361	5568	...	82	1369	1442	5073	9710	10641	11152	21793	...	3487	49449	52936	...	2340	19218	21558	42575	72534	95511	94092	189603

Table XVII.

OCCUPATION.

TABLE XVII.

Occupation:—*Continued.*

Class.	Order.	Sub-order and Group.	Number in Census Commissioner's List.	Serial Number.	OCCUPATION.	State Total. Workers. Males. 0–4	5–14	15 and over.	Total.	Females. 0–4	5–14	15 and over.	Total.	Dependents. Males.	Females.	Total. Males.	Females.	Total.
1	2	3	4	5	6	7	8	9	10	11	12	13	14	15	16	17	18	19
B. Commerce, Transport, Storage.	XVIII. Commerce.	54. Dealers in Money and Securities.	346	179	Bankers and Bank Managers	...	...	40	40	...	...	...	...	23	29	63	29	92
			347	180	Money Lenders and Pawn Brokers	...	...	78	78	...	...	7	7	67	195	145	202	347
			350	181	Money Changers and Testers	...	...	10	10	...	...	1	1	9	21	19	22	41
			351	182	Bank Clerks, Cashiers, Bill-Collectors Accountants &c.	...	...	25	25	...	...	...	...	11	32	36	32	68
					Total, Sub-order 54	...	...	153	153	...	...	8	8	110	277	263	285	548
		55. General Merchandise.	352	183	General Merchants	...	...	48	48	...	...	...	...	288	312	336	312	648
			353	184	Merchants' Managers, Accountants, Clerks &c.	...	2	438	440	...	...	24	24	234	425	674	449	1,123
					Total, Sub-order 55	...	2	486	488	...	...	24	24	522	737	1,010	761	1,771
		56. Dealing Unspecified.	354	185	Shopkeepers' Clerks, Salesmen &c.	...	19	363	382	...	2	39	41	416	783	798	824	1,622
			355	186	Shopkeepers and Money Lenders' Servants	...	21	862	883	...	4	260	264	652	1,504	1,535	1,768	3,303
			356	187	Shopkeepers Otherwise Unspecified	...	...	1,552	1,552	...	...	90	90	2,328	1,819	3,880	1,909	5,789
			357	188	Pedlars, Hawkers &c.	...	2	11	13	...	...	7	7	16	25	29	32	61
					Total, Sub-order 56	...	42	2,788	2,830	...	6	396	402	3,412	4,131	6,242	4,533	10,775

TABLE XVII.

Occupation:—*Continued.*

Serial Number.	Town.													Country.												
	Workers.								Dependents.		Total.			Workers.								Dependents.		Total.		
	Males.				Females.									Males.				Females.								
	0–4	5–14	15 and over.	Total.	0–4	5–14	15 and over.	Total.	Males.	Females.	Males.	Females.	Total.	0–4	5–14	15 and over.	Total.	0–4	5–14	15 and over.	Total.	Males.	Females.	Males.	Females.	Total.
	20	21	22	23	24	25	26	27	28	29	30	31	32	33	34	35	36	37	38	39	40	41	42	43	44	45
179	...	...	21	21	...	...	...	...	10	21	31	21	52	...	...	19	19	...	...	...	...	13	8	32	8	40
180	...	...	32	32	...	...	4	4	34	76	66	80	146	...	...	46	46	...	...	3	3	33	119	79	122	201
181	...	...	8	8	...	...	1	1	7	16	15	17	32	...	...	2	2	...	...	...	...	2	5	4	5	9
182	...	...	14	14	...	...	...	...	4	15	18	15	33	...	...	11	11	...	...	...	...	7	17	18	17	35
	...	...	75	75	...	...	5	5	55	128	130	133	263	...	...	78	78	...	...	3	3	55	149	133	152	285
183	...	...	32	32	...	...	...	...	254	297	286	297	583	...	...	16	16	...	...	...	...	34	15	50	15	65
184	...	...	37	37	...	...	18	18	30	59	67	77	144	...	2	401	403	...	...	6	6	204	366	607	372	979
	...	...	69	69	...	...	18	18	284	356	353	374	727	...	2	417	419	...	...	6	6	238	381	657	387	1044
185	...	9	104	113	...	...	12	12	98	163	211	175	386	...	10	259	269	...	2	27	29	318	620	587	649	1236
186	...	17	168	185	...	3	79	82	104	217	289	299	588	...	4	694	698	...	1	181	182	548	1287	1246	1469	2715
187	...	...	619	619	...	...	58	58	1112	1069	1731	1127	2858	...	...	933	933	...	...	32	32	1216	750	2149	782	2931
188	...	2	7	9	...	...	3	3	8	4	12	7	19	...	...	4	4	...	...	4	4	13	21	17	25	42
	...	28	898	926	...	3	152	155	1317	1453	2243	1608	3851	...	14	1890	1904	...	3	244	247	2095	2678	3999	2925	6924

TABLE XVII.

Occupation:-*Continued.*

Class.	Order.	Sub-Order and Group.	Number in Census Commissioner's List.	Serial Number.	Occupation.	State-Total. Workers. Males. 0–4	5–14	15 and over.	Total.	Females. 0–4	5–14	15 and over.	Total.	Dependents. Males.	Females.	Total. Males.	Females.	Total.
1	2	3	4	5	6	7	8	9	10	11	12	13	14	15	16	17	18	19
E. Commerce, Transport, Storage—(*Continued.*)	XVIII. Commerce—(*Continued.*)	57. Middlemen &c.	358	189	Brokers, Agents and Dubash	...	...	44	44	...	...	3	3	20	65	64	68	132
			359	190	House-Agents &c.	...	...	3	3	...	...	...	...	3	10	6	10	16
			360	191	Farmers of Tolls, Ferries &c.	...	...	19	19	...	...	...	...	10	18	29	18	47
			361	192	Farmers of Liquor, Opium &c.	...	...	11	11	...	...	...	...	7	12	18	12	30
			362	193	Lessees and Superintendents of Markets Stalls &c.	...	...	2	2	...	...	...	...	...	...	2	...	2
			363	194	Contractors Otherwise Unspecified.	...	...	19	19	...	...	...	...	28	39	47	39	86
			364	195	Contractors for Labour &c.	...	...	20	20	...	...	...	...	29	40	49	40	89
					Total, Sub-order 57	...	...	118	118	...	...	3	3	97	184	215	187	402
					Total, Order XVIII	...	44	3545	3,589	...	6	431	437	4,141	5,329	7,730	5,766	13,496
	XIX. Transport and Storage	59. Road.	375	196	Cart Owners and Drivers, Carting Agents &c.	...	28	481	509	...	...	22	22	278	495	787	517	1,304
			378	197	Palki, &c. Owners, Bearers &c.	...	...	34	34	...	...	...	...	10	15	44	15	59
			379	198	Pack Bullock Owners, Drivers &c.	...	24	602	626	...	...	20	20	396	762	1,022	782	1,804
			380	199	Pack Camel, Elephant &c. Owners and Drivers	...	...	72	72	...	...	...	...	69	82	141	82	223
					Total, Sub-order 59	...	52	1189	1,241	...	...	42	42	753	1,354	1,994	1,396	3,390

TABLE XVII.

Occupation:—*Continued.*

Serial Number.	Town.													Country.												
	Workers.								Dependents.		Total.			Workers.								Dependents.		Total.		
	Males.				Females.									Males.				Females.								
	0–4	5–14	15 and over.	Total.	0–4	5–14	15 and over.	Total.	Males.	Females.	Males.	Females.	Total.	0–4	5–14	15 and over.	Total.	0–4	5–14	15 and over.	Total.	Males.	Females.	Males.	Females.	Total.
	20	21	22	23	24	25	26	27	28	29	30	31	32	33	34	35	36	37	38	39	40	41	42	43	44	45
189	...	...	29	29	...	...	...	...	9	27	38	27	65	...	...	15	15	...	...	3	3	11	38	26	41	67
190	...	...	3	3	...	...	...	...	3	10	6	10	16	...	...	...	...	...	...	...	...	...	...	...	...	...
191	...	...	5	5	...	...	...	...	2	4	7	4	11	...	...	14	14	...	...	...	...	8	14	22	14	36
192	...	...	6	6	...	...	...	...	4	7	10	7	17	...	...	5	5	...	...	...	...	3	5	8	5	13
193	...	...	2	2	...	...	...	...	...	...	2	...	2	...	...	...	...	...	...	...	...	...	...	...	...	...
194	...	...	11	11	...	...	...	...	17	23	28	23	51	...	...	8	8	...	...	...	...	11	16	19	16	35
195	...	...	14	14	...	...	...	...	20	32	34	32	66	...	...	6	6	...	...	...	...	9	8	15	8	23
	...	...	70	70	...	...	...	...	55	103	125	103	228	...	...	48	48	...	...	3	3	42	81	90	84	174
	...	28	1112	1140	...	3	175	178	1711	2040	2851	2218	5069	...	16	[illegible]	[illegible]	...	3	256	[illegible]	2430	3289	[illegible]	[illegible]	8427
196	...	5	142	147	...	...	...	...	87	166	234	166	400	...	23	339	362	...	...	22	22	191	329	553	351	904
197	...	...	4	4	...	...	...	...	3	5	7	5	12	...	...	30	30	...	...	...	...	7	10	37	10	47
198	...	...	19	19	...	...	...	...	18	17	37	17	54	...	24	583	607	...	...	20	20	378	745	985	765	1750
199	...	...	4	4	...	...	...	...	4	6	8	6	14	...	...	68	68	...	...	...	...	65	76	123	76	209
	...	5	169	174	...	...	...	...	112	194	286	194	480	...	47	1020	1067	...	...	42	42	641	1160	1708	1202	2910

TABLE XVII.

Occupation.-*Continued.*

Class.	Order.	Sub-Order and Group.	Number in Census Commissioner's List.	Serial Number.	Occupation.	State-Total. Workers. Males. 0–4	5–14	15 and over.	Total.	Females. 0–4	5–14	15 and over.	Total.	Dependents. Males.	Females.	Total. Males.	Females.	Total.
1	2	3	4	5	6	7	8	9	10	11	12	13	14	15	16	17	18	19
E. Commerce, Transport, Storage—(*Continued.*)	XIX. Transport and Storage;—(*Continued.*)	60. Water.	383	200	Boat and Barge Owners &c.	...	1	12	**13**	...	...	4	**4**	4	23	**17**	**27**	**44**
			384	201	Ships' Officers, Mariners &c.	...	...	192	**192**	...	...	...	...	26	54	**218**	**54**	**272**
			385	202	Boat and Barge Men	...	58	1454	**1512**	...	...	7	**7**	879	1322	**2391**	**1329**	**3720**
			386	203	Pilots	...	...	5	**5**	...	...	...	...	3	11	**8**	**11**	**19**
			388	204	Dock and Harbour Service	...	2	28	**30**	...	...	21	**21**	26	29	**56**	**50**	**106**
					Total, Sub-order 60	...	61	1691	**1752**	...	...	32	**32**	938	1439	**2690**	**1471**	**4161**
		61. Messages.	390	205	Postal Directors, Post Masters&Clerks	...	...	20	**20**	...	...	...	...	6	8	**26**	**8**	**34**
			391	206	Postal Messengers, Runners &c.	...	...	63	**63**	...	...	...	...	36	55	**99**	**55**	**154**
			392	207	Messengers (*Unspecified*)	...	6	105	**111**	...	...	8	**8**	91	160	**202**	**168**	**370**
			393	208	Telegraph Officers &c.	...	...	2	**2**	...	...	...	...	...	...	**2**	...	**2**
			394	209	Telegraph Signallers & Messengers.	...	...	5	**5**	...	...	...	...	...	...	**5**	...	**5**
					Total, Sub-order 61	...	6	195	**201**	...	...	8	**8**	133	223	**334**	**231**	**565**
		62. Storage and Weighing.	398	210	Porters	...	61	1565	**1626**	...	21	599	**620**	1060	2019	**2686**	**2639**	**5325**
			399	211	Weighmen and Measurers	...	1	18	**19**	...	...	2	**2**	17	32	**36**	**34**	**70**
			400	212	Watchmen (*Not Village*)	...	...	33	**33**	...	...	...	...	24	18	**57**	**18**	**75**
					Total, Sub-order 62	...	62	1616	**1678**	...	21	601	**622**	1101	2069	**2779**	**2691**	**5470**
					Total, Order **XIX**.	...	181	4691	**4872**	...	21	683	**704**	2935	5085	**7807**	**5789**	**13596**
					Total, Class **E**.	...	225	8236	**8461**	...	27	1114	**1141**	7076	10414	**15537**	**11555**	**27092**

TABLE XVII.

Occupation:—*Continued.*

Serial Number.	Town.													Country.												
	Workers.								Dependents.		Total.			Workers.								Dependents.		Total.		
	Males.				Females.									Males.				Females.								
	0–4	5–14	15 and over.	Total.	0–4	5–14	15 and over.	Total.	Males.	Females.	Males.	Females.	Total.	0–4	5–14	15 and over.	Total.	0–4	5–14	15 and over.	Total.	Males.	Females.	Males.	Females.	Total.
	20	21	22	23	24	25	26	27	28	29	30	31	32	33	34	35	36	37	38	39	40	41	42	43	44	45
200	...	...	4	4	...	...	1	1	3	4	7	5	12	...	1	8	9	...	...	3	3	11	19	20	22	42
201	...	...	86	86	...	...	...	...	19	36	105	36	141	...	...	106	106	...	...	...	...	7	18	113	18	131
202	...	9	151	160	...	...	1	1	93	117	253	118	371	...	49	1303	1352	...	...	6	6	786	1205	2138	1211	3349
203	...	...	2	2	...	...	...	...	2	4	4	4	8	...	...	3	3	...	...	...	...	1	7	4	7	11
204	...	...	16	16	...	...	13	13	7	9	23	22	45	...	2	12	14	...	...	8	8	19	20	33	28	61
	...	9	259	268	...	...	15	15	124	170	392	185	577	...	52	1432	1484	...	...	17	17	824	1269	2308	1286	3594
205	...	...	8	8	...	...	...	...	2	5	10	5	15	...	...	12	12	...	...	...	...	4	3	16	3	19
206	...	...	7	7	...	...	...	...	2	6	9	6	15	...	...	56	56	...	...	...	...	34	49	90	49	139
207	...	...	15	15	...	...	...	...	4	11	19	11	30	...	6	90	96	...	...	8	8	87	149	183	157	340
208	...	...	2	2	...	...	...	...	...	...	2	...	2	...	...	...	...	...	...	...	...	...	...	...	...	...
209	...	...	5	5	...	...	...	...	...	...	5	...	5	...	...	...	...	...	...	...	...	...	...	...	...	...
	...	...	37	37	...	...	...	...	8	22	45	22	67	...	6	158	164	...	...	8	8	125	201	289	209	498
210	...	13	158	171	...	7	142	149	127	204	298	353	651	...	48	1407	1455	...	14	457	471	933	1815	2388	2286	4674
211	...	1	14	15	...	...	2	2	14	23	29	25	54	...	...	4	4	...	...	...	...	3	9	7	9	16
212	...	...	7	7	...	...	...	...	5	4	12	4	13	...	...	26	26	...	...	...	...	19	14	45	14	59
	...	14	179	193	...	7	144	151	146	231	339	382	721	...	48	1437	1485	...	14	457	471	955	1838	2440	2309	4749
XIX	...	28	644	672	...	7	159	166	390	617	1062	783	1845	...	153	4047	4200	...	14	524	538	2545	4468	6745	5006	11751
CL.E.	...	56	1756	1812	...	10	334	344	2101	2657	3913	3001	6914	...	169	6480	6649	...	17	780	797	4975	7757	11624	8554	20178

TABLE XVII.

Occupation—*Continued.*

Class.	Order.	Sub-order and Group.	Number in Census Commissioner's List.	Serial Number.	Occupation.	State Total. Workers. Males. 0–4	5–14	15 and over.	Total.	Females. 0–4	5–14	15 and over.	Total.	Dependents. Males.	Females.	Total. Males.	Females.	Total.
1	2	3	4	5	6	7	8	9	10	11	12	13	14	15	16	17	18	19
F. Professions.	XX Learned and Artistic Professions.	63 Religion.	401	213	Priests, Ministers, Preachers, Missionaries &c.	...	...	1048	1048	...	...	5	5	572	1095	1620	1100	2720
			402	214	Catechists, Readers, Zanana, Mission Service &c.	...	1	46	47	...	...	9	9	22	34	69	43	112
			403	215	Exorcists, Hail-Averters, Amulettiers &c.	...	...	174	174	...	...	45	45	120	153	294	198	492
			404	216	Religious Mendicants, Inmates of Monasteries Converts &c.	...	...	85	85	...	...	10	10	...	...	85	10	95
			405	217	Church, Temple, Muisjid, Pagoda, Ghat, Burial or Burning Ground Service, Pilgrim Conductors and Undertakers.	...	125	1424	1549	...	80	644	724	976	1701	2525	2425	4950
					Total, Sub-order 63	...	126	2777	2903	...	80	718	793	1690	2983	4593	3776	8369
		64. Education.	406	218	Administrative and Inspecting Officials.	...	...	5	5	...	...	...	...	15	16	20	16	36
			407	219	Principals, Professors, Teachers &c.	...	...	885	885	...	...	26	26	597	998	1482	1024	2506
			408	220	Clerks &c. on Educational Establishment.	...	...	39	39	...	...	7	7	17	34	56	41	97
					Total, Sub-order 64	...	...	929	929	...	...	33	33	629	1048	1558	1081	2639
		65. Literature.	409	221	Authors, Editors, Journalists, Ballad Makers	...	...	7	7	...	...	...	...	7	10	14	10	24
			410	222	Reporters, Short-Hand Writers, Book Copyists	...	...	4	4	...	...	...	...	2	7	6	7	13
			411	223	Private Secretaries and Clerks	...	15	568	583	...	...	...	...	412	621	995	671	1616
			412	224	Public Scribes and Copyists	...	...	258	258	...	...	...	...	64	282	322	282	604
			413	225	Service in Libraries and Literary Institutions	...	...	2	2	...	...	...	...	...	...	2	...	2
					Total, Sub-order 65	...	15	839	854	...	...	...	...	485	920	1339	920	2259

TABLE XVII.

Occupation.—Continued.

Serial Number.	Town.													Country.												
	Workers.								Dependents.		Total.			Workers.								Dependents.		Total.		
	Males.				Females.									Males.				Females.								
	0–4	5–14	15 and over	Total.	0–4	5–14	15 and over.	Total.	Males.	Females.	Males.	Females.	Total.	0–4	5–14	15 and over.	Total.	0–4	5–14	15 and over.	Total.	Males.	Females.	Males.	Females.	Total.
	20	21	22	23	24	25	26	27	28	29	30	31	32	33	34	35	36	37	38	39	40	41	42	43	44	45
213	...	...	165	**165**	...	...	...	...	107	169	**272**	**169**	**441**	...	...	883	**883**	...	...	5	**5**	465	926	**1348**	**931**	**2279**
214	...	1	21	**22**	...	...	8	**8**	14	29	**36**	**37**	**73**	...	...	25	**25**	...	...	1	**1**	8	5	**33**	**6**	**39**
215	...	...	21	**21**	...	...	9	**9**	19	34	**40**	**43**	**83**	...	...	153	**153**	...	...	36	**36**	101	119	**254**	**155**	**409**
216	...	...	34	**34**	...	...	6	**6**	...	...	**34**	**6**	**40**	...	...	51	**51**	...	...	4	**4**	...	...	**51**	**4**	**55**
217	...	...	204	**204**	...	...	75	**75**	161	335	**365**	**410**	**775**	...	125	1220	**1345**	...	80	569	**649**	815	1366	**2160**	**2015**	**4175**
	...	1	445	**446**	...	...	98	**98**	301	567	**747**	**665**	**1412**	...	125	2332	**2457**	...	80	615	**695**	1389	2416	**3846**	**3111**	**6957**
218	...	...	4	**4**	...	...	...	...	11	11	**15**	**11**	**26**	...	...	1	**1**	...	...	...	...	4	5	**5**	**5**	**10**
219	...	...	159	**159**	...	...	11	**11**	107	183	**266**	**194**	**460**	...	...	726	**726**	...	...	15	**15**	490	815	**1216**	**830**	**2046**
220	...	...	23	**23**	...	...	5	**5**	9	21	**32**	**26**	**58**	...	...	16	**16**	...	...	2	**2**	8	13	**24**	**15**	**39**
	...	...	186	**186**	...	...	16	**16**	127	215	**313**	**231**	**544**	...	...	743	**743**	...	...	17	**17**	502	833	**1245**	**850**	**2095**
221	...	...	3	**3**	...	...	...	...	4	5	**7**	**5**	**12**	...	...	4	**4**	...	...	...	...	3	5	**7**	**5**	**12**
222	...	...	...	...	...	...	...	...	...	...	...	...	...	...	...	4	**4**	...	...	...	...	2	7	**6**	**7**	**13**
223	...	4	110	**114**	...	...	...	...	106	183	**220**	**183**	**403**	...	11	458	**469**	...	...	...	...	306	438	**775**	**438**	**1213**
224	...	...	131	**131**	...	...	...	...	37	152	**168**	**152**	**320**	...	...	127	**127**	...	...	...	...	27	130	**154**	**130**	**284**
225	...	...	2	**2**	...	...	...	...	...	...	**2**	...	**2**	...	...	...	...	...	...	...	...	...	...	...	...	...
	...	4	246	**250**	...	...	...	...	147	340	**397**	**340**	**737**	...	11	593	**604**	...	...	...	...	338	580	**942**	**580**	**1522**

TABLE XVII.

Occupation:-*Continued.*

Class.	Order.	Sub-Order and Group.	Number in Census Commissioner's List.	Serial Number.	Occupation.	State-Total. Workers. Males. 0–4	5–14	15 and over.	Total.	Females. 0–4	5–14	15 and over.	Total.	Dependents. Males.	Females.	Total. Males.	Females.	Total.
1	2	3	4	5	6	7	8	9	10	11	12	13	14	15	16	17	18	19
F. Professions:-(*Continued.*)	XX. Learned and Artistic Professions:-(*Continued.*)	66. Law.	414	226	Barristers, Advocates and Pleaders.	...	...	182	182	...	...	...	...	292	383	474	383	857
			416	227	Articled Clerks and Other Lawyers' Clerks	...	...	27	27	...	...	...	...	15	29	42	29	71
			418	228	Stamp-Vendors	...	...	14	14	...	...	...	...	6	6	20	6	26
			419	229	Petition-Writers	...	...	24	24	...	...	...	...	14	23	38	23	61
					Total, Sub-order 66	...	...	247	247	...	...	...	...	327	441	574	441	1015
		67. Medicine.	421	230	Practitioners by Diploma	...	...	2	2	...	...	...	...	5	8	7	8	15
			422	231	Practitioners without Diploma	...	...	727	727	...	...	8	8	770	1006	1497	1014	2511
			424	232	Occulists	...	...	5	5	...	...	...	...	1	3	6	3	9
			425	233	Vaccinators	...	...	6	6	...	...	...	...	5	9	11	9	20
			426	234	Midwifery	...	...	2	2	...	...	14	14	3	2	5	16	21
			427	235	Hospital &c. Assistants and Apothecaries	...	...	6	6	...	...	...	...	15	16	21	16	37
			428	236	Compounders, Nurses, and Hospital and Dispensary Service	...	...	13	13	...	...	...	...	7	19	20	19	39
					Total, Sub-order 67	...	...	761	761	...	...	22	22	806	1063	1567	1085	2652

TABLE XVII.

Occupation:—*Continued.*

Serial Number.	Town.													Country.												
	Workers.								Dependents.		Total.			Workers.								Dependents.		Total.		
	Males.				Females.									Males.				Females.								
	0–4	5–14	15 and over.	Total.	0–4	5–14	15 and over.	Total.	Males.	Females.	Males.	Females.	Total.	0–4	5–14	15 and over.	Total.	0–4	5–14	15 and over.	Total.	Males.	Females.	Males.	Females.	Total.
	20	21	22	23	24	25	26	27	28	29	30	31	32	33	34	35	36	37	38	39	40	41	42	43	44	45
226	...	...	99	99	...	...	...	...	135	196	234	196	430	...	...	83	83	...	...	...	...	157	187	240	187	427
227	...	...	14	14	...	...	...	...	5	3	19	3	22	...	...	13	13	...	...	...	...	10	26	23	26	49
228	...	...	3	3	...	...	...	...	...	...	3	...	3	...	...	11	11	...	...	...	...	6	6	17	6	23
229	...	...	17	17	...	...	...	...	8	10	25	10	35	...	...	7	7	...	...	...	...	6	13	13	13	26
	...	...	133	133	...	...	...	...	148	209	281	209	490	...	...	114	114	...	...	...	...	179	232	293	232	525
230	...	...	2	2	...	...	...	...	5	8	7	8	15	...	...	...	...	...	...	...	...	...	...	...	...	...
231	...	...	71	71	...	...	1	1	68	121	139	122	261	...	...	656	656	...	...	7	7	702	885	1358	892	2250
232	...	...	1	1	...	...	...	...	...	...	1	...	1	...	...	4	4	...	...	...	...	1	3	5	3	8
233	...	...	3	3	...	...	...	...	5	7	8	7	15	...	...	3	3	...	...	...	...	...	2	3	2	5
234	...	...	2	2	...	...	3	3	3	2	5	5	10	...	...	...	...	...	...	11	11	...	...	...	11	11
235	...	...	4	4	...	...	...	...	5	4	9	4	13	...	...	2	2	...	...	...	...	10	12	12	12	24
236	...	...	9	9	...	...	...	...	5	10	14	10	24	...	...	4	4	...	...	...	...	2	9	6	9	15
	...	...	92	92	...	...	4	4	91	152	183	156	339	...	...	669	669	...	...	18	18	715	911	1384	929	2313

TABLE XVII.

Occupation:—*Continued.*

Class.	Order.	Sub-order and Group.	Number in Census Commissioner's List.	Serial Number.	OCCUPATION.	Workers: Males 0–4	Workers: Males 5–14	Workers: Males 15 and over.	Workers: Males Total.	Workers: Females 0–4	Workers: Females 5–14	Workers: Females 15 and over.	Workers: Females Total.	Dependents: Males.	Dependents: Females.	Total: Males.	Total: Females.	Total: Total.
1	2	3	4	5	6	7	8	9	10	11	12	13	14	15	16	17	18	19
F. Professions—(*Continued.*)	XX Learned and Artistic Professions.—(*Continued.*)	68. Engineering and Surveying.	430	237	Civil Engineers and Architects	...	...	2	2	...	...	...	...	4	3	6	3	9
			431	238	Topographical, Archæological and Revenue Surveyors	...	...	2	2	...	...	...	...	3	5	5	5	10
			432	239	Draughtsmen, Overseers &c.	...	...	7	7	...	...	...	...	8	12	15	12	27
			433	240	Clerks &c. in the Offices of the above	...	...	111	111	...	...	...	...	80	147	191	147	338
					Total, Sub-order 68	...	...	122	122	...	...	...	...	95	167	217	167	384
		69. Other Sciences.	437	241	Astrologers, Horoscope Casters &c.	...	...	364	364	...	...	3	3	320	628	684	631	1315
					Total, Sub-order 69	...	...	364	364	...	...	3	3	320	628	684	631	1315
		70. Pictorial Art and Sculpture.	440	242	Painters &c.	...	...	35	35	...	...	...	...	28	64	63	64	127
			442	243	Photographers	...	...	1	1	...	...	...	...	...	...	1	...	1
					Total, Sub-order 70	...	...	36	36	...	...	...	...	28	64	64	64	128
		71. Music, Acting Dancing.	443	244	Music Composers and Teachers	...	...	17	17	...	...	5	5	9	15	26	20	46
			444	245	Bandmasters and Players (*Not Military.*)	...	...	452	452	...	...	...	...	239	475	691	475	1166
			446	246	Actors, Singers and Dancers and Their Accompanists	...	2	77	79	...	1	13	14	43	88	122	102	224
					Total, Sub-order 71	...	2	546	548	...	1	18	19	291	578	839	597	1436
					Total, Order XX	...	143	6621	6764	...	81	789	870	4671	7892	11435	8762	20197

TABLE XVII.

Occupation:—*Continued.*

Serial Number.	Town.													Country.												
	Workers.								Dependents.		Total.			Workers.								Dependents.		Total.		
	Males.				Females.									Males.				Females.								
	0–4	5–14	15 and over.	Total.	0–4	5–14	15 and over.	Total.	Males.	Females.	Males.	Females.	Total.	0–4	5–14	15 and over.	Total.	0–4	5–14	15 and over.	Total.	Males.	Females.	Males.	Females.	Total.
	20	21	22	23	24	25	26	27	28	29	30	31	32	33	34	35	36	37	38	39	40	41	42	43	44	45
237	...	...	2	2	...	...	...	...	4	3	6	3	9	...	...	...	...	...	...	...	...	...	...	...	...	...
238	...	...	2	2	...	...	...	...	3	5	5	5	10	...	...	...	...	...	...	...	...	...	...	...	...	...
239	...	...	6	6	...	...	...	...	7	10	13	10	23	...	...	1	1	...	...	...	...	1	2	2	2	4
240	...	...	69	69	...	...	...	...	53	101	122	101	223	...	...	42	42	...	...	...	...	27	46	69	46	115
	...	...	79	79	...	...	...	...	67	119	146	119	265	...	...	43	43	...	...	...	...	28	48	71	48	119
241	...	...	27	27	...	...	...	...	13	28	40	28	68	...	...	337	337	...	...	3	3	307	600	644	603	1247
	...	...	27	27	...	...	...	...	13	28	40	28	68	...	...	337	337	...	...	3	3	307	600	644	603	1247
242	...	...	5	5	...	...	...	...	2	5	7	5	12	...	...	30	30	...	...	...	...	26	59	56	59	115
243	...	...	1	1	...	...	...	...	...	...	1	...	1	...	...	...	...	...	...	...	...	...	...	...	...	...
	...	...	6	6	...	...	...	...	2	5	8	5	13	...	...	30	30	...	...	...	...	26	59	56	59	115
244	...	...	10	10	...	...	2	2	2	11	12	13	25	...	...	7	7	...	...	3	3	7	4	14	7	21
245	...	...	66	66	...	...	...	...	36	134	102	134	236	...	...	386	386	...	...	...	...	203	341	589	341	930
246	...	...	6	6	...	...	2	2	2	3	8	5	13	...	2	71	73	...	1	11	12	41	85	114	97	211
	...	...	82	82	...	...	4	4	40	148	122	152	274	...	2	464	466	...	1	14	15	251	430	717	445	1162
XX	...	5	1296	1301	...	...	122	122	936	1786	2237	1908	4145	...	138	5325	5463	...	81	667	748	3735	6106	9198	6854	16062

TABLE XVII.

Occupation:-*Continued.*

Class.	Order.	Sub-Order and Group.	Number in Census Commissioner's List.	Serial Number.	Occupation.	State-Total. Workers. Males. 0–4	5–14	15 and over.	Total.	Females. 0–4	5–14	15 and over.	Total.	Dependents. Males.	Females.	Total. Males.	Females.	Total.
1	2	3	4	5	6	7	8	9	10	11	12	13	14	15	16	17	18	19
F. Professions:-(*Continued.*)	XXI. Sport and Amusements	72. Sport.	448	247	Shikaris, Falconers, Bird-Catchers	...	...	15	15	...	...	2	2	4	12	19	14	33
					Total, Sub-order 72	...	...	15	15	...	...	2	2	4	12	19	14	33
		73. Exhibition and Games.	450	248	Exhibitors of tamed Animals	...	...	4	4	...	...	...	...	3	9	7	9	16
			454	249	Story and Ballad Reciters	...	...	29	29	...	...	18	18	9	21	38	39	77
			455	250	Exhibitors of Puppets	...	...	3	3	...	...	1	1	1	4	4	5	9
			457	251	Tumblers, Acrobats &c.	...	...	106	106	...	...	69	69	160	205	266	274	540
					Total, Sub-order 73	...	...	142	142	...	...	88	88	173	239	315	327	642
					Total, Order XXI	...	...	157	157	...	...	90	90	177	251	334	341	675
					Total, Class F	...	143	6778	6921	...	81	879	960	4848	8143	11769	9103	20872
G. Indefinite and Independent.	XXIII. Indefinite.	74. Unskilled Labour.	462	252	Tank Diggers and Excavators	...	11	69	80	...	2	48	50	23	69	103	119	222
			463	253	Road Labourers	...	...	128	128	...	...	6	6	102	213	230	219	449
			464	254	Quarrymen (Stone-Splitters)	...	13	186	199	...	1	1	2	143	211	342	213	555
			466	255	Rice-Pounders and Huskers	...	61	275	336	...	378	3872	4250	937	1856	1273	6106	7379
			467	256	General Labour	...	5022	42433	47455	...	3823	30386	34209	27260	43648	74715	77857	152572
					Total, Sub-order 74	...	5107	43091	48198	...	4204	34313	38517	28465	45997	76663	84514	161177
		75. Undefined &c.	468 (*a*)	257	Undefined Means of Livelihood	...	172	1415	1587	...	58	558	616	785	1298	2372	1914	4286
			468 (*b*)	258	Disreputable Means of Livelihood	...	...	6	6	...	3	14	17	12	6	18	23	41
					Total, Sub-order 75	...	172	1421	1593	...	61	572	633	797	1304	2390	1937	4327
					Total, Order XXIII	...	5279	44512	49791	...	4265	34885	39150	29262	47301	79053	86451	165504

TABLE XVII.

Occupation:—*Continued.*

Serial Number.	Town.													Country.												
	Workers.								Dependents.		Total.			Workers.								Dependents.		Total.		
	Males.				Females.									Males.				Females.								
	0–4	5–14	15 and over.	Total.	0–4	5–14	15 and over.	Total.	Males.	Females.	Males.	Females.	Total.	0–4	5–14	15 and over.	Total.	0–4	5–14	15 and over.	Total.	Males.	Females.	Males.	Females.	Total.
	20	21	22	23	24	25	26	27	28	29	30	31	32	33	34	35	36	37	38	39	40	41	42	43	44	45
247	...	...	1	1	...	...	...	...	2	2	3	2	5	...	...	14	14	...	...	2	2	2	10	16	12	28
	...	...	1	1	...	...	...	...	2	2	3	2	5	...	...	14	14	...	...	2	2	2	10	16	12	28
248	...	...	1	1	...	...	...	...	1	3	2	3	5	...	...	3	3	...	...	...	...	2	6	5	6	11
249	...	...	4	4	...	...	2	2	6	12	10	14	24	...	...	25	25	...	...	16	16	3	9	28	25	53
250	...	...	...	...	...	...	...	...	...	...	...	...	...	...	...	3	3	...	...	1	1	1	4	4	5	9
251	...	...	7	7	...	...	2	2	6	10	13	12	25	...	...	99	99	...	...	67	67	154	195	253	262	515
	...	...	12	12	...	...	4	4	13	25	25	29	54	...	...	130	130	...	...	84	84	160	214	290	298	588
	...	...	13	13	...	...	4	4	15	27	28	31	59	...	...	144	144	...	...	86	86	162	224	306	310	616
	...	5	1309	1314	...	...	126	126	951	1810	2265	1936	4201	...	138	5469	5607	...	81	753	834	3897	6333	9504	7167	16671
252	...	4	13	17	...	...	9	9	6	11	23	20	43	...	7	56	63	...	2	39	41	17	58	80	99	179
253	...	...	17	17	...	...	...	...	19	33	36	33	69	...	...	111	111	...	...	6	6	83	180	194	186	380
254	...	...	9	9	...	...	...	...	6	12	15	12	27	...	13	177	190	...	1	1	2	137	199	327	201	528
255	...	7	51	58	...	28	427	455	67	209	125	664	789	...	54	224	278	...	350	3445	3795	870	1647	1148	5442	6590
256	...	28	574	602	...	6	151	157	328	623	930	780	1710	...	4994	41859	46853	...	3817	30235	34052	26932	43025	73785	77077	150862
	...	39	664	703	...	34	587	621	426	888	1129	1509	2638	...	5068	42427	47495	...	4170	33726	37896	28039	45109	75534	83005	158539
257	...	35	183	218	...	3	23	26	130	333	348	359	707	...	137	1232	1369	...	55	535	590	655	965	2024	1555	3579
258	...	...	3	3	...	2	8	10	3	2	6	12	18	...	...	3	3	...	1	6	7	9	4	12	11	23
	...	35	186	221	...	5	31	36	133	335	354	371	725	...	137	1235	1372	...	56	541	597	664	969	2036	1566	3602
XXIII	...	74	850	924	...	39	618	657	559	1223	1483	1880	3363	...	5205	43662	48867	...	4226	34267	38493	28703	46078	77570	84571	162141

TABLE XVII.

Occupation:—*Continued.*

Class.	Order.	Sub-order and Group.	Number in Census Commissioner's List.	Serial Number.	OCCUPATION.	State Total: Workers: Males: 0–4	5–14	15 and over.	Total.	Workers: Females: 0–4	5–14	15 and over.	Total.	Dependents: Males.	Females.	Total: Males.	Females.	Total.
1	2	3	4	5	6	7	8	9	10	11	12	13	14	15	16	17	18	19
G. Indefinite and Independent:—(Continued.)	XXIV. Independent of Work.	76. Property and Alms.	469	259	House-Rent, Shares and Other Property (*Not being Land.*) ...	17	42	287	346	16	36	268	320	265	524	611	844	1455
			470	260	Allowances from Pations or Relatives	...	2	32	34	...	...	18	18	37	46	71	64	135
			471	261	Educational and Other Endowments...	...	3	40	43	...	...	...	...	...	...	43	...	43
			472	262	Mendicancy (*Not Religious.*) ...	15	166	817	998	15	113	627	755	265	356	1263	1111	2874
					Total, Sub-order 76	32	213	1176	1421	31	149	913	1093	567	926	1988	2019	4007
		77. Supported at the Public Charge.	473	263	Pension, Civil Services ...	...	...	36	36	...	...	...	...	59	156	95	156	251
			476	264	Prisoners under Trial ...	...	...	10	10	...	...	...	...	...	...	10	...	10
			477	265	Prisoners for Debt ...	...	...	20	20	...	...	...	...	...	...	20	...	20
			478	266	Prisoners Convicted ...	...	...	256	256	...	...	4	4	...	...	256	4	260
					Total, Sub-order 77	...	...	322	322	...	...	4	4	59	156	381	160	541
					Total, Order XXIV.	32	213	1498	1743	31	149	917	1097	626	1082	2369	2179	4548
					Total, Class G.	32	5492	46010	51534	31	4414	35802	40247	29888	48383	81422	88630	170052
					Total, Class A to Class G.	53	13327	183458	196838	49	8555	72512	81116	163918	278709	360756	359825	720581
					Net Recognizeable ...	...	...	24	24	...	...	6	6	14	38	38	44	82
					Not Stated ...	32	98	741	871	28	56	867	951	...	...	871	951	1822
					Grand Total ...	85	13425	184223	197733	77	8611	73385	82073	163932	278747	361665	360820	722485

TABLE XVII.

Occupation.—*Continued.*

Serial Number.	Town. Workers. Males. 0–4	Town. Workers. Males. 5–14	Town. Workers. Males. 15 and over.	Town. Workers. Males. Total.	Town. Workers. Females. 0–4	Town. Workers. Females. 5–14	Town. Workers. Females. 15 and over.	Town. Workers. Females. Total.	Town. Dependents. Males.	Town. Dependents. Females.	Town. Total. Males.	Town. Total. Females.	Town. Total. Total.	Country. Workers. Males. 0–4	Country. Workers. Males. 5–14	Country. Workers. Males. 15 and over.	Country. Workers. Males. Total.	Country. Workers. Females. 0–4	Country. Workers. Females. 5–14	Country. Workers. Females. 15 and over.	Country. Workers. Females. Total.	Country. Dependents. Males.	Country. Dependents. Females.	Country. Total. Males.	Country. Total. Females.	Country. Total. Total.
	20	21	22	23	24	25	26	27	28	29	30	31	32	33	34	35	36	37	38	39	40	41	42	43	44	45
259	6	10	67	83	4	5	78	87	90	206	173	295	468	11	32	220	263	12	31	190	233	175	316	438	549	987
260	...	...	6	6	...	...	8	8	10	9	16	17	33	...	2	26	28	...	...	10	10	27	37	55	47	102
261	...	3	27	30	...	...	...	...	...	...	30	...	30	...	...	13	13	...	...	...	...	...	...	13	...	13
262	2	33	117	152	3	11	81	95	9	14	161	109	270	13	133	700	846	12	102	546	660	256	342	1102	1002	2104
	8	46	217	271	7	16	167	190	109	231	380	421	801	24	167	959	1150	24	132	746	903	458	695	1608	1598	3206
263	...	...	13	13	...	...	...	...	31	53	44	53	97	...	...	23	23	...	...	...	...	28	103	51	103	154
264	...	...	10	10	...	...	...	...	...	...	10	...	10	...	...	...	...	...	...	...	...	...	...	...	...	...
265	...	...	20	20	...	...	...	...	...	...	20	...	20	...	...	...	...	...	...	...	...	...	...	...	...	...
266	...	...	214	214	...	...	4	4	...	...	214	4	218	...	...	42	42	...	...	...	...	...	...	42	...	42
	...	...	257	257	...	...	4	4	31	53	288	57	345	...	...	65	65	...	...	...	...	28	103	93	103	196
F.	8	46	474	528	7	16	171	194	140	284	668	478	1146	24	167	1024	1215	21	133	746	903	486	798	1701	1701	3402
G.	8	120	1324	1452	7	55	789	851	699	1507	2151	2358	4509	24	5372	44686	50082	24	4359	35013	39396	29189	46876	79271	86272	165543
A. to G.	11	509	13036	13556	7	196	3330	3533	12162	20615	25718	24148	49866	42	12818	170422	183282	42	8359	69182	77583	151756	258094	335038	335677	670715
	...	...	...	...	...	...	...	...	...	...	...	...	...	...	...	24	24	...	...	6	6	14	38	38	44	82
	5	24	102	131	3	23	113	139	...	...	131	139	270	27	74	639	740	25	33	754	812	...	...	740	812	1552
	16	533	13138	13687	10	219	3443	3672	12162	20615	25849	24287	50136	69	12892	171085	184046	67	8392	69942	78401	151770	258132	335816	336533	672349

TABLE XVII.

Occupation:—*Continued.*

(British Military Limits.)

Class.	Order.	Sub-Order and Group.	Number in Census Commissioner's List.	Occupation.	Males.				Females.				Total.			
					0–4	5–14	15 and over.	Total.	0–4	5–14	15 and over.	Total.	0–4	5–14	15 and over.	Total.
1	2	3	4	5	6	7	8	9	10	11	12	13	14	15	16	17
A.	II. Defence.	4. Army.	12	Officers ...	3	4	6	13	2	2	4	8	5	6	10	21
"			13	Non-Commissioned Officers and Privates.	24	24	136	184	9	10	120	139	33	34	256	323
"			14	Followers ...	2	4	3	9	2	3	5	10	4	7	8	19
C.	VI.	14. Personal and Domestic Services.	59	Barbers ...	...	...	2	2	...	...	1	1	...	...	3	3
			63	Washermen ...	...	1	2	3	1	1	2	4	1	2	4	7
			66	Indoor-Servants ...	...	...	2	2	...	...	...	...	...	...	2	2
			67	Grooms, Coachmen, Dog-boys &c. ...	...	1	1	2	...	...	...	...	...	1	1	2
D.	VII.	17. Animal Food.	79	Butchers ...	...	...	4	4	...	1	2	3	...	1	6	7
"	XI.	29. Watches, Clocks &c.	163	Watch and Clock Makers &c. ...	...	...	1	1	...	...	1	1	...	...	2	2
F.	XX.	64. Education.	407	Teachers ...	...	1	1	2	...	1	1	2	...	2	2	4
G.	XXIV.	77. Supported at the Public Charge.	474	Pension, Military Services ...	1	4	12	17	2	3	9	14	3	7	21	31
				Total ...	30	39	170	239	16	21	145	182	46	60	315	421

OPTIONAL TABLE A.

Civil Condition by Caste and Age.

78 Males and 75 Females whose Civil Condition or Age or Both are not returned are not included in this Table.

OPTIONAL TABLE A.

Civil Condition by Caste and Age.

Caste, Race or Tribe.	Males.																			
	All Ages.				0—9				10—14				15—39				40 and over.			
	Total.	Unmarried.	Married.	Widowed.	Total.	Unmarried.	Married.	Widowed.	Total.	Unmarried.	Married.	Widowed.	Total.	Unmarried.	Married.	Widowed.	Total.	Unmarried.	Married.	Widowed.
1	2	3	4	5	6	7	8	9	10	11	12	13	14	15	16	17	18	19	20	21
Malayali—Brahmins ...	3469	2126	1273	70	570	569	1	...	387	375	11	1	1651	1017	625	9	861	165	636	60
Other Do ...	10475	5094	4981	400	2680	2674	6	...	1204	1168	36	...	4317	1175	3070	72	2274	77	1869	328
Kshatriyas ...	645	316	305	24	142	142	...	...	64	58	6	...	318	105	205	8	121	11	94	16
Vaisyas ...	239	119	111	9	51	51	...	...	31	29	2	...	104	38	64	2	53	1	45	7
Ampalavasis ...	3555	2148	1359	48	912	910	2	...	467	462	5	...	1504	716	782	6	672	60	570	42
Malayali—Sudras ...	58585	33412	24097	1076	15399	15379	20	...	7477	7376	100	1	24990	10085	14751	154	10719	572	9226	921
Other Do ...	24792	12249	11624	919	6018	6014	3	1	2728	2664	64	...	10890	3482	7185	223	5156	89	4372	695
Ainkuti Kammalars ...	17315	9198	7750	367	4775	4765	10	...	2182	2153	29	...	7119	2229	4817	73	3239	51	2894	294
Iluvans ...	85369	45761	37633	1975	23895	23881	14	...	10821	10717	102	2	35189	10925	23856	408	15464	238	13661	1565
Dasans ...	5521	2837	2503	181	1476	1475	1	...	681	671	10	...	2196	674	1484	38	1168	17	1008	143
Other Low Castes ...	3143	1475	1555	113	794	793	1	...	359	354	5	...	1305	313	966	26	685	15	583	87
Aborginal Tribes ...	36507	18061	17309	1137	9586	9580	6	...	4437	4353	84	...	14804	3972	10630	202	7680	156	6589	935
Total Hindus ...	249615	132796	110500	6319	66298	66233	64	1	30838	30380	454	4	104387	34731	68435	1221	48092	1452	41547	5093

OPTIONAL TABLE A.

Civil Condition by Caste and Age.

Caste, Race or Tribe.	Females.																			
	All Ages.				0—9				10—14				15—39				40 and over.			
	Total.	Unmarried.	Married.	Widowed.	Total.	Unmarried.	Married.	Widowed.	Total.	Unmarried.	Married.	Widowed.	Total.	Unmarried.	Married.	Widowed.	Total.	Unmarried.	Married.	Widowed.
	22	23	24	25	26	27	28	29	30	31	32	33	34	35	36	37	38	39	40	41
Malayali—Brahmins ...	2670	1046	1283	541	615	605	10	...	280	248	32	...	1142	169	868	105	833	24	373	436
Other Do ...	9685	3167	4707	1811	1990	1941	47	2	1520	963	552	5	4040	208	3275	557	2135	55	833	1247
Kshatriyas ...	573	211	302	60	156	154	2	...	54	38	16	...	232	14	210	8	131	5	74	52
Vaisyas ...	207	75	96	36	51	51	...	...	19	17	2	...	85	6	70	9	52	1	24	27
Ampalavasis ...	3625	1197	1977	451	787	763	24	...	394	305	89	...	1490	87	1368	35	954	42	496	416
Malayali—Sudras ...	62697	22312	32814	7571	15268	14846	422	...	6747	4744	2003	...	26637	2170	23349	1118	14045	552	7040	6453
Other Do ...	24112	8547	11230	4335	5927	5876	50	1	2288	1808	475	5	10847	753	8926	1168	5050	100	1779	3161
Ainkuti Kammalars ...	17815	7890	7931	1994	4958	4920	38	...	2015	1781	230	4	7538	1050	6106	382	3304	139	1557	1608
Iluvans ...	84569	38748	36934	8887	24952	24773	179	...	9894	8865	1024	5	35456	4571	29111	1774	14367	539	6620	7108
Dasans ...	5201	2388	2247	566	1548	1541	7	...	615	537	78	...	2075	287	1682	106	963	23	480	460
Other Low Castes ...	3192	1303	1436	453	844	837	7	...	251	198	53	...	1337	245	984	106	760	23	390	347
Aboriginal Tribes ...	37281	15770	18145	3366	10510	10453	54	3	3779	3419	357	3	16226	1683	14006	537	6766	215	3728	2823
Total Hindus ...	251827	102654	119102	30071	67606	66760	840	6	27856	22923	4911	22	107105	11243	89957	5905	49260	1728	23394	24138

Optional Table A.

CIVIL CONDITION BY CASTE AND AGE.

OPTIONAL TABLE A.

Civil Condition by Caste and Age.

Caste Race or tribe.	Males. All Ages. Total.	Unmarried.	Married.	Widowed.	0—9 Total.	Unmarried.	Married.	Widowed.	10—14 Total.	Unmarried.	Married.	Widowed.	15—39 Total.	Unmarried.	Married.	Widowed.	40 and over. Total.	Unmarried.	Married.	Widowed.
1	2	3	4	5	6	7	8	9	10	11	12	13	14	15	16	17	18	19	20	21
Mappilas ...	18499	10499	7720	330	5536	5535	1	...	2424	2418	6	...	7203	2470	4663	70	3336	26	3050	260
Ravuthans ...	3215	1796	1373	46	923	923	...	...	425	422	3	...	1319	440	867	12	548	11	503	34
Pathans ...	1163	621	524	18	302	302	...	...	131	131	...	...	495	181	310	4	235	7	214	14
Others ...	646	307	310	25	142	142	...	...	63	60	3	...	317	100	212	5	126	5	101	20
Total, Mussalmans...	[illegible]	[illegible]	[illegible]	[illegible]	[illegible]	[illegible]	1	...	3043	3031	12	...	9334	3191	6052	91	4245	49	3868	328
Europeans ...	27	19	7	1	7	7	...	...	2	2	...	...	9	7	2	...	9	3	5	1
Eurasians ...	155	93	58	4	41	41	...	...	18	16	2	...	63	33	29	1	33	3	27	3
Native Christians ...	87938	47062	38350	2526	25390	25367	23	...	11928	11712	215	1	34795	9668	24643	484	15825	315	13469	2041
Total, Christians...	88120	47174	38415	2531	25438	25415	23	...	11948	11730	217	1	34867	9708	24674	485	15867	321	13501	2045
Jews ...	566	314	233	19	130	130	...	...	57	57	...	...	235	123	108	4	144	4	125	15
Grand Total ...	361826	193457	159081	9288	98769	98680	88	1	45886	45198	683	5	148823	47753	99269	1801	68348	1826	59041	7481

OPTIONAL TABLE A.

Civil Condition by Caste and Age.

Caste, Race or Tribe.	Females.																			
	All Ages.				0—9				10—14				15—39				40 and over.			
	Total.	Unmarried.	Married.	Widowed.	Total.	Unmarried.	Married.	Widowed.	Total.	Unmarried.	Married.	Widowed.	Total.	Unmarried.	Married.	Widowed.	Total.	Unmarried.	Married.	Widowed.
	22	23	24	25	26	27	28	29	30	31	32	33	34	35	36	37	38	39	40	41
Mappilas ...	**17878**	8540	7464	1874	**5520**	5514	6	...	**2042**	1945	96	1	**7407**	991	6012	404	**2909**	90	1350	1469
Ravuthans ...	**3271**	1376	1420	475	**910**	904	6	...	**376**	305	71	...	**1433**	151	1140	142	**552**	16	203	333
Pathans ...	**1127**	425	554	148	**278**	274	4	...	**118**	92	26	...	**505**	54	406	45	**226**	5	118	103
Others ...	**569**	263	215	91	**159**	159	...	...	**113**	91	22	...	**190**	10	157	23	**107**	3	36	68
Total, Musalmans ...	22845	10604	9653	2588	**6867**	6851	16	...	**2649**	2433	215	1	**9535**	1206	7715	614	**3794**	114	1707	1973
Europeans ...	11	5	5	1	**3**	3	...	...	**2**	2	...	...	**5**	...	5	...	**1**	...	1	...
Eurasians ...	115	57	45	13	**36**	35	1	...	**11**	11	...	...	**37**	8	27	2	**31**	3	17	11
Native Christians ...	85553	30724	36986	8843	25995	25932	61	2	**10855**	9841	1008	6	**34124**	3444	28935	1745	**14579**	507	6982	7090
Total, Christians ...	85679	30786	37036	8857	26034	25970	62	2	10868	9854	1008	6	**34166**	3452	28967	1747	**14611**	510	7000	7101
Jews ...	**576**	231	271	74	**145**	144	1	...	**48**	46	2	...	**243**	39	192	12	**140**	2	76	62
Grand Total ...	560927	153275	166062	41590	**100652**	99725	919	8	**41421**	35256	6136	9	**151049**	16040	126831	8278	**67805**	2354	32177	33274

OPTIONAL TABLE B.

Education by Caste.

OPTIONAL TABLE B.

Education by Caste.

Serial Number.	Group of Caste, Race or Tribe.	State—Total.												Kanayanur.							
		Total.			Learning.			Literate.			Illiterate.			Total.		Learning.		Literate.		Illiterate.	
		Total.	Males.	Females.	Total.	Males.	Females.	Total.	Males.	Females.	Total.	Males.	Females.	Males.	Females.	Males.	Females.	Males.	Females.	Males.	Females.
1	2	3	4	5	6	7	8	9	10	11	12	13	14	15	16	17	18	19	20	21	22
1	Malayali--Brahmins ...	6344	3474	2870	474	363	111	2887	2312	575	2978	799	2179	501	326	42	10	370	85	89	231
2	Other Do. ...	20024	10408	9616	203	2063	140	5733	5513	220	12092	2827	9265	2023	1671	517	33	1063	79	443	1559
3	Kshatriyas ...	1218	645	573	205	122	83	440	331	109	573	192	381	268	289	90	68	111	43	67	178
4	Vaisyas ...	447	240	207	26	22	4	147	137	10	274	81	193	13	12	1	3	12	7	...	2
5	Ampalavasis ...	7187	3560	3627	746	519	227	2843	1969	874	3598	1072	2526	485	388	92	29	242	121	151	238
6	Malayali Sudra (Superior)...	101691	48950	52761	8429	6396	2033	26513	21184	5329	66740	21350	45390	6942	6889	1018	307	3528	1071	2396	5511
7	Do. (Inferior) ...	19623	9663	9960	608	511	97	2074	1897	177	16939	7253	9686	747	730	43	11	183	69	521	650
8	Other Sudras ...	48899	24785	24114	1124	993	131	3985	3826	159	43798	19976	23822	2335	1944	148	79	458	84	1729	1781
9	Ainkuti Kammalars ...	35140	17321	17819	1154	1029	125	4823	4524	299	29156	11765	17391	2035	1972	125	38	606	166	1304	1768
10	Iluvans ...	169949	85375	84574	3984	3471	513	14591	13604	987	151363	68298	83065	9366	9088	477	144	1784	310	7105	8634
11	Dasans ...	10723	5522	5201	212	176	36	1010	906	104	9501	4440	5061	1619	1458	57	12	245	59	1317	1387
12	Other Low Castes ...	6340	3146	3194	300	218	82	1131	922	209	4904	2001	2903	194	189	26	11	77	25	91	153
13	Aborginal Tribes ...	73813	36522	37291	89	35	54	780	556	224	72880	35908	36972	6175	6059	...	19	434	205	5720	5794
14	Not Stated ...	138	67	71	...	...	...	12	8	4	126	59	67	4	5	...	...	4	4	...	1
	Total Hindus ...	501536	249658	251878	19554	15918	3636	66969	57689	9280	422722	176821	245901	32707	31020	2636	764	9117	3328	20933	27887

OPTIONAL TABLE B.

Education by Caste.

Serial Number.	Cochin. Total. Males.	Total. Females.	Learning. Males.	Learning. Females.	Literate. Males.	Literate. Females.	Illiterate. Males.	Illiterate. Females.	Kotungallur. Total. Males.	Total. Females.	Learning. Males.	Learning. Females.	Literate. Males.	Literate. Females.	Illiterate. Males.	Illiterate. Females.	Mukundapuram. Total. Males.	Total. Females.	Learning. Males.	Learning. Females.	Literate. Males.	Literate. Females.	Illiterate. Males.	Illiterate. Females.
	23	24	25	26	27	28	29	30	31	32	33	34	35	36	37	38	39	40	41	42	43	44	45	46
1	**101**	**46**	9	4	67	6	25	36	**89**	**45**	12	3	58	11	19	31	**997**	**922**	95	26	596	143	306	753
2	**2688**	**2280**	307	15	1467	42	914	2222	**489**	**423**	74	3	198	8	217	412	**958**	**818**	154	3	545	11	259	804
3	**174**	**79**	5	...	91	13	78	66	**37**	**33**	8	8	26	11	3	14	**48**	**74**	2	3	35	22	11	49
4	**181**	**141**	16	1	95	3	70	137	...	...	...	...	...	...	...	...	...	...	...	...	...	...	...	...
5	**97**	**44**	12	4	67	19	18	21	**77**	**70**	4	4	39	12	34	54	**756**	**757**	93	39	446	195	217	523
6	**2276**	**2301**	387	182	1284	507	605	1612	**1374**	**1495**	224	71	623	143	527	1281	**9456**	**10208**	1036	300	3650	722	4770	9180
7	**300**	**281**	15	7	84	4	201	270	**160**	**153**	3	...	27	...	130	153	**1011**	**1053**	59	6	224	7	727	1040
8	**2965**	**2584**	118	19	601	28	2246	2537	**858**	**780**	27	1	85	3	746	776	**2400**	**2082**	30	1	202	4	2168	2077
9	**907**	**890**	62	17	330	16	515	857	**283**	**311**	13	1	58	...	212	310	**4159**	**4320**	238	29	1127	50	2792	4241
10	**10102**	**9734**	543	117	2760	206	6797	9409	**5027**	**5003**	214	5	776	7	4037	4991	**20765**	**20633**	849	76	3034	129	16882	20426
11	**3009**	**2852**	102	24	580	44	2327	2784	**688**	**687**	11	...	66	1	611	686	**206**	**204**	6	...	15	...	185	204
12	**28**	**33**	4	2	15	6	9	25	**22**	**34**	1	...	6	6	15	28	**797**	**770**	42	13	328	35	422	722
13	**4145**	**4000**	33	32	97	14	4015	3954	**960**	**958**	...	...	...	...	960	958	**7696**	**7776**	...	2	3	...	7693	7774
14	...	...	...	...	...	...	...	...	...	...	...	...	...	...	...	...	**63**	**66**	...	...	4	...	59	66
Total Hindus.	**26073**	**25265**	1613	424	7738	908	17820	23930	**10064**	**9992**	591	96	1962	202	7511	9694	**49312**	**49683**	2604	498	10209	1318	36491	47859

OPTIONAL TABLE B.

Education by Caste.

Serial Number.	Trichur. Total. Males.	Trichur. Total. Females.	Trichur. Learning. Males.	Trichur. Learning. Females.	Trichur. Literate. Males.	Trichur. Literate. Females.	Trichur. Illiterate. Males.	Trichur. Illiterate. Females.
	47	48	49	50	51	52	53	54
1	**1025**	**837**	94	35	720	183	211	614
2	**933**	**822**	226	31	490	35	213	756
3	**73**	**45**	11	1	44	13	18	31
4	**12**	**6**	...	...	8	...	4	6
5	**1089**	**1236**	167	88	614	319	308	829
6	**10779**	**11834**	1334	526	4580	1102	4865	1206
7	**3511**	**3483**	185	34	690	47	2626	3402
8	**1578**	**1446**	81	5	231	12	1266	1428
9	**4203**	**4312**	293	24	1247	37	2663	4251
10	**17079**	**16993**	714	85	3064	209	13301	16699
11	...	...	...	...	...	...	...	...
12	**637**	**606**	74	27	268	78	295	501
13	**5214**	**5401**	1	1	21	5	5192	5396
14	...	...	...	...	...	...	...	...
Total Hindus.	**46133**	**47021**	3180	857	10977	2040	30962	35119

Serial Number.	Talappilli. Total. Males.	Talappilli. Total. Females.	Talappilli. Learning. Males.	Talappilli. Learning. Females.	Talappilli. Literate. Males.	Talappilli. Literate. Females.	Talappilli. Illiterate. Males.	Talappilli. Illiterate. Females.
	55	56	57	58	59	60	61	62
1	**745**	**692**	111	33	487	147	147	512
2	**1623**	**1571**	350	9	882	14	391	1548
3	**25**	**33**	6	3	14	7	5	23
4	...	...	...	...	...	...	...	...
5	**1037**	**1119**	151	63	551	206	335	850
6	**15011**	**16756**	1793	486	5940	1141	7278	15126
7	**3227**	**3431**	161	29	582	40	2484	3362
8	**2776**	**2628**	66	13	267	7	2443	2607
9	**4120**	**4296**	255	16	883	25	2981	4252
10	**13525**	**13360**	481	85	1430	116	11614	13154
11	...	...	...	...	...	...	...	...
12	**916**	**961**	59	29	216	57	641	875
13	**7926**	**8706**	1	...	1	...	7924	8706
14	...	...	...	...	...	...	...	...
Total Hindus.	**50931**	**53553**	3434	766	11253	1760	36243	51015

Serial Number.	Chittur. Total. Males.	Chittur. Total. Females.	Chittur. Learning. Males.	Chittur. Learning. Females.	Chittur. Literate. Males.	Chittur. Literate. Females.	Chittur. Illiterate. Males.	Chittur. Illiterate. Females.
	63	64	65	66	67	68	69	70
1	**16**	**2**	...	...	14	...	2	2
2	**1694**	**2031**	435	46	869	31	390	1954
3	**20**	**20**	...	...	10	...	10	20
4	**34**	**48**	5	...	22	...	7	48
5	**19**	**13**	...	...	10	2	9	11
6	**3092**	**3278**	604	161	1579	643	909	2474
7	**717**	**829**	45	10	107	10	564	809
8	**11883**	**12650**	523	13	1982	21	9378	12616
9	**1614**	**1718**	43	...	273	5	1298	1712
10	**9511**	**9763**	193	1	756	10	8562	9752
11	...	...	...	...	...	...	...	...
12	**552**	**601**	12	...	12	2	528	599
13	**4404**	**4390**	...	...	...	...	4404	4390
14	...	...	...	...	...	...	...	...
Total Hindus.	**33556**	**31343**	1860	231	5634	724	26081	34387

OPTIONAL TABLE B.

Education by Caste.

Serial Number.	Group of Caste Race or Tribe.	State—Total.												Kanayanur.							
		Total.			Learning.			Literate.			Illiterate.			Total.		Learning.		Literate.		Illiterate.	
		Total.	Males.	Females.	Total.	Males.	Females.	Total.	Males.	Females.	Total.	Males.	Females.	Males.	Females.	Males.	Females.	Males.	Females.	Males.	Females.
1	2	3	4	5	6	7	8	9	10	11	12	13	14	15	16	17	18	19	20	21	22
15	Mappilas ...	36393	18510	17883	753	666	87	3015	2799	216	32567	15029	17538	2330	2151	150	24	551	41	1627	2086
16	Ravuthans ...	6486	3215	3271	171	169	2	1554	1546	8	5761	2500	3261	14	14	...	...	...	...	14	14
17	Pathans ...	2291	1163	1128	105	91	14	384	333	51	1799	738	1061	216	189	23	...	93	18	160	171
18	Others ...	1217	650	567	82	59	23	270	259	11	863	332	531	92	72	3	...	15	...	74	72
	Total, Mussalmans...	46387	23538	22849	1111	985	126	5223	4937	286	40990	18599	22391	2652	2426	176	24	659	59	1875	2843
19	Europeans ...	38	27	11	4	2	2	28	21	7	6	4	2	4	3	..	1	3	1	1	1
20	Eurasians ...	270	155	115	62	40	22	132	79	53	76	36	40	36	32	9	4	18	16	9	12
21	Native Christians.	173523	87952	85571	9438	7044	2394	28168	24309	3859	135616	56554	79062	16834	15892	1250	411	4640	1116	10944	14365
	Total, Christians...	173831	87134	85697	9504	7086	2418	28328	24409	3919	135698	56594	79104	16874	15927	1259	416	4661	1133	10954	14378
22	Jews ...	1142	566	576	62	50	12	264	181	83	816	335	481	221	206	19	6	40	51	162	149
	Grand Total ...	722896	360896	361000	30232	24040	6192	100787	87219	13568	600292	252415	347877	52454	49579	4090	1210	14477	4571	33924	44757

OPTIONAL TABLE B.

Education by Caste.

Serial Number.	Cochin.								Kotungallur.								Mukundapuram.							
	Total.		Learning.		Literate.		Illiterate.		Total.		Learning.		Literate.		Illiterate.		Total.		Learning.		Literate.		Illiterate.	
	Males.	Females.	Males.	Females.	Males.	Females.	Males.	Females.	Males.	Females.	Males.	Females.	Males.	Females.	Males.	Females.	Males.	Females.	Males.	Females.	Males.	Females.	Males.	Females.
	23	24	25	26	27	28	29	30	31	32	33	34	35	36	37	38	39	40	41	42	43	44	45	46
15	2480	2444	113	31	752	122	1615	2258	3187	3088	86	1	410	...	2691	3087	3205	3110	120	10	412	22	2672	3077
16	54	34	3	...	24	...	27	34	1	...	...	...	...	...	1	...	189	173	15	1	43	...	131	172
17	36	45	2	2	12	5	22	38	8	4	...	...	4	...	4	4	120	108	15	5	41	6	64	97
18	277	228	11	2	165	4	101	222	92	108	13	...	40	...	39	103	67	69	1	...	3	...	63	69
	2847	2751	129	35	953	131	1765	2552	3288	3195	99	1	454	...	2735	3194	3581	3460	151	16	499	28	2930	3415
19	...	...	...	...	...	...	...	...	...	...	...	...	...	...	...	...	...	...	...	...	...	...	...	...
20	41	33	8	9	22	12	11	12	...	...	...	...	...	...	...	...	25	12	10	3	9	4	6	5
21	24239	22808	2179	920	7467	1295	14579	20354	759	667	29	...	185	11	545	656	19847	19680	1478	384	4681	495	13682	18789
	24280	22841	2187	929	7489	1307	14590	20366	759	667	29	...	185	11	545	656	19872	19692	1488	387	4690	499	13688	18794
22	296	329	31	6	133	32	132	291	...	...	...	...	...	...	...	...	49	41	...	...	8	...	41	41
Grand Total.	53496	51186	3960	1394	16313	2378	34307	47139	14111	13854	719	97	2601	213	10791	13544	72814	72876	4243	901	1546	1845	53150	70109

OPTIONAL TABLE B.

Education by Caste.

Serial Number.	Trichur. Total. Males.	Total. Females	Learning. Males.	Learning. Females.	Literate. Males.	Literate. Females.	Illiterate. Males.	Illiterate. Females.
	47	48	49	50	51	52	53	54
15	1805	1786	104	11	311	25	1390	1749
16	71	65	2	...	9	3	60	62
17	226	228	23	6	72	13	130	208
18	108	87	31	21	33	6	44	58
	2210	2166	160	38	425	47	1624	2077
19	8	2	2	...	6	2	...	...
20	33	26	13	6	14	13	6	7
21	15606	15759	1271	499	4465	770	9845	14485
	15647	15787	1286	505	4485	785	9851	14492
22	...	...	...	...	...	...	...	...
Grand Total.	63990	64974	4626	1400	15987	2772	42437	51688

Serial Number.	Talappilli. Total. Males.	Total. Females.	Learning. Males.	Learning. Females.	Literate. Males.	Literate. Females.	Illiterate. Males.	Illiterate. Females.
	55	56	57	58	59	60	61	62
15	5262	5058	93	10	347	6	4809	5035
16	654	669	50	1	126	1	478	667
17	50	50	...	...	12	...	38	50
18	6	3	...	...	...	...	6	3
	5972	5780	143	11	485	7	5331	5755
19	...	...	...	...	...	...	...	...
20	2	2	...	...	1	1	1	1
21	8814	8840	731	166	2452	160	5631	8514
	8816	8842	731	166	2453	161	5632	8515
22	...	...	...	...	...	...	...	...
Grand Total.	65719	68175	4308	943	14191	1928	47205	19585

Serial Number.	Chittur. Total. Males.	Total. Females.	Learning. Males.	Learning. Females.	Literate. Males.	Literate. Females.	Illiterate. Males.	Illiterate. Females.
	63	64	65	66	67	68	69	70
15	241	246	...	...	16	...	225	246
16	2232	2316	99	...	344	4	1789	2312
17	507	504	28	1	99	9	380	493
18	8	5	...	...	3	1	5	4
	2988	3071	127	1	462	14	2399	3055
19	15	6	...	1	12	4	3	1
20	18	10	...	...	15	7	3	3
21	1853	1925	106	14	419	12	1328	1899
	1886	1941	106	15	446	23	1834	1903
22	...	...	...	...	...	...	...	...
Grand Total.	38430	36355	2093	247	6542	761	29814	39345

APPENDIX I.

ALPHABETICAL LIST OF CASTES.

APPENDIX I.

Alphabetical List of Castes.

Group No.	Caste Number.	Sub-Division of Caste.	Strength. Total.	Males.	Females.
1	2	3	4	5	6
5	6	Acharyar	20	10	10
2 (a)	1	Akamudiyan	255	123	132
2 (a)	1	Akamudiyan Pillai	10	4	6
1	6	Alikkara Nayar	9	4	5
5	9	Aluvar	9	5	4
7	1	Ammanampattu Kuruppu	90	50	40
7	2	Ampalavanavar	13	9	4
18	1	Ampattan	849	447	402
6	1	Andi	259	102	157
2 (a)	2	Angani	2	...	2
1	6	Anthuran	1569	682	887
2 (a)	2	Arasu	126	55	71
35	1	Aravan	3093	1568	1525
20	1	Asari	14439	7121	7318
20	1	Asari Kurruppu	99	65	34
1	6	Athikkurissi	3490	1692	1798
1	6	Athikkurissi Marar	263	116	147
7	1	Atikal	34	20	14
7	1	Atiyoti	14	6	8
1	6	Atiyoti	16	7	9
5	1	Ayyankar	50	26	24
5	8	Ayyar	890	468	422
6	4	Bairagi	98	80	18
14	2	Balija	8	5	3
14	2	Banya	147	88	59
1	6	Bhagavathi Atiyar	249	117	132
47	2	Bharatha Kuravan	38	22	16
5	7	Bhattathiri	127	57	70
1	1	Bhattiya	155	97	58
1	6	Chakkala	3	3	...
27	1	Chakkan	930	431	499
38	1	Chakkiliyan	696	362	334
13	1	Chakkiyar	8	8	...
23	1	Chaliyan	1586	806	780
36	1	Chanan	101	45	56
1	6	Charnavan	9096	4272	4824
10	1	Chavala Kaniyan	62	30	32
2 (c)	3	Chavara Kanakkan	538	268	270
14	4	Chaya Chetti	18	11	7
1	6	Cheethikan	1063	507	556
1	6	Chembottil Nayar	27	15	12
7	1	Chengali Nampiyar	137	68	69
2 (c)	1	Cheruman	9645	4773	4872
23	2	Chetan	924	451	473
23	2	Chetan Chayakkaran	24	9	15
23	2	Chetan Thevankan	768	384	384
24	1	Chetti	1202	655	547
14	4	Chetti Mannan	47	28	19
14	4	Chetti Vadhyar	129	64	65
5	8	Choliya Pattar	44	29	15
2 (a)	27	Choliya Vellalan	200	98	102
1	6	Chovathara Nayar	22	11	11
41	3	Chunnamp-Ottan	429	199	230
6	3	Dasar	16	10	6
45	1	Dasi	86	31	55
14	4	Desanka Chetti	17	13	4
5	9	Desikar	28	15	13
45	1	Devadasi	40	18	22
5	9	Dravida Brahmanan	136	77	59

APPENDIX I.

Alphabetical List of Castes.

Group Number.	Caste Number.	Sub-Division of Caste.	Strength. Total.	Males.	Females.
1	2	3	4	5	6
1	6	Elamkiriyam	43	30	13
1	6	Elamkori Nayar	11	3	8
1	6	Elayatam	66	33	33
30	1	Eluthachan	672	354	318
5	3	Empranthiri	495	390	105
1	6	Eruma Sudran	196	94	102
26	1	Etayan	52	34	18
26	2	Golla	5	3	2
2 (a)	7	Golla Kapu	7	3	4
2 (a)	4	Goundan	2676	1290	1386
2 (a)	2	Goundan Mutharasu	31	18	13
5	9	Gujaratti Brahmin	17	12	5
2 (a)	9	Irivathinalu Manayar	1605	809	796
10	1	Iluva Kaniyan	179	81	98
36	2	Iluvan	167121	83967	83154
12	1	Iluva Panan	39	18	21
36	2	Iluva Panikkar	168	88	80
36	2	Iluva Parisha	178	96	82
23	3	Kaikolan	3543	1731	1812
23	3	Kaikolan Muthali	43	24	19
1	6	Kaimal	240	114	126
41	1	Kallan	254	133	121
40	1	Kallandi	138	53	85
2 (a)	6	Kallar	32	14	18
41	2	Kallasari	1210	574	636
7	1	Kallattu Kuruppu	127	60	67
40	1	Kallu Muppan	145	71	74
2 (a)	22	KambolathanThottiyan	159	65	94
5	5	Kammathi	149	89	60
2 (b)	1	Kammatiyar	56	33	23
2 (c)	3	Kanakkan	3761	1832	1929
10	1	Kaniyan	902	461	441
10	1	Kaniyara Kurruppu	683	347	336
10	1	Kaniyara Panikkar	669	328	341
21	1	Kannan	243	127	116
1	6	Kannathevan	48	24	24
1	6	Kannori Nayar	10	4	6
2 (a)	7	Kapu	12	5	7
2 (a)	18	Kapu Reddi	8	4	4
2 (a)	27	Karakkattu Vellalar	28	15	13
1	2	Karnataka Kshatriya	6	2	4
1	6	Karthavu	146	75	71
19	1	Karuvan	2741	1356	1385
19	2	Katachi Kollan	60	24	36
4	1	Katar	221	94	127
14	3	Katuka Chetti	9	4	5
30	1	Katuppattan	10996	5445	5551
14	3	Kavara Chetti	321	167	154
10	1	Kavara Kaniyan	27	14	13
2 (a)	25	Kavara Vatukan	218	111	107
2 (a)	4	Kaviliya Goundan	41	22	19
18	3	Kavuthiyan	10	6	4
2 (c)	7	Kichata Pulayan	87	44	43
1	6	Kiriyam	20028	9709	10319
46	2	Kiruthala Kurruppu	42	18	24
1	6	Kolankori Nayar	161	83	78
19	2	Kolla Kurruppu	17	13	4
19	2	Kollan	3560	1749	1811
14	3	Komatti	84	44	40
26	3	Konan	206	98	108
20	1	Konga Asari	80	44	36
14	3	Konga Chetti	31	18	13

APPENDIX I.

Alphabetical List of Castes.

Group Number.	Caste Number.	Sub-Division of Caste.	Strength. Total.	Males.	Females.
1	2	3	4	5	6
45	1	Konga Dasi	26	9	17
19	2	Konga Kollan	67	36	31
28	1	Konga Kusavan	87	45	42
4	3	Konga Malayan	129	67	62
24	1	Konga Mannan	255	130	125
41	3	Konga Naickan	93	46	47
2 (c)	6	Konga Parayan	68	40	28
17	1	Konga Thattan	309	130	179
5	5	Konkani	5389	2822	2567
5	5	Konkani Vadhyar	18	9	9
46	1	Kotanki	57	26	31
2 (a)	8	Kotikkar	30	17	13
2 (a)	17	Kotuka Pillai	157	76	81
45	1	Kovil Dasi	100	28	72
1	2	Kshatriya	16	7	9
18	1	Kshurakan	193	91	102
2 (c)	7	Kulamari	145	81	64
47	1	Kuravan	368	203	165
7	1	Kurukkal	35	17	18
30	1	Kurukkal	128	67	61
4	2	Kurumbar	150	73	77
1	6	Kuruppal	34	19	15
1	6	Kurruppu	141	70	71
46	2	Kuruppu	242	121	121
1	6	Kuruppu Charnathu	6	2	4
1	6	Kuruppu Pallichan	6	2	4
1	6	Kuruppu Vellayma	43	18	25
28	1	Kusavan	1901	984	917
2 (c)	1	Kuta Cheruman	2241	1007	1234
4	3	Kuta Malayan	121	58	63
2 (c)	5	Kutan	520	259	261
14	3	Kutikkara Chetti	73	40	33
14	3	Kutumi Chetti	10158	5397	4761
1	2	Mahratta Kshatriya	77	39	38
1	3	Mahratta Sudra	75	71	4
14	7	Mahratta Vaisya	19	11	8
14	3	Mala Chetti	14	8	6
7	3	Malakkaran	70	38	32
2 (a)	4	Malaraya Goundan	92	41	51
4	8	Malayar	2247	1155	1092
5	5	Mallan	203	103	100
4	3	Malser	564	294	270
1	6	Manakkal Sudran	718	354	364
7	1	Manavalan	60	31	29
2 (a)	9	Manayar	74	29	45
1	6	Mannatiyar	52	27	25
24	1	Mannan	4560	2216	2344
26	1	Mannetayan	51	31	20
41	3	Mann-Ottan	666	330	336
35	3	Marakkan	37	24	13
7	1	Marar	1307	654	653
1	4	Maravar	57	24	33
1	6	Matampi Nayar	42	19	23
1	6	Matathil Nayar	581	304	277
2 (a)	10	Mathiya	7	4	3
35	4	Mukkuvan	1436	753	683
2 (a)	12	Mupan	1	...	1
2 (a)	11	Mupanar	1	1	...
21	2	Musari	786	378	408
5	7	Mussathu	57	34	23
2(a)	13	Muthaliyar	137	71	66
2(a)	2	Mutharasan	157	81	76
7	1	Muthathu	135	72	63

APPENDIX I.

Alphabetical List of Castes.

Group Number.	Caste Number.	Sub-Division of Caste.	Strength.		
			Total.	Males.	Females.
1	2	3	4	5	6
1	5	Naickar	133	67	66
1	6	Naluveetan	28	13	15
1	9	Nampati	227	108	119
7	1	Nampati	251	132	119
7	1	Nampi Kuruppu	40	23	17
1	6	Nampiyar	119	53	66
13	2	Nampiyar	39	14	25
1	6	Nampiyarku Charnathu	6	3	3
7	1	Nampiyassan	1502	770	732
5	7	Nampuri	4541	2397	2144
5	7	Nampuripad	263	150	113
1	6	Nanjinattu Pillai	183	107	76
18	1	Nasuvan	35	19	16
1	6	Natathalli	92	41	51
2 (a)	15	Nayadu	126	61	65
1	6	Nayar (*Unspecified.*)	7929	4001	3928
4	4	Nayati	123	61	62
1	9	Netungati	6	2	4
2 (a)	4	Okkiliya Goundan	8	4	4
2 (a)	16	Okkiliyan	73	42	31
5	2	Onnamparisha Elayathu	31	19	12
28	2	Otan	657	342	315
1	6	Otathu Nayar	56	31	25
5	7	Othikkan Nampuri	14	9	5
41	3	Otta Naickan	1293	686	607
6	1	Pakkanandi	59	31	28
1	6	Pallichan	18568	8835	9733
47	1	Pana Kuravan	52	24	28
12	1	Panan	2312	1159	1153
5	4	Pancha Gauda	68	39	29
1	9	Pandala	6	3	3
5	10	Pandaram	134	62	72
27	1	Pandi Chakkan	138	76	62
14	3	Pandi Chetti	70	34	36
47	1	Pandi Kuravan	17	7	10
41	3	Pandi Naickan	203	106	97
2 (a)	17	Pandi Pillai	103	58	45
5	4	Pandithar	50	25	25
17	1	Pandi Thattan	1423	735	688
2 (a)	27	Pandi Vellalan	104	52	52
1	6	Panikkar	23	14	9
1	6	Panikkar Charnathu	77	45	32
1	6	Panikkar Kiriyam	69	28	41
1	6	Panikkar Sudran	84	46	38
1	6	Panikkar Vattekkatan	8	5	3
14	3	Pappata Chetti	2542	1281	1261
35	6	Paravan	28	10	18
2 (c)	6	Parayan	6044	3082	2962
19	2	Parisha Kollan	47	18	29
1	6	Pathrani Nayar	226	100	126
14	3	Pathukuti Chetti	241	120	121
23	3	Patnulkaran	59	27	32
5	8	Pattar	11204	5730	1474
2 (c)	3	Patunna Kanakkan	2565	1270	1295
6	1	Payandi	69	38	31
24	1	Peru Mannan	116	58	58
19	2	Perumkollan	53	27	26
2 (a)	17	Pillai	312	176	136
1	6	Pindiyan	121	63	58
7	1	Pisharoti	987	459	528
18	3	Pittilan	11	4	7
1	6	Polakkal Nayar	16	11	5
35	7	Pondan	155	82	73

APPENDIX I.

Alphabetical List of Castes.

Group Number.	Caste Number.	Sub-Division of Caste.	Strength. Total.	Males.	Females.
1	2	3	4	5	6
5	5	Prabhu	163	93	70
18	1	Pranopakari	277	153	124
2 (c)	3	Pulaya Kanakkan	329	158	171
2 (c)	7	Pulayan	36215	17913	18302
12	1	Puli Panan	47	24	23
47	2	Pulluvan	111	53	58
2 (a)	4	Puluva Goundan	18	9	9
2 (c)	8	Puluvan	53	22	31
5	10	Puppandaran	165	84	81
6	1	Pusari	16	8	8
7	1	Puthuval	307	153	154
6	1	Puvandi	29	12	17
1	7	Rajput	64	55	9
1	8	Raju	88	38	50
5	1	Rayar	20	10	10
2 (a)	18	Reddi	32	13	19
14	7	Sadhu	7	5	2
1	9	Samanthan	35	17	18
2 (a)	20	Sami	7	3	4
2 (c)	6	Sankha Parayan	129	68	61
5	4	Saraswatha Gauda	1188	612	576
2 (a)	19	Sathan	1	1	...
5	5	Shenai	164	92	72
1	6	Sudran	23279	11212	12067
1	6	Swarupam	28	14	14
5	8	Thaliyalcha Pattar	13	8	5
1	2	Thampan	119	55	64
1	2	Thampuran	77	37	40
36	4	Thandan	1690	820	870
14	6	Tharaka Kurukkal	513	239	274
14	6	Tharakan	80	39	41
17	1	Thattan	3179	1575	1604
2 (a)	21	Thelenga	6	3	3
23	2	Thelunka Chetan	317	150	167
14	3	Thelunka Chetti	1404	695	709
17	1	Thelunka Thattan	38	18	20
		Thevanka Chetti	1393	716	677
2 (c)	10	Thevar	17	13	4
1	2	Thirumulpad	607	302	305
36	5	Thiyyan	111	48	63
38	3	Tholkollan	698	360	338
2 (a)	22	Thottiyan	159	82	77
4	5	Ullatan	439	208	231
2 (a)	4	Uluva Goundan	23	11	12
1	6	Unithiri Nayar	75	36	39
7	1	Unni	38	25	13
7	1	Unniyathiri	21	10	11
2 (c)	11	Uppiliyan	15	9	6
14	3	Uppilu Chetti	4	2	2
2 (a)	4	Urumala Goundan	5	3	2
2 (a)	23	Utayar	53	26	27
2 (a)	9	Utumanayar	17	9	8
14	7	Vaisya	35	18	17
14	3	Vala Chetti	271	125	146
35	8	Valan	6157	3177	2980
5	12	Valluvan	565	262	303
27	2	Vaniyan	683	360	323
7	1	Variyar	2011	970	1041
2 (a)	4	Vatayachi Goundan	61	31	30
18	6	Vathi	514	268	246
18	6	Vathi Kuruppu	178	87	91

APPENDIX I.

Alphabetical List of Castes.

Group Number.	Caste Number.	Sub-Division of Caste.	Strength. Total.	Males.	Females.
1	2	3	4	5	6
1	6	Vattekatan	8452	4038	4414
14	3	Vatuka Chetti	338	171	167
47	1	Vatuka Kuravan	80	44	36
2 (a)	25	Vatukan	758	356	402
41	3	Vatuka Naickan	35	19	16
1	5	Vatuka Naickar	14	7	7
1	6	Veettil Nayar	863	390	473
18	7	Velakkathalan	2299	1083	1216
2 (a)	26	Velambar	21	11	10
24	3	Velan	2524	1269	1255
1	6	Veliyathu Nayar	34	18	16
14	3	Vellala Chetti	291	147	144
2 (a)	4	Vellala Goundan	25	16	9
26	3	Vellala Konan	17	8	9
28	1	Vellala Kusavan	180	114	66
1	6	Vellalan	38	17	21
2 (a)	27	Vellalar	2510	1227	1283
5	10	Vellala Pandaram	42	20	22
2 (a)	17	Vellala Pillai	733	345	388
2 (a)	25	Vellala Vatukan	12	5	7
1	6	Vellayma	2989	1425	1564
2 (c)	7	Velluva Pulayan	108	54	54
24	4	Veluthetan	2989	1390	1599
2 (c)	1	Vettuva Cheraman	3034	1468	1566
2 (a)	4	Vettuva Goundan	87	41	46
2 (c)	3	Vettuva Kanakkan	3733	1931	1802
2 (c)	12	Vettuvan	747	367	380
2 (c)	7	Vettuva Pulayan	8	6	2
46	2	Vil Kuruppu	803	396	407
		Not Stated	138	67	71
		Total Hindus ...	501544	249666	251878

APPENDIX II.

LIST OF DESAMS OR VILLAGES WITH POPULATION.

APPENDIX II.

List of Desams or Villages with Population.

Pravirthi	Village or Desam.	No. of occupied Houses.	Population. Total.	Males.	Females.
1	2	3	4	5	6
KANAYANNUR.	1 Irimbanam	353	1865	880	985
	2 Thiruvankulam	302	1534	760	774
	3 Vatavakode	123	635	306	329
	4 Chottanikara	81	419	212	207
	5 Katungamangalam	114	596	284	312
	6 Kurikad	92	475	244	231
	7 Kanayannur	350	1748	862	886
	8 Mulanthuruthu	309	1646	862	784
	9 Karikode	217	1148	602	546
	10 Pangarapilly	112	559	279	280
	11 Perumpilly	157	896	464	432
	12 Thuruthikara	78	408	202	206
	13 Kanjiramittam	166	1385	684	701
	14 Pappakode	56	261	113	148
	15 Kuliathikara	31	170	75	95
	16 Veetangara	43	244	120	124
	17 Puthuvashery	77	408	204	204
	18 Mambala	89	477	252	225
	19 Pilappilli	47	257	138	119
	20 Karimalappatty	51	269	129	140
	21 Thottara	52	275	136	139
	22 Keechery	88	481	255	226
	23 Amballoor	226	1175	596	579
	24 Kunnappilly	49	266	138	128
	25 Chettikode	40	208	108	100
	26 Valiyil-Patinjara	38	198	110	88
	27 Kattimuttam	37	197	96	101
	28 Oolakata	30	152	81	71
	29 Netuvayal	16	86	42	44
	30 Etakattuvayal	63	292	135	157
	31 Kanayikode	33	182	102	80
	32 Kaypattoor	65	338	166	172
	33 Alakattoor	14	73	38	35
	34 Thottoor	37	194	105	89
	35 Thirumarayoor	39	212	100	112
	36 Mangatappilly	69	357	172	185
	37 Oorakam	46	231	117	114
	38 Veliyanad	114	563	276	287
	39 Elippuram	15	80	39	41
	40 Ayyukunnam	11	59	32	27
	41 Kanjirhappilly	14	75	32	43
	42 Motavakata	24	115	64	51
	43 Thalapana	57	303	157	146
	Total ...	4025	21512	10769	10743
NETTOOR.	1 Kumbalam	534	2874	1465	1409
	2 Panangata	451	2400	1210	1190
	3 Udayathuvathal	84	449	230	219
	4 Chathammal	48	251	125	126
	5 Cheppanam	151	828	449	379
	6 Vaittila	192	1116	572	544
	7 Kundannoor	155	840	433	407
	8 Matavana	72	399	215	184
	9 Punnurinny	184	993	503	490
	10 Poonithura	332	1800	912	888
	11 Nettoor	368	2064	1063	1001
	12 Marata	667	3495	1786	1709
	13 Karanakode	86	447	234	213
	14 Palarivattam	209	1109	556	553
	15 Vennala	225	1275	662	613
	16 Cheru Punnurinny	183	984	510	474
	Total ...	3941	21324	10925	10399

APPENDIX II.

List of Desams or Villages with Population.

Pravrithi	Village or Desam.		No. of occupied Houses.	Population.		
				Total.	Males.	Females.
1	2		3	4	5	6
NEENDA-KARA.	1	Natamel	1107	**5325**	2928	2397
	2	Eravoor	948	**4713**	2405	2308
	3	Thekumbhagam	837	**4056**	2068	1988
		Total ...	2892	**14094**	7401	6693
ERNAKULAM.	1	**Ernakulam** (*Town*)	1124	**7283**	4083	3200
	2	Thevara	43	**241**	127	114
	3	Chenganad	192	**1017**	535	482
	4	Perumanoor	687	**3406**	1763	1643
	5	Komanthuruthu	49	**256**	129	127
	6	Katavanthra	207	**1032**	534	498
	7	Chilavannoor	82	**433**	226	207
	8	Karithala	364	**1723**	898	825
	9	Kathrakatavu	57	**290**	147	143
	10	Thrikanarvattam	1048	**5458**	2785	2673
	11	Vatuthala	698	**3676**	1859	1817
	12	Kaloor	522	**2616**	1296	1320
	13	Elamkulam	181	**925**	474	451
	14	Palathurutha	59	**307**	153	154
	15	Chittur	307	**1590**	814	776
	16	Etakunnam	108	**541**	280	261
	17	Palam	29	**158**	84	74
	18	Cheranelloor	617	**3137**	1682	1455
		Total ...	6374	**34089**	17869	16220
VELLARAPILLI.	1	Chowera	375	**1895**	953	942
	2	Edanad	221	**1208**	582	626
	3	Thekumbhagam	383	**2031**	1021	1010
	4	Vatakumbhagam	208	**1080**	534	546
	5	Kilakumbhagam	353	**1965**	1016	949
	6	Thoravankara	107	**594**	301	293
	7	Chengala	141	**762**	370	392
	8	Malayattoor	261	**1479**	713	766
		Total ...	2049	**11014**	5490	5524
COCHIN.	1	**Mattanchery** (*Town*)	2978	**17254**	9028	8226
	2	Edacochy	484	**2175**	1142	1033
	3	Vatakummuri	866	**4365**	2334	2031
	4	Mundamveli	346	**1820**	924	896
	5	Moolamkuli	708	**3576**	1830	1746
	6	Venduruthy	342	**1967**	1041	926
		Total ...	5724	**31157**	16299	14858
CHERIANANDA-PURAM.	1	Andikatavu	698	**3614**	1843	1771
	2	Kandakatavu	193	**709**	368	341
	3	Chellanam	585	**2911**	1484	1427
	4	Ganapathikatu	68	**386**	209	177
	5	Maravakatu	269	**1171**	630	541
	6	Cheriakatavu	289	**1440**	731	709
	7	Mananchery	151	**781**	407	374
	8	Kumbalangy	1452	**7444**	3769	3675
	9	Thekummuri	882	**4071**	2036	2035
		Total ...	4587	**22527**	11477	11050
VYPEEN.	1	Sanketham	168	**844**	418	426
	2	Malippuram	148	**756**	375	381
	3	Elankunnapula	506	**2706**	1358	1348
	4	Narakal	996	**5135**	2565	2570
	5	Nayarambalam	778	**3783**	1914	1869
	6	Etavanakad	859	**3849**	2020	1829

APPENDIX II.

List of Desams or Villages with Population.

Pravritti	Village or Desam.	No. of occupied Houses.	Population. Total.	Males.	Females.
1	2	3	4	5	6
VYPEEN (*Continued.*)	7 Netunkad	239	1266	650	616
	8 Mundankad	46	202	90	112
	9 Pookad	77	401	197	204
	10 Manjanakad	52	281	179	102
	11 Aleekal	290	1674	876	798
	12 Muthikanapatam	174	883	479	404
	13 Ochanthuruthu	449	2418	1217	1201
	Total ...	4782	24198	12338	11860
PALLIPPURAM.	1 Kuluppilly	337	1719	877	842
	2 Ayyampilly	278	1442	738	704
	3 Cherayi	1085	4832	2526	2306
	4 Pallippuram	283	1390	705	685
	5 Chathetam	80	436	211	225
	6 Kotithuruthu	408	1885	996	889
	7 Vatakumpuram	359	2307	1169	1138
	8 Kilakumpuram	76	502	249	253
	9 Thekumpuram	208	1123	583	540
	10 Kutumkad	120	583	298	285
	11 Palathuruthu	224	1256	646	610
	12 Manakotam	127	769	356	413
	Total ...	3585	18244	9354	8890
MULAVUKAD.	1 Ponjikara	141	746	376	370
	2 Ponnarimangalam	213	1080	559	521
	3 Mulavukad	327	1771	919	852
	4 Vallarpatam	125	553	300	253
	5 Valia Katamakuti	185	912	502	410
	6 Cheria Katamakuti	28	141	74	67
	7 Pilala	116	640	331	309
	8 Kothata	99	498	268	230
	9 Moolampilli	130	651	325	326
	10 Chennoor	119	647	339	308
	11 Puthushery	2	5	3	2
	12 Korampatam	83	459	241	218
	13 Panambukatu	224	1043	543	500
	14 Kandanatu	12	65	31	34
	15 Karikat Thuruthu	42	245	117	128
	Total ...	1846	9456	4928	4528
KOTUNGALLUR.	1 Aleekode	897	4924	2474	2450
	2 Eriyad	574	3240	1622	1618
	3 Matavana	673	3547	1736	1811
	4 Methala	1468	7872	3914	3958
	5 Lokamaleswaram	1002	5751	2950	2801
	6 Pulloot	366	2094	1069	1025
	7 Narayanamangalam	76	437	246	191
	Total ...	5056	27865	14011	13854
PALAM.	1 Kolathoor	36	205	102	103
	2 Pailoor	36	219	103	116
	3 Nandikara	215	1386	681	705
	4 Puthranikara	110	752	342	410
	5 Rappal	118	803	390	413
	6 Alathoor	81	528	269	259
	7 Aloor	316	1885	921	964
	8 Chengaloor	321	1965	984	981
	9 Anandapuram	219	1313	656	657
	10 Pathaloor	112	663	311	352
	11 Kotakara	882	4507	2228	2279
	12 Nandipulam	181	1105	548	557

APPENDIX II.

List of Desams or Villages with Population.

Pravrithi	Village or Desam.		No. of occupied Houses.	Population. Total.	Males.	Females.
1	2		3	4	5	6
PALAM (*Continued.*)	13	Parappukara	149	**816**	405	411
	14	Maravanchery	41	**279**	149	130
	15	Manjoor	123	**739**	365	372
	16	Muppiliam	95	**412**	227	185
	17	Peetikapparamba	11	**65**	37	28
	18	Varandarapilli	221	**990**	510	480
	19	Netuval	179	**1080**	536	544
	20	Mattathoor	496	**2262**	1155	1107
	21	Thottipal	134	**898**	439	459
	22	Mulangoor	66	**439**	218	221
	23	Nellayi	94	**532**	270	262
		Palappilli	70	**383**	188	195
		Total ...	4306	**24224**	12034	12190
MUKUNDAPURAM.	1	Pallivattam	388	**2180**	1139	1041
	2	Thekunkara	581	**3198**	1691	1507
	3	Karumathra	78	**283**	144	139
	4	Vadakunkara	315	**1784**	895	889
	5	Vellookara	338	**2097**	1017	1080
	6	Kottalloor	254	**1567**	787	780
	7	Vatakattukara	37	**228**	121	107
	8	Thumbore	166	**1033**	509	524
	9	Katalayi	77	**294**	162	132
		Total ...	2184	**12664**	6465	6199
PATHI-NETTARA-YALAM.	1	Etavilanga	376	**1932**	980	952
	2	Kathiyalam	344	**1736**	887	849
	3	Kara	259	**1333**	673	660
	4	Tiruvanchikulam	30	**238**	135	103
		Total ...	1009	**5239**	2675	2564
AREEPALAM.	1	Patiyoor	361	**2020**	1030	990
	2	Areepalam	218	**1157**	630	527
	3	Poomangalam	193	**1067**	555	512
	4	Manavalashery	168	**1033**	521	512
	5	Etakkulam	283	**1626**	805	821
	6	Etathirinji	511	**2877**	1430	1447
	7	Thannishery	291	**1683**	840	843
	8	Kattoor	769	**4393**	2202	2191
	9	Korambishery	91	**498**	246	252
	10	Cheloor	218	**1256**	619	637
		Total ...	3113	**17610**	8878	8732
MAPRANAM.	1	**Irinjalakuta** (*Town*)	869	**52117**	2638	2579
	2	Irinjalakuta	25	**123**	76	47
	3	Manavalashery	170	**961**	488	473
	4	Parathishery	227	**1292**	618	674
	5	Thaliakonam	101	**588**	293	295
	6	Matayikonam	127	**793**	389	404
	7	Kulikathekonam	80	**473**	247	226
	8	Karivannoor	259	**1421**	688	733
	9	Moorkanatu	189	**1043**	507	536
	10	Kiluthani	196	**1271**	628	643
	11	Vellani	121	**673**	344	329
	12	Karalam	282	**1643**	822	821
	13	Mapranam	18	**105**	47	58
	14	Chemminga	122	**690**	354	336
	15	Pichampillikonam	105	**626**	290	336
		Total ...	2951	**16919**	8429	8490

APPENDIX II.

List of Desams or Villages with Population.

Pravrithi	Village or Desam.	No. of occupied Houses.	Population. Total.	Males.	Females.
1	2	3	4	5	6
PUTHUKAD.	1 Cheruval	14	249	125	124
	2 Paluva	105	625	279	346
	3 Amballoor	121	712	373	339
	4 Nemminikara	52	331	158	173
	5 Thoravunkara	384	2083	1005	1078
	6 Kalloor	220	1138	537	601
	7 Vengore	36	200	103	97
	8 Pookode	84	399	225	174
	9 Pattanathara	126	605	294	311
	10 Matavakara	46	304	156	148
	11 Eravakad	44	246	135	111
	12 Chittishery	77	372	183	189
	13 Thalore	82	404	206	198
	14 Paleekara	37	181	91	90
	15 Thalopanikara	57	246	108	138
	16 Konikara	87	459	244	215
	17 Trikoor	206	941	461	480
	18 Mannampotta	135	687	356	331
	Total ...	1940	10182	5039	5143
KODASHERY.	1 Palookara	143	761	374	387
	2 Karur	193	1073	554	519
	3 Annalloor	163	885	456	429
	4 Patinarai-Chalakuti	348	1896	916	980
	5 Annamanata	159	1031	518	513
	6 Muringoor	220	1226	599	627
	7 Kilakai-Chalakuti	518	2985	1498	1487
	8 Perumpra	226	1287	623	664
	9 Potta	304	1771	850	921
	10 Elinjipra	137	716	351	365
	11 Melur	567	2900	1398	1502
	12 Pariyaram	529	2828	1381	1447
	13 Kotashery	54	264	129	135
	Total ...	3561	19623	9647	9976
KORATTY.	1 Kundoor	184	1129	559	570
	2 Thirumukulam	31	186	105	81
	3 Airanikulam	49	332	172	160
	4 Patinarai-Bhagam	222	1290	635	655
	5 Kunpidi	129	615	310	305
	6 Kalloor-Thekummuri	206	1153	570	583
	7 Kalloor-Vatakummuri	187	1004	497	507
	8 Palishery	141	730	381	389
	9 Puvathishery	164	815	424	391
	10 Eravathoor	67	359	179	180
	11 Poyya	146	876	433	443
	12 Vayanattukara	18	95	49	46
	13 Melattoor	126	717	366	351
	14 Alathur	109	606	301	305
	15 Kiluthur	65	359	188	171
	16 Karuvilashery	205	1274	632	642
	17 Champaloor	85	464	242	222
	18 Vainthala	131	666	337	329
	19 Vennoor	145	817	392	425
	20 Kakkad	90	489	245	244
	21 Katankutti	120	620	315	305
	22 Cheruvaloor	88	478	236	242
	23 Annamanata	113	618	308	310
	24 Muringoor	199	961	470	491
	25 Valoor	78	425	209	216
	26 Thuruthu	68	346	180	166
	27 Matathumpadi	127	739	370	369
	28 Kilakemuri	389	1915	994	921

APPENDIX II.

List of Desams or Villages with Population.

Pravrithi	Village or Desam.	No. of occupied Houses.	Population.[1] Total.	Males.	Females.
1	2	3	4	5	6
KOBATTY (*Cont:*)	29 Patinjaramuri	120	**698**	329	369
	30 Mampra	101	**545**	257	288
	31 Erayamkuti	64	**339**	158	181
	32 Kathrikotam	57	**305**	149	156
	33 Etayattur	59	**312**	159	153
	34 Thainnishery	45	**266**	143	123
	35 Kakulishery	220	**1244**	635	609
	36 Thekummury	276	**1522**	718	804
	Total ...	4624	**25309**	12607	12702
THALAKAD.	1 Muriyad	221	**1227**	590	637
	2 Kallettumkara	207	**1167**	572	595
	3 Thalakad	196	**1083**	565	518
	4 Kulikattushery	229	**1362**	685	677
	5 Vatama	242	**1302**	672	630
	6 Vatakumbhagam	324	**1624**	842	782
	7 Naithukkudi	31	**150**	85	65
	8 Poyya	43	**236**	116	120
	9 Pallippuram	176	**959**	483	476
	10 Katuppishery	209	**976**	514	462
	11 Oorakam	158	**817**	407	410
	12 Pullore	214	**1199**	613	586
	13 Avittathore	137	**774**	369	405
	14 Mala	189	**1044**	527	517
	Total ...	2576	**13920**	7040	6880
TRICHUR.	1 **Trichur** (*Town*)	2070	**12945**	6592	6353
	2 Chettupula	117	**678**	326	352
	3 Pulla	40	**304**	146	158
	4 Cherikkalam	18	**115**	60	55
	5 Olarikkara	40	**226**	112	114
	6 Puthurkara	67	**428**	220	208
	7 Ayyanthol	159	**890**	448	442
	8 Poothol	35	**202**	99	103
	9 Poonkunnu	52	**276**	140	136
	10 Kanattukara	27	**142**	66	76
	11 Laloor	71	**395**	199	196
	12 Karyattukara	72	**435**	204	231
	13 Aranattukara	375	**2016**	980	1036
	14 Angati	41	**238**	108	130
	15 Koorkancheri	111	**759**	377	382
	16 Patukkara	20	**153**	75	78
	17 Vellannoor	49	**315**	168	147
	18 Kannankulangara	76	**464**	233	231
	19 Netupula	115	**645**	324	321
	20 Panamukku	66	**519**	265	254
	21 Kanimangalam	110	**768**	367	401
	22 Chiyyaram	156	**1078**	524	554
	23 Chelakkattukara	64	**335**	169	166
	24 Kilakumpattukara	297	**1836**	907	929
	25 Paramekkavu	16	**95**	51	44
	26 Chembukkavu	52	**341**	170	171
	27 Peringavu	57	**215**	103	112
	28 Trikkumarankutam	50	**138**	69	69
	29 Veluthur	7	**30**	13	17
	Total ...	4429	**26981**	13515	13466
VIJAYAPURAM.	1 Kuttoor	170	**1057**	504	553
	2 Kottekkatu	155	**906**	442	464
	3 Attore	55	**290**	141	149
	4 Pottore	127	**743**	348	395
	5 Kolikkunnu	78	**487**	226	261

APPENDIX II.

List of Desams or Villages with Population.

Pravrithi	Village or Desam.	No. of occupied Houses.	Population. Total.	Males.	Females.
1	2	3	4	5	6
VIJAYAPURAM (*Continued.*)	6 Kolali	118	723	344	379
	7 Patukkad	55	341	183	158
	8 Viyyore	141	910	432	478
	9 Killannoor	175	1121	567	554
	10 Tiroor	93	473	240	233
	11 Mannookad	14	99	52	47
	12 Evannoor	28	90	48	42
	13 Pandikavu	3	22	13	9
	14 Cheroor	81	456	209	247
	15 Vilwattam	172	979	475	504
	16 Nellikad	43	230	107	123
	17 Kurichikara	61	241	129	112
	Total ...	1569	9168	4460	4708
ARIMPOOR.	1 Veluthoor	68	404	209	195
	2 Erava	98	640	307	333
	3 Kaippulli	92	495	262	233
	4 Manakkoti	43	275	155	120
	5 Thachampilli	9	69	35	34
	6 Kilakumpuram	39	256	138	118
	7 Vatakumpuram	49	283	140	143
	8 Parakad	76	423	230	193
	Total ...	479	2845	1476	1369
PARAVATTANI.	1 Kainoor	76	464	259	205
	2 Kolukully	76	437	206	231
	3 Murkanikara	136	815	379	436
	4 Mulayalam	49	196	96	100
	5 Nallenkara	42	298	144	154
	6 Mukkattukara	144	854	415	439
	7 Ollookara	323	2025	1010	1015
	8 Pananchery	395	1893	974	919
	9 Vellanikara	79	437	215	222
	10 Matakathara	220	1181	596	585
	11 Nettishery	56	352	152	200
	12 Pattikkad	37	256	135	121
	Total ...	1633	9208	4581	4627
PERINGOTTUKARA.	1 Kurunpilava	371	2139	1050	1089
	2 Kiluppillikara	235	1606	861	745
	3 Thaniyam	197	1099	539	560
	4 Vaittilashery	23	141	67	74
	5 Muthetathara	87	482	239	243
	6 Karukappilli	40	260	126	134
	7 Puthumanakara	16	85	44	41
	8 Painoor	110	659	352	307
	9 Pitayanad	74	397	220	177
	10 Patinjaramuri	213	1208	595	613
	11 Vatakemuri	279	1433	704	729
	12 Thekkemuri	114	678	336	342
	13 Kilakemuri	253	1468	726	742
	14 Chettukulam	126	730	374	356
	15 Chaloor	182	1010	505	505
	16 Paluvam	295	1514	762	752
	17 Purathoor	247	1176	579	597
	18 Alappad	119	698	334	364
	19 Pulla	63	434	220	214
	Total ...	3044	17217	86633	8584

APPENDIX II.

List of Desams or Villages with Population.

Pravrithi	Village or Desam.	No. of occupied Houses.	Population. Total.	Males.	Females.
1	2	3	4	5	6
ENAMAKAL.	1 Puthoor	56	335	155	180
	2 Kallattupula	44	300	147	153
	3 Kilakan Kallattupula	26	130	64	66
	4 Muttichool	141	854	441	413
	5 Patiyam	132	751	380	371
	6 Etathiri	61	336	170	166
	7 Cherianthikad	51	259	138	121
	8 Irimprayoor	139	725	339	386
	9 Anthikad	314	1700	840	860
	10 Palloor	78	427	211	216
	11 Thrithani	45	284	137	147
	12 Ponalloor	344	1857	910	947
	13 Manaloor	476	2783	1424	1359
	14 Mangattukara Thekkemuri	256	1524	765	759
	15 Mangattukara Vatakemuri	249	1325	663	662
	16 Karamukku	453	2635	1282	1353
	Total ...	2865	16225	8066	8159
CAITTILAPPILLI.	1 Atad	156	889	438	451
	2 Kolangattukara	72	484	225	259
	3 Naranathra	31	246	115	131
	4 Choolishery	49	291	149	142
	5 Velappaya	161	981	468	513
	6 Manithra	31	209	107	102
	7 Avanoor	91	581	293	288
	8 Etakkulam	35	214	102	112
	9 Thangaloor	58	337	156	181
	10 Karore	17	122	54	68
	11 Varatiyam	96	678	322	356
	12 Chittilappilli	123	763	364	399
	13 Mulloor	24	154	72	82
	14 Chalakal	109	663	325	338
	15 Parappoor	101	637	301	336
	16 Tholloor	45	288	140	148
	17 Etakulathoor	186	833	426	407
	18 Ponore	68	456	244	212
	19 Puthoor	107	764	353	411
	20 Kaiparamba	36	268	121	147
	21 Kolathoor	36	191	98	93
	22 Puttekara	103	649	325	324
	23 Puranattukara	177	1078	516	562
	24 Pulakal	41	216	107	109
	25 Muthuvara	96	539	266	273
	26 Choorakattukara	138	747	371	376
	27 Peramangalam	327	2090	1036	1054
	28 Peringandoor	46	276	129	147
	29 Palayamukku	47	296	153	143
	30 Anhoor	89	469	239	230
	Total ...	2646	16409	8015	8394
OORAKAM.	1 Cheruvathery	84	523	270	253
	2 Palishery	74	382	166	166
	3 Cherashery	44	285	127	158
	4 Avanishery	79	650	311	339
	5 Perinchery	130	706	362	344
	6 Vellushery	121	742	377	365
	7 Vellukumathashery	34	131	75	56
	8 Cherushery	78	482	240	242
	9 Thekattushery	98	640	326	314
	10 Etakkuni	209	1388	665	723
	11 Perumanam	71	452	214	238
	12 Cherpu	452	2673	1338	1335
	13 Inchumuty	125	686	348	338

APPENDIX II.

List of Desams or Villages with Population.

Pravrithi	Village or Desam.	No. of occupied Houses.	Population. Total.	Males.	Females.
1	2	3	4	5	6
OORAKAM (*Continued.*)	14 Chenam	66	370	184	186
	15 Perumpillashery	267	1797	871	926
	16 Oorakam	230	1445	695	750
	17 Etumuna	153	880	452	428
	18 Panankulam	112	630	316	314
	19 Pallishery	109	575	292	283
	20 Arattupula	85	585	295	290
	21 Nerivashery	28	224	107	117
	22 Katalashery	85	609	278	331
	23 Chathakutam	46	303	137	166
	24 Vallachira	91	646	309	337
	25 Perimpatupuncheri	35	249	126	123
	26 Panrinyam	63	472	238	234
	27 Paralam	155	807	425	382
	28 Pallippuram	114	704	354	350
	29 Vattekad	51	344	163	181
	30 Kotannoor	131	840	411	429
	31 Elad	51	309	162	147
	32 Chakiarakad	31	189	96	93
	33 Penginashery	32	212	106	106
	34 Perukkara	63	460	222	238
	35 Chevoor	111	650	318	332
	Total ...	3708	22990	11376	11614
KUTTANELLOOR.	1 Ancheri	159	1052	523	529
	2 Natathra	73	483	231	252
	3 Erivimangalam	160	1022	529	493
	4 Kuttanelloor	85	521	253	268
	5 Elanthurithy	77	524	240	284
	6 Olloor	352	1931	921	1010
	7 Marathakara	210	1157	566	591
	8 Puthoor	226	1204	579	625
	9 Manangalam	9	20	16	4
	Total ...	1351	7914	3858	4056
MACHAD.	1 Wadakanchery	123	719	367	352
	2 Kumaranelloor	258	1371	662	709
	3 Kanjirakode	122	817	425	392
	4 Thekumkara	260	1466	685	781
	5 Mangalam	82	493	243	250
	6 Trikanapathiyaram	174	1153	555	598
	7 Karumathra	103	589	220	319
	8 Enkakad	420	1962	946	1016
	9 Kumbalangad	213	1225	599	626
	10 Manalithra	116	626	291	335
	11 Viruppakka	97	466	240	226
	12 Chittanda	122	826	407	419
	13 Machad Hills	12	49	28	21
	Total ..	2102	11762	5718	6044
CHENGALIKODE.	1 Arangottukara	82	530	253	277
	2 Katukashery	50	321	161	160
	3 Thalashery	67	350	189	161
	4 Muringathery	56	321	150	171
	5 Kuttanchery	59	442	200	242
	6 Parinjaram	29	185	96	89
	7 Thichoor	111	590	281	309
	8 Thalli	136	749	375	374
	9 Pelakad	131	835	426	409
	10 Varavur	326	1703	863	840
	11 Nelluvaya	116	654	301	353
	12 Vengilashery	191	1133	588	545

APPENDIX II.

List of Desams or Villages with Population.

Pravrithi	Village or Desam.		No. of occupied Houses.	Population.		
				Total.	Males.	Females.
1	2		3	4	5	6
CHENGALIKODE (*Continued.*)	13	Veloor	236	**1373**	672	701
	14	Thalakkottukara	190	**950**	479	471
	15	Chiranelloor	134	**712**	353	359
	16	Kurumal	56	**400**	203	197
	17	Palavoor	67	**444**	227	217
	18	Thayyore	126	**782**	380	402
	19	Kunnathery	28	**192**	95	97
	20	Thippallore	29	**137**	69	68
	21	Erumappatty	49	**328**	161	167
	22	Kariyannoor	43	**352**	168	184
	23	Thonnalloor	42	**227**	103	124
	24	Pathramangalam	44	**256**	125	131
	25	Karuvennoor	32	**247**	108	139
	26	Puliyannoor	32	**227**	107	120
	27	Vellattanjoor	104	**602**	295	307
	28	Thandilam	88	**535**	267	268
		Total ...	2654	**15577**	7695	7882
EYYAL.	1	Eyyal	169	**1052**	508	544
	2	Aroor	68	**418**	199	219
	3	Vellithirithy	98	**595**	291	304
	4	Panthalloor	68	**435**	218	217
	5	Kavanan Chittur	136	**841**	408	433
	6	Chemmanthatta	40	**224**	84	140
	7	Puthiamathoor	51	**308**	140	168
	8	Palanthana	120	**732**	359	373
	9	Puthushery	104	**535**	264	271
	10	Kurunellipparampa	16	**98**	57	41
	11	Chiramangad	183	**1042**	504	538
	12	Vellarakad	95	**648**	302	346
	13	Chovannoor	137	**849**	393	456
	14	Kitangoor	70	**430**	209	221
	15	Kurangoor	50	**367**	178	189
	16	Paliyode	21	**118**	58	60
	17	Kotakuly	12	**70**	29	41
	18	Katangode	290	**1722**	865	857
	19	Mandamparampa	33	**212**	93	119
		Total ...	1761	**10696**	5159	5537
KUNNANKULAM.	1	Chiralayam	193	**1060**	534	526
	2	Kunnankulam	602	**3287**	1576	1711
	3	Keeloor	174	**975**	474	501
	4	Kakkad	56	**310**	157	153
	5	Manchery	134	**703**	344	359
	6	Kaniampal	214	**904**	412	462
	7	Kanippayyoor	240	**1329**	658	671
	8	Chemmandoor	122	**617**	298	319
	9	Porkalangad	59	**366**	179	187
	10	Anayakal	50	**307**	159	148
	11	Irinjippuram	59	**367**	175	192
	12	Arthat	103	**575**	278	297
	13	Chittanjoor	110	**692**	353	339
	14	Alathoor	69	**394**	213	181
	15	Anjoor	65	**358**	168	190
	16	Vatuthala	121	**624**	323	301
	17	Cheruvathani	86	**469**	237	232
	18	Muthuvammal	64	**318**	162	156
	19	Maugat	157	**879**	439	440
		Total ...	2678	**14544**	7179	7365

APPENDIX II.

List of Desams or Villages with Population.

Pravrithi	Village or Desam.	No. of occupied Houses.	Population. Total.	Males.	Females.
1	2	3	4	5	6
PORKOLAM.	1 Kotta	63	404	194	210
	2 Katavalloor	340	1901	958	943
	3 Kollanchery	40	231	122	109
	4 Korattikara	124	745	383	362
	5 Mainarkode	47	258	132	126
	6 Karuvatal	27	157	71	86
	7 Pathaykara	55	312	150	162
	8 Perumpilava	211	1209	626	583
	9 Thippilashery	86	524	254	270
	10 Katakampal	343	1931	960	971
	11 Perumthuruthy	91	543	284	259
	12 Pangamukku	219	1242	642	600
	13 Palanji	395	2108	1031	1077
	14 Patimuri	59	397	207	190
	15 Kongandoor	58	293	157	136
	16 Poravore	58	297	152	145
	17 Karikad	49	280	151	129
	18 Akathiyoor	100	725	372	353
	19 Pulikkode	37	209	104	105
	20 Porkolam	207	1145	593	552
	21 Ayyamparampa	37	198	102	96
	22 Cheruthuruthy	98	557	286	271
	Total ...	2754	15666	7931	7735
CHOONDAL.	1 Pelakkattupayyoor	114	633	308	325
	2 Kariyannoor	30	191	99	92
	3 Chovalloor	81	474	225	249
	4 Aloor	228	1332	686	646
	5 Vatuthala	38	219	121	98
	6 Kandanishery	205	1083	555	528
	7 Atayoor	20	150	74	76
	8 Nampalikad	50	288	141	147
	9 Mattam	150	754	396	358
	10 Perumanna	153	968	483	485
	11 Choondal	242	1476	741	735
	12 Thuvanoor	28	182	89	93
	13 Eranelloor	75	442	232	210
	14 Pannishery	99	581	284	297
	15 Maluvanshery	52	283	143	140
	16 Parannoor	84	518	254	264
	17 Ariyannoor	111	642	309	333
	Total ...	1760	10216	5140	5076
MUNDATHIKODE.	1 Minaloor	151	798	375	423
	2 Mangad	112	702	343	359
	3 Chittalikara	151	906	465	441
	4 Paralikad	97	568	274	294
	5 Attithra	79	404	206	198
	6 Puthurithy	22	129	61	68
	7 Mundathikode	205	1327	657	670
	8 Peringandoor	95	576	296	280
	9 Kiraloor	99	569	272	297
	10 Kottappuram	115	663	315	348
	11 Thiruthipparampa	94	578	287	291
	12 Irrippakkunna	73	473	232	241
	Total ...	1289	7693	3783	3910

APPENDIX II.

List of Desams or Villages with Population.

Pravrithi	Village or Desam.	No. of occupied Houses.	Population. Total.	Males.	Females.
1	2	3	4	5	6
CHERUTHIRUTHY	1 Attoor	205	1296	599	697
	2 Panjal	173	1229	591	638
	3 Netumpura	301	1928	944	984
	4 Puthushery	145	871	422	449
	5 Cheruthiruthy	301	1137	547	590
	6 Mulloorkara	259	1526	751	775
	7 Kanjirashery	122	804	375	429
	8 Kondayoor	107	714	339	375
	9 Kuttampattoor	46	269	129	140
	10 Cherukad	15	94	44	50
	11 Palloor	156	837	382	455
	12 Kalavarakode	38	234	108	126
	13 Pallikal	103	618	291	327
	14 Desamangalam	207	1261	616	645
	15 Paravattoor	29	198	92	106
	Total ...	2247	13016	6230	6786
PALAYANNOOR.	1 Kaniyarkode- Kilakummuri	589	3302	1573	1729
	2 Kaniyarkode- Patinjaranmuri	799	4274	2080	2194
	3 Thekkethra	641	3650	1776	1874
	4 Vatakethra	329	1782	877	905
	5 Mayannore– Thekummuri	404	2440	1194	1246
	6 Mayannore– Vatakummuri	325	2008	993	1015
	7 Pampady	184	1124	585	539
	8 Chelakode	139	839	404	435
	Total ...	3410	19419	9482	9937
CHELAKARA	1 Pulakode	180	974	447	527
	2 Vennoor	85	427	208	219
	3 Elanad	154	650	337	313
	4 Pangarappilly	123	701	334	367
	5 Kolathoor	35	220	100	120
	6 Venganelloor	370	2244	1089	1155
	7 Chelakara	389	2278	1075	1203
	8 Painkolam	406	2589	1284	1305
	9 Killimangalam	369	2365	1146	1219
	10 Thonnoorkara	325	1947	954	993
	11 Kurumala	152	910	428	482
	Total ...	2588	15305	7402	7903
CHITTUR.	1 **Chittur** (*Town*)	1472	7848	3737	4111
	2 Chittur	858	4147	2060	2087
	3 Kunnankattupathy	253	913	460	453
	4 Moolathara	515	2133	1105	1028
	5 Kolippathy	354	1904	930	974
	6 Valiavallampathy	428	2161	1077	1084
	7 Thekke-Desam	521	2562	1258	1304
	Total ...	4401	21668	10627	11041
THATHA-MANGALAM.	1 Thathamangalam	1729	9336	4689	4647
	2 Pattanchery	1078	5683	2769	2914
	3 Perumatty	997	4503	2279	2224
	Total ...	3804	19522	9737	9785

APPENDIX II.

List of Desams or Villages with Population.

Pravrithi	Village or Desam.		No. of occupied Houses.	Population.		
				Total.	Males.	Females.
1		2	3	4	5	6
NALLEPPILLI.	1	Nalleppilli	904	**5063**	2347	2716
	2	Vatakke-Desam	609	**3409**	1635	1774
	3	Kolinjampara	829	**4765**	2297	2468
	4	Eruthenpathy	359	**1850**	883	967
	5	Vanchikunnampathy	94	**491**	251	240
	6	Attempathy	56	**304**	147	157
	7	Olalapathy	301	**1631**	804	827
	8	Vatakarapathy	255	**1472**	731	741
	9	Thenampathy	35	**182**	97	85
	10	Eravattapparapathy	119	**600**	303	297
		Total ...	3561	**19767**	9495	10272
NENMARAI.	1	Nenmarai	1170	**5550**	2589	2961
	2	Vallangy	516	**2472**	1178	1294
	3	Vithanashery	395	**2080**	968	1112
	4	Ailoor	732	**4029**	1863	2166
	5	Tiruvaliyad	507	**2488**	1213	1275
	6	Nelliampathies	311	**1209**	760	449
		Total ...	3631	**17828**	8571	9257